The Pacific Crest Trailside Reader

CALIFORNIA

THE PACIFIC CREST TRAILSIDE READER

ADVENTURE, HISTORY, AND LEGEND ON THE LONG-DISTANCE TRAIL

CALIFORNIA

EDITED BY REES HUGHES AND COREY LEE LEWIS

ORIGINAL WOODCUT ILLUSTRATIONS BY AMY UYEKI

THE MOUNTAINEERS BOOKS

THE MOUNTAINEERS BOOKS
is the nonprofit publishing arm of The Mountaineers,
an organization founded in 1906 and dedicated to the exploration,
preservation, and enjoyment of outdoor and wilderness areas.

1001 SW Klickitat Way, Suite 201, Seattle, WA 98134

First edition: first printing 2011, second printing 2018

Distributed in the United Kingdom by Cordee, www.cordee.co.uk

Manufactured in the United States of America

Copy Editor: Julie Van Pelt
Cover, book design, layout, and map: John Barnett/4 Eyes Design
Illustrations © by Amy Uyeki

Library of Congress Cataloging-in-Publication Data
The Pacific Crest trailside reader, California : adventure, history, and legend on the long-distance trail / edited by Rees Hughes and Corey Lewis.
    p. cm.
Includes index.
ISBN 978-1-59485-508-5 (pbk.)—ISBN 978-1-59485-510-8 (ebook)
1. Pacific Crest Trail—Guidebooks. 2. Trails—California—Guidebooks. 3. California—Guidebooks. I. Hughes, Rees. II. Lewis, Corey Lee, 1972-
GV199.42.P3P34 2011
917.94—dc23
                            2011022381

ISBN (paperback): 978-1-59485-508-5

To Robert Brandenburg,
whose inspiration has often reminded me that there are few limits to
what a determined person can do.

—Rees Hughes

In loving memory of Tim "Bear" Pyles,
whose lifelong loyalty and friendship to me were matched only by his
love for building and being on backcountry trails.

—Corey Lee Lewis

OREGON

Siskiyou Mountains

Preston Peak
Kangaroo Springs
Seiad Valley/Klamath River
Somes Bar
Mt Shasta
Eagle Creek
Castle Crags
Burney Falls

Old Station
Hideaway and the Heitmans
Lassen Peak
Little Haven and the Braatens
Beckwourth Trail
Bucks Summit

North Yuba River/Sierra City
Peter Grubb Hut
Donner Pass

Barker Pass

Border Ruffian Pass and Flats
Ebbetts Pass
Sonora Pass

NEVADA

Matterhorn Peak

SAN FRANCISCO

Lyell Fork Creek
Mt Lyell
Ritter Range
Muir Pass
Le Conte Canyon/Little Pete Meadow
Forester Pass
Mt Whitney
Rock Creek

CALIFORNIA

Rockhouse Basin
Walker Pass

Mojave Desert

PACIFIC CREST TRAIL
NATIONAL SCENIC TRAIL

Tehachapi-Willow Springs Road

Los Angeles Aqueduct

Deep Creek Hot Springs

Agua Dulce and Hiker Heaven

LOS ANGELES

Mt San Jacinto

Scissors Crossing

Mt Laguna

Lake Morena

The Pacific Crest Trail
CALIFORNIA

SAN DIEGO

Campo

MEXICO

WA
OR
CA

CONTENTS

CASCADES AND THE KLAMATH KNOT: THE REALM OF FIRE 227
Covering Section N–Section R
Belden—Feather River Canyon—Lassen Peak—Burney Falls
Castle Crags—Etna Summit—Seiad Valley—Siskiyou Summit

PREFACE

The Pacific Crest Trail has loomed large in both of our lives, ever since we first set foot on it. Like most PCT hikers and high-country travelers who went before us, we have found ourselves continually pulled back to the Pacific Crest, returning again and again, either through repeated trips or revisited stories. When unable to be on the trail, we find ourselves at home, scanning maps as we plan future trips, looking at pictures as we remember past journeys, and vicariously enjoying the memories and experiences of others. We have also found that we are not alone in this regard, that many other PCT hikers, like us, are called back irresistibly to that wild and rugged country snaking its way along the back of the American West.

As lovers of the trail, and of the stories surrounding it, we decided to compile a trailside reader that could stand as a testament to the PCT and those who have hiked it. Thus began a long and arduous literary journey, full of as many blisters and hardships as any PCT hike but also with just as many moments of inspiration, insight, and wonder. We sifted through countless historical accounts of exploration in the region, enjoyed reading the stories of contemporary PCT hikers, and collected some of the best work of our most well-known regional writers. We hope you will find this eclectic collection of stories to be as varied and enriching as your experiences on the PCT itself.

Perhaps, like many before, you will be inspired to write or tell your own story and will pass the PCT fever on to another lucky traveler. And if you are new to the trail, if *The Pacific Crest Trailside Reader* is your first exposure to the Pacific Crest, we hope that you too will be bitten by the bug and will find yourself compelled to explore the wilderness without as well as the wilderness within. For both of us, our first steps on the trail have come to stand out as significant moments in our lives, turning points and peak experiences, occasions for insight that have remained with us ever since. These first steps have led to countless others, both physical and intellectual journeys along the trail, to ultimately arrive as the book that you now hold in your hand. This volume is paired with its companion book, *The Pacific Crest Trailside Reader: Oregon and Washington*, which contains stories from the northern half of the trail. Although each volume can be read alone, we see them, like the trail, as two parts of a whole that are meant to be read together.

Rees's Story: The Beginning of a Thirty-Year Relationship

I have relived my first exposure to the Pacific Crest Trail countless times since 1981. The three of us, naïve young men, hoisted our packs and began the relentless 3000-foot climb to the rounded top of Big Huckleberry Mountain, just north of the Columbia River as the PCT enters Washington State. Upon reaching the grassy knoll near the summit, we each collapsed, dropping our too-heavy packs to the ground. I wrote in my journal, "The 50 pounds of food, clothes, and gear was devastating to my un-indoctrinated body." But around us was "a carpet of flowers and a panorama of the Gorge, mountains, and the awesome spire of Mount Hood." To this day I remember the overwhelming majesty of that view. However, we barely had the strength to eat and erect a tent. "All that beauty," I wrote, "could not mask the ache of my muscles. We pray for more good weather and quick relief for our beleaguered bodies."

A month later we reached Rainy Pass—leaner, wiser, and much more connected with the rhythm of the wilderness. We had crossed the deathly quiet blanket of ash blasted from Mount St. Helens the prior year that had smothered all life across a twenty-mile swath. We had camped in awestruck silence on a snowy flank of Mount Adams as we watched the setting sun illuminating distant Mount Rainier. We had supported each other across the precarious and icy Egg Butte ridgeline. We had endured days of soaking rain, snow, surging rivers, and lightning storms. We had watched the full moon rise over Waptus Lake. We had experienced the serenity of the mossy-backed Douglas fir forests in the valleys below Glacier Peak. We had witnessed the miracle of the dipper as its shadow danced along the water's surface. It is not hyperbole to say that we would never be the same. The Pacific Crest Trail was indelibly part of us.

On the final day of that trip I wrote that "the cleansing that I sought in the solace, the sweat, and the stimulation by nature has certainly occurred in the past four weeks. I feel renewed and aware, once again, of my purpose and vitality." I concluded,

Rushing stream; verdant forest glade,
Silent mountains, erupt with spectral colors,
The marmot whistle breaks the spell of the pilgrim.
Walking, walking, walking, walking, walking.
He has found his answer.

Since that first hike, Jim moved to Maine, Howard stayed in western Washington, and I relocated to California. But, as work and families have permitted, we have reunited to walk new sections of the PCT for a week or two at a time in the years since. Within a couple of days of our return to the trail, our bodies seem to rise to the demands we place upon them, we marvel at the view of Lake Tahoe or Mount Shasta, and we return to the familiar rhythm of the mountains. This bond begun nearly three decades ago has forever connected us with each other and the PCT.

COREY'S STORY: A SPIRITUAL QUEST

I first encountered the Pacific Crest Trail in the summer of 1998 shortly after having moved to the University of Nevada, Reno, to attend graduate school. Little did I know then that the next decade would find me taking countless expeditions along the PCT: backpacking alone or with my friends, day hiking with my young boys, and leading both trail-construction crews and classes of environmental studies students among its high peaks and ridgelines. Although an experienced backpacker and outdoorsman, I was new to the Sierras, having spent most of my mountaineering days in the Rockies of Wyoming and Colorado.

I entered the Desolation Wilderness, alone and expectant, hiking west from the Tahoe basin and then following the trail north toward Donner Pass. This area of the PCT is dominated by sparkling granite and clear water, blue sky and green pine. The first thing that struck me, as I hiked in silent awe, was the light. Great white shafts were everywhere: sparkling off quartz-studded granite, cascading through long feathery pine needles, reflecting off still mountain lakes, and raining down constantly from the cloudless western sky.

Lake Aloha held in its still reflection the perfect picture of the granite ridges of Mount Price and Pyramid Peak behind it. Without a schedule to keep or hiking partners to consider, I found myself drawn almost hypnotically to sit and watch the rippling mirror image for a long, meditative hour. In contrast to such stillness, Middle Velma Lake had me whooping and shouting as I jumped from lakeside cliffs into its icy waters.

As I headed north, through the Granite Chief Wilderness, and my gaze fell from the horizon line to the trail underneath my feet, I slowly became aware of the vast number and amazing variety of wildflowers bordering the trail. I marveled at the mountain sorrel and jewelflowers, along with the Lobb's buckwheat that clung so bravely to the tiniest cracks in cliffs and crevasses in rock. In the open pine forests, I sat down to study the saprophytic pinedrops and snow plants, while the moist meadows had me harvesting marsh marigold and Sierra onion. Everywhere I looked, the ground was studded with bright splashes of color, as if the artist had been tasked to use every hue on her palette.

Already, on that first trip, I was planning future hikes along the Pacific Crest Trail, camping trips with friends, field classes for students, and solo expeditions for spiritual solace. For weeks afterward, I walked long miles in my dreams, haunted by the desire to return and plagued by thoughts of starting preparations for a future thru hike.

After having walked more than sixty miles with a forty-pound pack on my back, and having weathered a brutally wild summer hail storm, I found myself walking and meditating on the conflict between freedom and security. At lunch breaks and campsites, after dropping my pack, I reveled in the freedom and weightlessness of packless hiking, bouldering, and rock climbing. But then, cold starry nights, and that long evening hailstorm that alternated between freezing rain and icy hailstones, filled me with gratitude for the forty pounds of tarp, sleeping bag, food, and gear that created my safe little port in the storm. As I headed off for the horizon of Donner Pass, I sang out loud to the world this hiking haiku that I wrote in my journal:

> I am the ship
> and all that I own
> the anchor

YOUR STORIES

Our stories are not unique. They are, however, deeply personal stories. Stories, we suspect, that will strike familiar chords with those that emerge from your own journeys along the Pacific Crest Trail. These may come from a day hike in the Laguna Mountains, a week in the Pasayten, or a month in the Sierras. We all share the themes of discovery, insight, challenge, and success. We hope that the *Trailside Reader* will both complement your next hike and inspire you to share your stories with others.

—REES HUGHES AND COREY LEWIS
Arcata, California

ACKNOWLEDGMENTS

When we embarked upon this project after a lunchtime walk into the Arcata Community Forest some years ago, neither of us had any idea of what we were really undertaking. It has been a wonderful partnership. Much like taking a long hike on the PCT with a good partner, we learned from each other, came to trust and appreciate each other, and above all emerged from the experience as friends.

No endeavor of this complexity is possible without the contributions and support of many. These books have become much better because of the suggestions, the feedback, the editing, the encouragement, and the patience of family, friends, colleagues, and the staff of The Mountaineers Books. We are eternally grateful for the many authors who submitted stories for inclusion in this anthology, including those we were unable to use. Great thanks go out to those hiker-authors included here, for their willingness to donate their stories in support of the PCT and for their patience and flexibility with us throughout the entire publication process. We would like to offer a special note of appreciation to Julie Van Pelt for her careful edits, and to the Department of English at Humboldt State University for its support of this project. Similarly, thanks go to the Association for the Study of Literature and Environment (ASLE) and the Pacific Crest Trail Association (PCTA) and all of their members, for their organizational support for this project in particular and for environmental writing and for the PCT in general.

Many have generously lent their talents and loving critique to individual stories, early drafts of sections, and to the publishing process itself: Rick and Susan Benoit, Bob Birkby, Barry Blake, Jan and Ingrid Brink, Joy Hardin, Michele McKeegan, Riley Quarles, Claire Reynolds, John Schafer, Kathy Statzer, Annie Stromquist, and Buzz and Judy Webb. And a special thanks to Cheryll Glotfelty for her professional advice on editing, anthologizing, and publishing. Your contributions have meant far more than any of you could ever realize.

REES'S ACKNOWLEDGMENTS

First and foremost, I would like to thank my wife, Amy Uyeki, who has patiently embraced this project as her own and has been willing to shoulder a backpack for nearly four decades to share the backcountry with me; my daughters, Chisa and Mei Lan, for understanding and supporting their crazy father; and the ever loving and nurturing Hughes and Uyeki clans.

I would also like to acknowledge my Pacific Crest Trail hiking partners from over the years, as well as the drivers and trail angels who have made it possible to be a section hiker. Howard "Rocky" Shapiro, Jim "Pierre" Peacock, and I grew up on the PCT. Over the past three decades of walking together, we have developed a passion for the trail and an unbreakable bond of friendship. In addition, I have had the good fortune to share trail time with my nephew, Taylor "Anti-Gravity" Smith, Steve "Crosscut" Benoit, Jim "The Epicurian" Elferdink, Gary "Nightcap" Fox, Steve Gustaveson, Chisa Hughes, Bruce and Nathan Johnston, Bob "Birdman" Lockett, Eli Robinson, Don Seifert, Kathy and Emily Shapiro, and my wife, Amy. I cherish each of these PCT experiences.

COREY'S ACKNOWLEDGMENTS

I offer a heartfelt thanks to my parents, Lon and Nancy Lewis, as well as to Grandad Lee and Grandma Dot Brunk, for instilling in me a love for the land and for backcountry adventure—thanks for all of those hiking, horsepacking, and backpacking trips that filled my childhood and adolescence with such amazing experiences. Thanks also to Bart Lewis and Tim Pyles for teaching me to love a good story and how to tell a good tale, as well as for their constant camping companionship and long, laughter-filled fireside conversations.

I would also like to thank Jerry Keir and everyone from the Great Basin Institute and the Nevada Conservation Corps for the opportunity to build hiking trails, lead university classes along the PCT, and gain valuable editorial experience and skill. Thank you, also, to Marge Sill, Roger Scholl, Sharon Netherton, and everyone else at Friends of Nevada Wilderness for mentoring me in wilderness advocacy and showing by your example how to live one's life on behalf of our wildlands. And a special thanks to Gary Snyder for connecting me to so many bioregional authors, to the bioregion itself, and to the mythopoetic power of literature. Your work has enriched both my life and our world.

INTRODUCTION

Those who have hiked the long miles and rugged terrain that the Pacific Crest Trail traverses understand well the wisdom of Lao-tzu's famous words: "The journey of a thousand miles begins with a single step." A Chinese hermit and philosopher who lived during the sixth century BC, and author of the *Tao Te Ching*, Lao-tzu was also a legendary traveler who, even as an old man, walked thousands of miles spreading his simple wisdom. Those who have made similar journeys of a thousand miles, or a hundred, or even ten, along the Pacific Crest Trail know well the significance of that first step. We all can point to that first powerful experience that led to countless others along the PCT. But what exactly constitutes that first step? Was it the first time our feet hit dirt and we began trudging or tearing up that long single-track trail? Or did it come months earlier, when we were poring over maps, reading trail descriptions in books, and mailing food and supplies to post offices along the way? Or did our journey begin all those years ago in a public library or friend's living room, reading or listening to tales of the high trail until we were hooked and heard the siren song of the Pacific Crest for ourselves?

Over the years, as we have hiked the Pacific Crest Trail, talked with hikers of every ilk, and read countless stories of traveling along its corridor, we have discovered a common feature among all those who have encountered the long trail: the only thing that matches a PCT hiker's enthusiasm for being on the trail is sharing stories about the trail. Whether this takes the form of a well-rehearsed campfire story, the often-told tall tale, or public trail blog, PCT hikers are generally PCT writers and readers as well. Similarly, whether you read these tales at home—to provide inspiration for returning to the high country— or on the trail itself, *The Pacific Crest Trailside Reader* promises to connect the magic of the footpath to the power of the page.

As one of our eight National Scenic Trails, the Pacific Crest Trail has offered unique and outstanding opportunities for taking the "thousand-mile journey" to countless travelers. Although American Indians and early immigrants had been exploring the PCT's high-country corridor for centuries, the idea of a high-elevation, or crest-line trail, was first envisioned by Catherine Montgomery in 1926. By 1937, Fred Cleator, supervisor for Region 6 of the US Forest Service, had overseen the completion of the Oregon and Washington sections of the PCT, but it would take fifty-six more years for the California section to be finished. The PCT spans the length of California, Oregon, and Washington, traveling 2650 miles from Mexico to Canada.

The California PCT

As the PCT bisects California lengthwise, it crosses the deserts and mountains of southern California, the high passes of the Sierra Nevada, and the dense forests and volcanic peaks of the Klamath Knot and the Cascades. PCT hikers come to know these bioregions intimately, each with its own distinct community of inhabitants and canon of stories. Accordingly, this first volume of the *Trailside Reader* is organized into four sections, each corresponding to its associated California section of the trail.

Starting in the south, as we hike the PCT and read the essays in this volume, we are first introduced to creosote, sage, and bitterbrush, all seemingly immortal members of America's southwestern deserts. From the charismatic Joshua tree, that lives in complete symbiosis with the pronuba moth, to the ugly horned lizard, that defends itself by shooting streams of blood from its eyes, the PCT's southernmost stretches contain exotic and wild inhabitants that often lend a surreal quality to the sand- and rock-dominated landscape. The trail stories from this "land of little rain" are filled with light and heat and are often preoccupied with thirst, shade, and the deep joys of vast space, overwhelming silence, and complete solitude.

Soon we are moving through juniper and pinyon pine as we hike through high-elevation desert and begin to climb into the southern Sierra. This stunningly diverse landscape contains a wide variety of wildlife—from the drought-tolerant desert rat, that goes its whole life without ever drinking a drop of water, to the wave-jumping water ouzel, a bird that calls both sky and stream home. The stories of this country are similarly varied. They range from ill-fated expeditions to dramatic backcountry rescues. This country is also replete with tales of trail magic and trail angels that have helped the beleaguered on their way, as well as with stories of high-elevation inspiration.

As we cross the central portion of the California PCT, we enter the alpine country of the High Sierra. Sparkling granite spires, glacially polished domes, and brilliantly white snowfields bounce sunbeams around hikers' heads, making this the aptly named Range of Light. From the giant sequoia to the delicate tiger lily, from the common black bear and manzanita to the rare cougar and sugar pine, this region of the PCT is full of the scenic vistas and plentiful wildlife that have become symbolic of American wilderness areas. The hardships of historical travelers, rock climbers, and mountaineers fill the tales of this high country just as often as they tell of exhilaration in the high mountain air.

And finally, we walk through the PCT's final California section. We leave the high and dry Sierra, moving through a volcanic country that steadily leads toward the wet and dense Cascades and landscape of the Klamath Knot. Surrounded now by fir and hemlock, moss and fern, we often find ourselves fording small streams, tramping down muddy trails, and discovering forested secrets along the way. From the wildly colored mushrooms and salamanders, and the plentiful huckleberries and blackberries, to the secretive spotted owls and pine martens, the depth of these northern forests holds treasures that PCT hikers will know well. Historic tales of mountain men and forgotten battles in the backcountry, as well as local legends of Lemuria and Bigfoot, haunt both the shadows of these dark forests and the stories that have grown out of them.

Regardless of where we start our journey along the PCT, past or present, north or south, we are sure to return home with memories and stories as worthy of retelling as our sore muscles and blisters are of forgetting. The PCT is truly one of the world's premier trails, combining so many magical elements into one experience that there is little wonder it has touched the very soul of so many. Aesthetically, historically, spiritually, physically, and emotionally, we are pulled to return again and again to this high crest of the Pacific Rim as day hikers, section hikers, or even thru hikers.

WALKING AND THE PACIFIC CREST TRAIL

Walking is at the very core of what defines our relationship with the PCT. We suspect that there is something about walking along the PCT that touches our subconscious, our primordial pedestrian being. Walking is what allows us to develop an intimacy, a special connection with a place.

In the long history of humankind, it has only been in the last few moments that walking has not been the primary means of getting from here to there. Our distant ancestors spread across the land, populating virtually every corner of the globe on foot. It is easy to imagine primitive people—who shaped their walking around issues of food, safety, and shelter—migrating with the change of seasons or movement of animal life.

Beginning some ten thousand years ago, people began to integrate animal power into transportation and work demands. But over the ensuing years, there was no alternative to walking for the vast majority of people. In *On Foot: A History of Walking* (NYU Press, 2004), Joseph Amato observed that society "worked, warred, traveled, explored, played, romanced, and carried out its religious processions afoot." By the Middle Ages, no one epitomized this more than the pilgrim. The journeys to Jerusalem, Rome, or along the Compostella trail across France and Spain serve as antecedents to contemporary thru hikes along the Appalachian, Pacific Crest, or Continental Divide Trails.

Similarly, walking figures prominently in American history and culture. As the United States expanded west beyond the coastal fringe of the North American continent, intrepid explorers were soon followed by trappers, fur traders, and ultimately emigrants. Lewis and Clark and Jedediah Smith were soon followed by the pedestrian migration of the Mormons in 1846–47 and the thousands of settlers who made their way to California and the Oregon Territory beginning in the 1840s.

While walking was a pragmatic necessity for most people during these times, others began to rearticulate the historical connection between spirituality and the practice of putting one foot in front of the other. As Thoreau noted in his journal entry dated January 7, 1857, "I come home to my solitary woodland walk as the homesick go home. I thus dispose of the superfluous and see things as they are, grand and beautiful" (*The Journal of Henry David Thoreau*, Peregrine Smith Books, 1984).

With the advent of the automobile, a highway system whose tentacles touch virtually every inch of our country, and our recent emphasis on time as money, walking has lost its important place in our culture and our lives. But walking is too much a part of our fundamental evolutionary design to be forgotten. We think at walking speed. "Walking," according to Rebecca Solnit, "is how the body measures itself against the earth. Walking, ideally, is a state in which the mind, body, and the world are aligned, as though they were three characters finally in conversation together, three notes suddenly making a chord" (*Wanderlust: A History of Walking*, Viking Penguin, 2000).

Given the clutter of our contemporary world, it should not be surprising that we have lost an appreciation for the simple elegance of walking. Walking requires nothing outside of ourselves—no gasoline, no saddle, no tires. Little special equipment is needed, and no special skill, expertise, or experience is necessary to become competent. Walking provides optimum independence and freedom of movement, and it is sustainable, nonpolluting, and minimally invasive. In much the same way that walking strengthens our bodies with a minimum amount of strain, long-distance walking clears the mind with its meditative quality. And as the PCT illustrates, there are few places on our marvelous planet that are not accessible by foot.

The length of the Pacific Crest Trail provides us with great incentive to walk and think, where time follows its own natural rhythms. It provides countless opportunities for day hikes, section hikes, and the ultimate commitment, the thru hike in terrain virtually unequaled in its access to diverse mountain scenery. Simply said, being able to walk on the PCT is a gift. And as every PCT hiker knows, so are the stories we return home with to share with others.

READING THIS BOOK

Each of us who has hiked along the PCT knows that our experiences mirror those of the thousands who have walked the trail before us. While the stories differ, the end result is the same. The trail is in our blood. Our feelings are not dissimilar to those who fell in love with the Cascades, the Sierras, the Siskiyous, and the San Gabriel Mountains long before there was a PCT.

We tread the same passes and cross the same rivers as the intrepid emigrants, mountain men, and native peoples of the West. The PCT winds its way through country that has inspired tall tales and has been inhabited by personalities larger than life. Its route includes sites of courage and cowardice, as well as triumph and tragedy. These tales of the trail capture the unique mystique and power that the American wilderness has held throughout time.

In the *Trailside Reader* we have collected three types of stories. Half of the anthology is comprised of contemporary real trail tales contributed by PCT day, section, and thru hikers. Some of these stories capture the humor of the trail, such as Gary Funk's "The Mystery of the Apple Pie" or Chuckie Veylupek's "Air Streaming off the Crest." Others provide a glimpse into PCT trail culture, such as Barney Mann's "The Many Faces of Trail Magic." Others recall encounters with wildlife, like Susan Alcorn's "When Deer Go Bad," from her battles with salt-starved deer in the Siskiyous, to Krystal Rogers's "The Bear at Lyell Fork Creek." There are stories of wild weather. Stories of being lost and found. Stories of conquering fear. Stories of camaraderie and conflict.

In working with the authors of these real trail tales, we emphasized the importance of telling a story. We have worked hard to preserve the unique narrative voice of each hiker-writer. As a result, these stories tend to be easy to read, and they explore themes familiar to all of those who have experienced the trail.

We have complemented these tales with others that, because of their historical significance, enrich our understanding and appreciation of certain stretches of the PCT. Read Moses Schallenberger's recollections about his winter spent in the Donner Pass area in 1844–45, for example, when you walk the PCT as it drops north from Tinker Knob; or Joaquin Miller's account in his "Battle of Castle Crags" as you follow the PCT up and around Castle Crags. Andy Hammond's profile of mountain man Jim Beckwourth is the perfect story to help you appreciate the trail as it intersects the old Beckwourth Trail east of Bucks Lake in the Feather River drainage. These rich stories are reminders of the many layers of history that exist in the land now occupied by the PCT. They tend to draw extensively from journal excerpts, often reflect the vernacular of an earlier time, and can benefit from being read and reread slowly and thoroughly.

The final element in this anthology has been the selective inclusion of the writings of classic environmental authors such as Mary Austin, whose "Land of Little Rain" captures the arid mystique of the PCT's southern deserts in beautiful prose; or John Muir, whose "Windstorm in a Sierra Forest" introduces us to both the diverse trees and wild weather of the region. Other well-known writers included here, such as Wallace Stegner and Gary Snyder, have helped define the way we think about the wilderness, walking, and the PCT itself. Unlike the real trail tales with their strong narrative thread, these stories demand to be read differently. Savor them like the glorious color of an alpine sunset. Read them like a love letter. Underline passages. Write in the margins.

In their sum, these stories are a tribute to the Pacific Crest Trail. They capture a slice of the spirit and culture, the people and places, and the philosophy and history of this national treasure.

Although these stories are organized parallel to the geographical sections of the PCT so that you can read about a particular stretch of trail while you are hiking it, each story stands alone. You might also elect to pick and choose, moving across regions and types of stories. This, the first volume in the set, covers California, beginning at the Mexican border and proceeding north. The second volume focuses on the Oregon and Washington sections of the PCT and concludes at the Canadian border. The *Trailside Reader* is intended to be an inspiring literary companion for day hikers and, for section and thru hikers, as indispensable as a stove or sleeping bag, worthy of the additional weight.

SOUTHERN CALIFORNIA
LAND OF LITTLE RAIN

COVERING SECTION A–SECTION F

Campo—Warner Springs—San Gorgonio Pass—Cajon Pass
Agua Dulce—Tehachapi Pass—Walker Pass

DAY ONE: COMFORT COMES IN SMALL DOSES

By Ben Wielechowski

Generally the first significant psychological revelation, or emotional experience, that Pacific Crest Trail hikers have derives from physically adjusting to the simplicity and rigor of life on the trail. Everyday life is reframed and seen from an entirely new perspective after a few days of living out of a pack. We quickly learn the ease of going without, of reducing our desires and finding pleasure in the simple, joy in the ordinary. Instead of needing recliner chairs and silk sheets, we find ourselves rejoicing in the opportunity to drink clean water without restraint or to rest weary muscles. The first few days spent on the trail can be the most difficult as we struggle to adjust, but they often bring special memories and insights as well. In this piece, Ben Wielechowski captures the challenge of this transition as well as the simple joys of trail life.

Although we reviewed a number of stories that talked about the elaborate preparations necessary for a section or a thru hike on the PCT, and many others that focused on the long walk from Campo to Lake Morena, this was our choice to begin the collection. It is not just the element of drama and hardship that makes this story compelling, but the recognition that first days necessitate adjustment to the Spartan realities of trail life. Regardless of where you begin your hike along the PCT, those early miles on the trail are often defined by this experience. In fact, for those poor souls, like us, who find themselves compelled to repeatedly return to the PCT, it is perhaps this expected adjustment, this forced flexibility and dropping of desires, that pulls us back again and again, one season after another.

By the time the bus rolled into Campo, California, the sun blazed high noon and we still had twenty-one miles to hike. We had taken the bus from San Diego that morning and had spent the three-hour trip watching the landscape change from plains of sagebrush to winding mountain passes.

One year prior, my friend Paul Niemi and I had decided that we wanted to spend the summer hiking the Pacific Crest Trail. Paul had never been on an extended backpacking trip. I had hiked the Appalachian Trail in 2006, but the desert climate of the PCT was new to me. We both embarked as beginners, excited yet naïve about what the adventure might hold.

Two other PCT hikers boarded the bus at El Cajon Transit Center in San Diego along with us: Todd, a young man from Santa Barbara who had delayed his start date by two weeks due to wildfires burning through Santa Barbara; and an older gentleman from Finland, who sat quietly several rows ahead of Todd, Paul, and me. The bus slowly filled as we headed east along the dusty highway, moving out of the city and into the rural villages. By the time we reached Tecate, the remaining local commuters emptied out, leaving us four behind.

We had been warned about the desert. We knew about the unbearable heat and the lack of shade. We knew to carry lots of water. But once we loaded up several liters from a nearby public restroom, we thought, well, maybe we don't need quite this many. Seven turned into five for me. Paul somehow managed six. We applied sunscreen, shifted and squirmed under the weight of our packs, and headed for the border. It was already 1:00 PM.

Paul and I both knew time was an issue, mainly because the next reliable water source lay at camp, twenty-one miles ahead. However, the excitement of finally touching the trail with our own feet after months of planning seemed to trump any potential worries. We staged poses and took pictures at the monument marking the southern terminus. We pointed to the helicopters and hollered at the border patrol kicking up dust in the distance. We laughed. We celebrated. The adventure had begun.

So we hiked north. Lizards skittered across the trail. We wound up and around massive boulders, up mountains and down into valleys. We rounded cliffs and walked along ridges. We crossed dusty roads and a set of railroad tracks cutting through the bronze landscape. All the while, the sun beat down. We rested every couple miles. Slugged water when we needed it. Five miles into the hike, we passed the one sure source of water between the Mexican border and Lake Morena Campground. We found Todd filling up on water. He smiled awkwardly, and upon seeing the water source we understood why. The pool was shallow and seemingly stagnant, filled with algae and debris. Paul and I took one look, checked our water bladders, and agreed to move on to the next potential source, which we thought was a short mile and a half away.

An hour passed. No water. Instead we continued to switchback up the mountainside. Then we followed the crest for miles, trekking past sagebrush, scrub oak, and yucca plants. The sun radiated off the rocks and sweat soaked my back. Paul began to have coughing fits the higher we ascended into the mountains. He said he felt fine; he was just having trouble breathing at the higher elevation.

By 4:00 PM, I began to feel dizzy and nauseous. We had hiked only nine miles, and with twelve remaining I was hesitant to stop for lunch. Yet I had reached a point on the trail where massive boulders sheltered us from the burning sun. When Paul rounded the corner, I saw his shoulders slacken and a smile spread across his face.

"I was hoping you'd stop soon," he said and shrugged his pack off. We both sat down in the shade, quiet and contemplative. I thought about my water rations as I slugged down half a liter, hot from the sun. I felt sick, but after the rest and a couple tuna and cream cheese sandwiches, my headache went away. Paul snacked on tuna and honey and the color returned to his face as well. We joked a bit before heaving our forty-pound packs back on our shoulders.

Lunch rejuvenated me and I asked Paul if I could hike ahead. We agreed to meet up every hour to check on one another.

Before the descent to Hauser Canyon, we weighed our options. We had an hour left of sunlight, and it was still over five miles to reach Lake Morena Campground. "I think we should try to get out of the canyon and over that next peak before sunset," I said, pointing to the massive rock face straight across the canyon. "Think we can do it?"

"Yeah, but I'm going to be moving slower. You go on ahead," Paul said, followed by a violent coughing fit. He looked exhausted, his face and white polyester shirt covered in the dust and dirt he had kicked up. But he said so convincingly, so I moved on ahead.

The climb out of Hauser Canyon was our last big climb of the day, in fact, our biggest climb of the day—a hefty 1000-foot ascent over a mile and a half. I had caught my second wind and attacked the climb fully energized. The big oaks that filled the canyon thinned out, and sagebrush and chamise lined the trail once again. The dwarf-sized vegetation allowed for a spectacular view west into the canyon as the sun descended.

This desert sunset was like nothing I had ever seen before. No clouds hung near the horizon like in the Midwest where I was from. The sky stretched clear and blue and all the colors appeared individually, vivid and deep, until the sun dipped below the horizon and all colors swirled to rainbow. I was so taken aback by the view and so full of adrenaline, I ripped up the mountainside. When I reached the top, my throat was dry and sweat beaded off my face and arms. I had lost too much water in the ascent.

I sucked down my last half liter and waited for Paul. I adjusted my head-lamp and aimed the beam at the ground, watchful for scorpions, rattlesnakes, or tarantulas. Crow-sized bats swooped down. I continued to wait, my imagi-nation growing, my dehydration deepening. Eventually, I ran back down the trail to check on Paul. I could see the beam of his headlamp roving back and forth as he tackled the endless switchbacks. He arrived at the summit out of breath, talking somberly and moving gingerly.

"I need to sit down. I've got nothin' left."

We sat in silence. Paul took sips from his water bladder. His coughing fits worsened. I was worried—about hiking the next three miles in the dark, about Paul making it to camp without throwing up blood, about running out of water—so I nervously moved small stones back and forth with my feet.

"Alright. I think I'm ready. But I'm going to be moving real slow," Paul said after a while. In the triangle glow of his head lamp, he looked just as exhausted as he had when he'd arrived, but we both knew we had to keep moving.

"We'll hike together the rest of the way, okay?"

We moved. The trail leveled out and widened as we wound north. The night sky stretched in all directions, an endless kaleidoscope, twinkling. A heli-copter thumped in the distance. I imagined an army of SUVs suddenly shining us with floodlights—two innocent PCT hikers mistaken for illegal immigrants lurking in the shadows of scrub oak. But the heathland remained quiet, except for desert mice skittering across the trail, their beady eyes catching the light of our headlamps.

It was the longest night hike I'd ever experienced—the trip was turning out to be a series of firsts. Before this night, I absolutely dreaded night hiking. The idea of strolling through an unfamiliar landscape filled with creatures terrified me, especially in the dark. Night hiking in the desert was much different. We towered over the desert shrubs. The stars lit up the vast expanse enough to offer me comfort, tricking me into believing the unknown was somehow less ominous. I thought, well this isn't too bad. But then I thought dehydration had started to affect my brain.

"I have to stop, Ben. I have to stop here," Paul said, and suddenly I was back on the trail, back in reality. "I feel nauseous. I've got to eat a snack." His breathing was labored and he shrugged his pack off and laid down in the middle of the trail, resting his head on his pack.

"You okay? You been drinking enough water?"

"Yeah, I just got to sit." Paul flipped off his headlamp and coughed violently in the darkness, his silhouette convulsing with each fit. I paced up and down the trail, trying to figure out what to do next. It must have been ten already. We had no water. Paul was fading fast—his energy, his attitude, his will. I had to do something. Hike to camp without him and come back to retrieve his pack? Hike to camp and return with water? Carry his stuff? Carry him? The one thing I was sure of was that we had to make it to camp. We had to. But then he said what I had feared all night.

"I don't know if I can make it. I might just sleep here. I can sleep here," he said, followed by another fit so violent I thought he had puked.

"No way, man. I'm sorry. We can't do that. We have to keep moving." The situation had become dire. I knew it, and I'm pretty sure Paul knew it.

"I know it," he said. "Just keep pushing me man. Keep an eye on me." I unfastened his pack and grabbed his tent and cooking gear and stuffed the items in my pack.

We hiked on. After fifteen minutes or so, Paul started talking again. "I feel much better. I just needed that food. I can't keep doing that. I have to listen to my body."

"Well, we shouldn't have far to go." Lights from a town nearby, hopefully Lake Morena, glimmered in the valley below. We were close. I started to lighten up, but every time Paul erupted into another coughing fit, I cringed. We're not out of it yet, I thought. Things could worsen at any moment. The entire day had been this lesson over and over again—when we missed the water source, when I almost puked from lack of food, when Paul didn't make it out of the canyon before dark, when I started to suffer from dehydration, and especially when Paul almost quit in the middle of the trail.

We arrived at the campground some time after eleven. Fortunately, Todd, the gentleman from Santa Barbara had staked out a campsite fairly close to the trail and was still awake by the time we arrived. I set my pack down and ran to the restroom to chug several liters of water. Paul moved a bit slower, but our needs were identical: water, food, and rest.

When I returned from the restroom, I sat down and inhaled. I must have been holding my breath for the past three hours, for I had not noticed the drop in temperature until the cold desert air bit my throat. It felt good. Then I exhaled and watched my breath slowly unfold toward the stars. And while looking into the open expanse above me, the vastness of the unknown, the uncertainty, I suddenly felt relieved—I had reached camp. I had Paul and Todd to laugh and joke with about the tribulations of the day. For a brief moment, I had found certainty. I knew, however, that the morning would inevitably arrive, and that when it did I would once again walk back out into the vastness, content within the unknown.

SIX MOON TRAIL

By Tom Marshburn

*Tom Marshburn turned twenty while walking the Pacific Crest Trail in
1980. The son of a Presbyterian minister from Georgia, Tom began his
PCT journey following his sophomore year at Davidson College, starting
at the Canadian border. He struggled with the hardships of the lingering winter in the north and an agreement with his family to always
walk with others. By the time Marshburn reached Crater Lake, he was
prepared to quit, a topic often on his mind during his first two months
on the trail—only to be encouraged by his family to complete his journey
even if it meant doing so solo. The determination to finish occupies his
thoughts to the very conclusion of his walk, as can be seen in his final two
journal entries.*

*Marshburn went on to complete medical school, and he ultimately
joined NASA in 1994 as a flight surgeon, assigned to Space Shuttle Medical Operations and to the joint US/Russian Space Program. He served
as a part of the Endeavor crew in 2009, which orbited Earth 248 times,
traveling 6,547,853 miles in 15 days, 16 hours, 44 minutes, and 58 seconds—staggering in its contrast to the distance traveled in his five and a
half months on the PCT.*

*In the first story in this volume, the Mexican border is the beginning,
but for a number of thru hikers Campo is the ultimate destination. It
seemed appropriate to include a story in which the southern border is the
much-anticipated conclusion. It should also be noted that, like many early
PCT hikers, Marshburn, often had to improvise because the PCT was, at
times, little more than a line on a piece of paper.*

SOURCE: Excerpted from *Six Moon Trail: Canada to Mexico along the Pacific Crest*, by Tom Marshburn
(Robert K. Leishman, 1985). Reprinted by permission of the author.

NOVEMBER 15, 1980

I just kept telling myself this was the next to the last day. Walking had become so hard. I couldn't understand it. I guess my mind realized that I was about to finish, so it released my body from its grip, and I felt extremely languid. I cried that morning as I walked. My feet and hands ached from the cold, and yet I knew soon I wouldn't have to wake up like this every morning. As usual, the cry was a good release, and I felt relaxed enough to pull out the old physics book and read some as I walked. No cars, just me, the morning sun, the highway, and the hills. At the tiny resort of Mount Laguna I bought a day's supplies. When I told someone where I was headed, he offered me a ride. "We'll be there in thirty minutes," he said. I declined, of course; these last miles were mine. If I hiked no others, I had to hike these. I was really that close!

For some reason I was not as excited as I thought I'd be. My emotions were draining out. I had been excited for the past month and a half, and the White-water and San Jacinto ordeals gave me reason to cry and yell in rage, and but now I was having trouble generating emotions. Also, I had been walking so long by then that I really wasn't able to believe I would be through until I was actually there. The next twenty-five miles might as well have been six hundred, because I was still walking.

But I had made good mileage and I'd worked hard, so with a slight glow inside and a little grin outside, I walked over the top of the Lagunas. The Anza-Borrego desert steamed to the east: miles and miles of land to the horizon without a blade of grass, just brown cracked earth.

I still walked in oak trees and tall grass, though, and the familiar ritual of weaving through some confusing dirt roads put me on the trail down Long Canyon. I wanted so badly to put myself in good standing for the next day, so that I could reach the border before sunset, that I pushed on into the night. The moon was bright; my last full moon.

For some reason my feet hurt terribly. I kept getting blisters where I'd never had them before. My feet seemed to be giving up on me. At a dirt road I hobbled to a stop, sat in the grass, and let the tears stream. "Won't it ever end? Will it ever, ever end?" I kept whispering. The entire family was on my mind, and I directed my words to them. "I can't wait to see you again."

The road led me to Cibbets Flat Campground, a small sectioned-off portion of grass which was heaped with campers, tents, and trailers. As I passed a ring of beer-drinkers, one asked, "Where you hiking?"

"The border."

"Where'd you come from?"

"Canada." That felt so good to say that I didn't care what their response was. One guy just said, "Damn." And after exchanging a few words, I moved on. I felt like camping alone, so I decided to push on a few more miles. My feet grated in my boots painfully. I slowly approached a small rushing creek and eyed it for awhile with my flashlight. My third step missed, and I ended up sprawled in the water, my pack hanging up over my neck, pinning me up to my waist in water. With a torrent of curses I climbed out like a fat man hauling himself out of a bathtub.

And then it came. My spurts of tears during the morning and earlier in the night were nothing compared to this outburst. I laughed and cried bitterly at nature's last demeaning slap. For about five minutes I stared at a moon blurred by tears and pumped out every bit of pressure and frustration I could. The emotion came in waves. I then sat, sighing heavily, and decided this should be my camp. My soaked shirt draped heavily over the crook of a tree, and I ate cereal for dinner, the last dinner I had.

NOVEMBER 16

My shirt had frozen, but I pulled it on anyway. In the early light I could see an easier way to cross the stream, and soon I was pounding over Yellow Rose Spring. I stopped at the low shallow pass to eat a banana. My eyes followed the road down the last hill, down across Interstate 8, and up the yellow grasses of Cameron Valley. Six miles past there was Mexico; I could see the tops of a few low green hills.

My pack broke. The front zipper popped off; and I noticed my flashlight was gone. I had vainly searched for it the previous night, and in the morning I still couldn't find it. Everything was falling apart; at least my feet felt all right. I was not excited, not elated, just calm. A mile later at a ranger station by the highway, I checked out conditions at the border.

The only way to cross the highway was to go under it. I climbed over a fence and headed for a drainage culvert. This was hard; I couldn't stand up, and crawling was too slow, so I duck-walked through as thumps from cars passing overhead resounded about my head. Another problem. I ended up on the wrong side of the creek. The trail followed a dirt road on the opposite side. Naturally, this watercourse was broad and deep. After thrashing around for a while in eroded, yellow grassy pasture, I resigned myself to removing my boots and sloshing across. I resorted again to hissing, "Will this ever end?" over and over. Now I headed up Cameron Valley and stopped to eat my last lunch: apple, crackers, and peanut butter. Little things were special about that lunch: the cool lightness of taking off my pack, the taste of apple and peanut butter while just sitting by the road under a large bush, a pleasantly warm sun.

At the top of the hill—the last hill—I looked across six miles of green brush and houses to the hills of Mexico. Probably the last six miles were the last thing I wanted to do. My fatigue with hiking came in a rush, and I read pieces of my physics book as I slowly stomped out three miles of paved road. At an intersection sat Cameron Corners, a town of a few buildings. It was busy enough, though, and I ate two soft ice cream cones at a corner ice cream stand.

It was cold those last three miles. A chill wind blew strong over the flat valley, and the piercing yellow sun just hurt my eyes. I was cold. Past a few pink stucco and adobe homes with squat cacti in the front yard, and then to the empty little corner of Campo. No traffic, no people, just a border guard station and a small bar.

A young girl appeared walking across the street. She looked at me. "Where are you going?"

"The border."

"Oh. Where are you hiking from?"

"Canada."

"Why'd you do that?" Good question. I mumbled a few things like oh, because I wanted to, it was fun, and crap like that. I just wanted to get there. But she smiled and was nice; I imagine she's seen a lot of hikers through here and understands things better than I realize.

She said she was the border guard's daughter. So I parted, half expecting some gun-toting uniformed man trundling out after me. But all I passed was a boys' home with a group playing volleyball behind a fence. "Hey," one guy shouted, "where you headed?"

"The border," I shouted back.

That was enough for him, and he turned and continued playing. The sun sat lower and yellowed the sky as I followed a dirt road. One mile from the border I came to a fork and had to check my maps just once more. Then I came upon a dilapidated trailer home surrounded by muddy pig pens, a few rusty, wheelless cars, and two chained and frantic dogs. A long-haired guy, a little younger than I, was feeding the pigs.

Out of the door stepped a huge, heavy black man the size of a boiler. He stomped to one of the trucks and leaned up against it. We waved. He pointed south and said, "The border's about two hundred yards that way. Where are you hiking from?" My answer produced a smile. "Well," he said, "Go on up there and come back, and by then I'll have some spaghetti ready for you." I smiled and said, "Thank you, I'll do that," and then I walked on up.

There was the border. A long and rusty barbed wire fence stood with a plastered but roofless hut behind it. I set my pack against the wooden PCT sign with THE START OF THE PCT and CANADA OR BUST written all over it, and then sat down for a while. A passerby may have thought I was about to fall asleep. I wasn't tired, just calm. I had already used up my emotions and felt like an empty vessel. Not that it was a bad feeling, just a very relaxed one. I was just happy that the day's hike was over. Washington and Oregon seemed so far away—I tried hard to string it all together, to say, okay, I began in Canada, crossed three states and snow and desert and mountains and—but I couldn't do it. The day's hike was over. I smiled at the memory of the times in the first few months when I dreamed of the border, picturing myself crying with delight and dancing around. I now just sat there, slowly gazing around at the low green and brown hills. And then I performed the rituals I had planned so perfectly, grasping the barbed fence with both hands, sticking my foot and then my hand through and touching the ground, and taking a few pictures. It was over. When walking away I looked back to study the scene. This was a place I never wanted to forget. I started back to the trailer, a warm feeling cradled inside.

WALKING DOWN A DREAM

By Natasha Carver

*Written from the thru-hiker perspective, Natasha Carver's essay intro-
duces a number of themes—the growing numbers of Pacific Crest Trail
hikers from other countries (England, in Carver's case), the inevitability
of being caught in a compromising position after seeing no one on the trail
for hours, and the challenge of dealing with different walking styles, blisters, water scarcity, and fear. Notably, this is not fear of the cougar, bear,
or snake, but the fear that stems from encounters with humans along the
margins of civilization.*

*The profile of the thru-hiking community has changed significantly
since Teddi Boston's solo thru hike in 1976. Increasingly, women make
up a sizable number of those on the PCT. As a result, many stories chosen
for these volumes are written by women, beginning with this story from
Carver's book,* Walking Down a Dream.

*Carver also references Ray Jardine throughout her account. Jardine
is an author and adventurer, who, with his wife Jenny, advocated and
popularized the philosophy of ultralight backpacking. His name reappears
periodically throughout the stories in these volumes.*

We have walked 42.2 miles. That's not a lot.
Kris wants to take a rest day. We're at Mount Laguna, our first
mail drop, where we have lost all shame and are trying to completely Jardine. We sent home extra socks, torches, compasses, spare top and now Kris

Source: Excerpted from *Walking Down a Dream: Mexico to Canada on Foot*, by Natasha Carver (Xlibris,
2002). Reprinted by permission of the author.

is even cutting the side off her sneakers (bought because Jardine points out that trainers are lighter than boots, and what you wear on your body, you are effectively carrying) to fit her toes better. This, she claims, is the advantage of cheap gym-shoes; my leather boots are not easily cut. I have to admit to being slightly horrified at the thought. Other hikers who pass rapidly by, keep telling us to cut the spare straps off our backpacks. I would like to lose weight from my pack—they must weigh around five pounds each when empty—but this really seems a bit vandalous.

There's a post office here, a campground and not much else. Naively we think we can just eat our camping food even in town-stops (this will change at the next stop). My blisters are large and unattractive. Everyday Kris and I spend a good half an hour plus sewing holes in our feet, so that the puss can drain out. The idea is to leave the thread in the foot, and walk on it, so that they keep on draining. It's not nice. My back and shoulders are at the point of crunching into a heap of knots and twists that would keep three chiropractors in business. OK, I admit it; I tried to break the end off my toothbrush. Unfortunately my nice, kind, this-is-ridiculous mother made sure that I was well equipped with what she considered essentials, the result is an expensive toothbrush which is designed to bend and won't, therefore, break.

And yet I feel like I'm being reined in. I feel guilty. You can't stop on Day Four. We'll get behind schedule. We have to keep moving. I can't stop. I must go. Walk walk walk says my mind as though this is some kind of duty one has to fulfill. I'm here to walk. I can't just hang out.

The ladder-backed woodpeckers hammer away at the pinyon pines and squawk noisily, and the jays, a shiny blue with black tufts on their heads, swoop from tree to tree. We spend the day watching the birds and washing socks. And it is good to relax. The post office is a hiker hangout. People queue for the one telephone, exchange blister stories and mileage. They are all lads, boasting of their testosterone, which in this 'sport' translates into number of miles per day. Most of them started at the border the day before. We comfort ourselves with 'it's not a competition' thoughts.

And then there is water. A great lady turned up just to tell us which 'cricks' (as they call them) still had water and where they had cached water for us.

"There's 29 gallons before that gate, 40 gallons up by so and so," she said, pointing at the map sprawled out on her car bonnet [hood]. It's amazingly hospitable. People just drive out and hoist gallons of water up into the hills for the hikers. […]

Day Seven is a fairly typical day. We have walked about six or seven miles and it is 10:30 in the morning; we stop to have a break and eat some nuts. I find this enormous rock for us to shelter under—the last bit of shade for miles. First things first and the blisters come out to be inspected and admired. Every minute or so the ground is banged with a pole to keep the rattlers away (rattlesnakes are deaf, they react to vibrations in the ground). Not that we've actually seen any yet, but Kris is taking no chances. We eat nuts—soya nuts today, which turn out to be like big dry lentils. That is, we force soya nuts down our poor dry throats into our poor dry stomachs. We rest for about an hour then decide to leave. Something becomes obviously, painfully wrong—my shorts are stuck to my bottom by millions, trillions of tiny tiny cactus spines. Ow. Well the shorts have to come off, no way round it, and there I am tenderly extracting each and every spine by feel, when round the corner comes a jolly hiker wearing a wide-brimmed floppy hat.

"What you do?" he asks, astonished, in a thick French accent.

"Um, errr, well, we're sheltering from the sun," I say, frozen into position.

Well we were, amongst other things.

"Ahh!" he says, "You are Engleeeesh."

And that explains everything.

We cross the San Felipe Valley, panic for a bit when the cached water isn't quite where it is meant to be, and stumble on to the creek of the same name, which unbelievably is still flowing. Here you have two bedraggled hikers who have not washed for six days (cached water can only be used as desperately needed drinking water). So the clothes came off: socks, bra, top, sarong, and shorts. That's everything. So what to wear while you're washing? A headscarf. Obviously. So there I am scrubbing away daintily and ladylike under a head-scarf when three beefy Americans stride round the corner.

"I'm English?" say I (well it worked the last time).

But they study the ground intently and bumble on by. Kris now claims that if we are ever in need of help, all I have to do is start undressing, and someone will appear....

We are at present sitting with our feet in the stream. Kris has hurt her ankle or tendon or some such body part. She is replacing the duct tape which she'd put round to stop the stones getting in. She has cut a small corner off our building wrap which she is sewing into her trainers with dental floss. Ray Jardine would be proud of her.

Here is Scissors Crossing where several main roads and the trail cross the

San Felipe Creek. The wash has been in vain, the dust is insidious and we are quickly coated with a fresh layer of orange powder as the wind blows.

That night I am even more paranoid than usual, sleeping right beside the road. I am grateful for our lack of a tent which makes us less conspicuous. [...] Kris can't believe I have never seen a shooting star and calls me a 'city kid' with some contempt. That's fighting talk. It does seem to be an embarrassing gap in my ever-so-countrified upbringing. I take my contact lenses out and realize I can't see any stars let alone ones that are dying. This could explain quite a lot.

The traffic grows less and less and by midnight it is almost quiet. And that's when the headlights swoop over our sleeping-bags and pull off the road to park just twenty feet away. They just miss illuminating our horizontal figures and light the shrub behind us. Two doors slam and the glow of cigarettes act out a complicated, violent dance through the air. There is an argument going on in low muttered voices. I strain to hear if they are speaking English or Spanish but can decipher nothing. I put my glasses on silently and wake Kris. We lie, rigid, unnerved.

Probably they have every excuse to be here—a hundred innocent explanations should be possible, only I can't think of any of them right now. And why would they be interested in two scruffy hikers anyway? Time ticks by and Kris goes back to sleep. Sleep is very important to Kris, even the thought of being hacked to pieces beside a road somewhere not that far from San Diego doesn't stop her sleeping. Or maybe she's just a whole heap more sensible than me. I stay awake and watch. Cigarette after cigarette dances around, sometimes inside the car, sometimes outside, sometimes walking towards us, sometimes away from us. Are they waiting for someone? Coyotes picking up illegals? Drug dealers waiting for cocaine brought all the way from Colombia?

Sleep is a luxury that people in houses can afford. The grime of not washing for six days through the sweltering heat has yet to get to me (it will), although I have to separate my thighs at night which is quite a challenge in a straight-jacket sleeping-bag, to try to find relief from the chafing from my shorts. The dry nuts and unappetizing peanut butter has yet to get so completely revolting that I can't stomach it (it will). Even blisters don't seem too bad. But sleep ... sleep. I crave sleep.

At around 4:30 AM they slam the doors, reverse and drive back on to the road. All that for nothing. At five I wake Kris up. Sometime after six we leave, laden with water, to climb up out of the valley into the shadeless hills.

We walk our 13 miles to the next water cache. Only there is no water left, just gallon bottles all tied together hanging around the bottom of a giant asparagus that looms taller than everything out of the orange hills. This is actually a Desert Agave, a plant that grows 10 to 15 foot tall. Once in a while (between 9 and 20 years), after a rain storm they burst into flower but otherwise they are tall, straight, giant asparagus. One begins to understand why there are so many alien sightings in the States. There is an option of walking another ten miles to Barrel Spring, which is not really an option. Or I can walk down off-trail to the W-W Ranch somewhere below us in the scrub. I park Kris under a tree where she rests her ankle and set off down a track with some vague directions in my head.

There's something comforting about walking along a trail, I realize, now off-trail, even an unmarked trail which is little more than a faint groove in a desert. Walking down what was once possibly a dirt road is slightly alarming. You feel lost instantly. Luckily for me, I take all the right turnings and arrive at the ranch. I wander through the (turned-off) watering system to the huge pile of junk that eventually evaporates into a house + caravan + old falling-apart trucks. The dogs wait in the shadows until I am almost on top of them and then leap out barking. I stand still. Guns, cowboys and drive-by shootings flash through my head in one petrifying second. I walk back down the drive. Then think about Kris and being thirsty. Turn round, walk back up the drive. The dogs growl. I walk back down the drive. This is ridiculous. So I walked instead in the other direction and come upon the ranch house proper and its owner, Richard. Richard is not the kind of guy to participate in a gangland killing. He is a kindly retired man who becomes a real Trail Angel. He lets me fill up the water bags and the bottles and then fills up some empties of his own and attempts to drive me back up the road to the trail. I did try to warn him that the road wasn't really a road, but he determinedly pushes on in the jeep until some scrub comes through the glass window and convinces him that walking might be easier.

Will my feet ever be the same again? I guess not. Blisters have formed on top of blisters beside blisters. I have tried to moisturize life back into my heels. Hoping they don't crack, that would be painful. I'm tired. Feet are tired. Bruised. Ingrained dirt, callused feet, raw thighs, worn shoulders. All in a week.

.

SOMETIMES THEY COME BACK

By Ryan Forsythe

The PCT follows the spine of the San Jacinto Mountains on the eastern perimeter of the Los Angeles basin. Despite being within an easy drive for millions of Angelenos, this thirty-mile range is surprisingly wild, rugged, and empty. As the trail climbs through the dense chaparral, it transitions into thick stands of forest made possible by the precipitation caught by the nearly 11,000-foot Mount San Jacinto. Ravines drop precipitously to both the east and west. Despite the searing desert heat nearby, it is not unusual for snow to remain in this high country until well into the summer. Over the years, day hikers and backpackers have found themselves struggling at times against the heat, other times against the cold, and most often with the rugged and disorienting terrain in this area.

A spring storm blanketed the San Jacintos with eight inches of snow in May 2005 and began a sequence of tragic events that culminated a year later. Ryan Forsythe explores this intersection in the existence of three people brought together by chance or fate or, perhaps, divine intervention.

Not until we are lost do we begin to understand ourselves.
—*Henry David Thoreau*

There are two types of stories of lost hikers. First are those the hikers themselves tell of being stuck or stranded, perhaps due to injury or horrific weather, before somehow miraculously finding their way out. And then there are those stories that others must tell, of friends or loved ones lost forever, perhaps gone off course in a rugged gorge or still missing on a mountain pass.

What follows combines both of these stories. It is also a story of the connections between hikers—even those who have never met.

In May 2006, Gina Allen and Brandon Day of Dallas were in Palm Springs for a financial group's biannual sales convention. On the conference's third day, the nearby San Jacinto Mountains beckoned. According to John Muir—who knew a thing or two about mountain vistas—"the view from San Jacinto is the most sublime spectacle to be found anywhere on this earth!" Topping out at 10,834 feet, the range is the second highest in southern California and is known for its subalpine forests, craggy granite peaks, and high mountain meadows. This was to be a welcome change of scenery from the manufactured walls and shadow-suppressing fluorescent lights of the conference resort.

Along with forty-one other conference attendees, the couple climbed onto the aerial tram in Chino Canyon, which took them nearly 6000 feet up in less than twenty minutes. Upon exiting at Mountain Station that Saturday afternoon, some of the group meandered to the state park visitor center, some to the snack bar and gift shop, while others made their way to one of the popular nature trails. Allen and Day took a few photos and began strolling down the Desert View Trail, with its stunning panoramas of the high-country peaks and the desert below.

Clad in light jackets and tennis shoes, and with no food, Allen and Day were prepared for little more than this quick day trip—an hour enjoying the view, a short hike in the San Jacinto Mountains, and then back to the conference.

It was close to 2:45 PM when they started on the trail. At one point they stepped off to photograph a waterfall. What Allen and Day did not realize was how quickly the few nature trails at the top of the tram connect to a vast network, leading to trails with names like Devil's Slide and Suicide Rock. It's just a few miles from Mountain Station to the Pacific Crest Trail. Once confused by the complex network of interchanging paths, they struggled to find their way back to the main trail. By 3:30, they knew they were lost.

Even experienced hikers have been known to get lost in the area pretty regularly. Just a year earlier, John Joseph Donovan, a fifty-nine-year-old retired social worker, thought he was prepared for these cold desert mountains. A veteran hiker, he had logged more than ten thousand miles, including both the Appalachian and the Colorado Trails. Four years earlier, he had completed sections of the PCT through Oregon and Washington to Manning Provincial Park, Canada.

Donovan walked everywhere—eight miles to and from work at Central State Hospital in Virginia, even in the rain. His plodding gait earned him the nickname "El Burro." After thirty years at the hospital, Donovan retired on April 19, 2005. The very day of his retirement, he left for the West Coast and his dream trip: finally completing the PCT.

In the end, Donovan was not much more prepared than Allen and Day. He was traveling as light as he could, carrying a small yellow backpack in which he'd stuffed a simple green tarp in place of a more protective tent. Against the advice of friends and other backpackers, he had wandered into some of the heaviest snowfall the San Jacintos had seen in nearly half a century. And another storm was heading his way.

Donovan was almost 180 miles into his trip when he was last seen near Saddle Junction, where the PCT crosses the Devil's Slide Trail. Like other thru hikers, Donovan had mailed himself boxes of provisions—to post offices in Anza, Cabazon, Big Bear, Agua Dulce, and points north. He picked up boxes in Anza on May 2 and signed the PCT register. When a friend back home hadn't heard from him for a while, she checked with all the post offices to see if he had picked up his supplies. Donovan had never made it to Cabazon. By the time a search party was organized and scouring the region, it was Memorial Day—nearly a month after he had last been seen. After several days, the search was called off. Nothing of his had been found. No gear or green tarp. No body.

John Donovan and his yellow backpack had vanished.

❧

Up on the mountain, Allen and Day heard voices, so they felt reassured. They couldn't be too far from the tram. But their fear rose as they seemed to be going in circles. And the voices were no more than echoes. When night descended and the temperature began to fall, they had to make a decision: either keep moving in hopes of finding their way back, or stay in one place in case a search party was trying to find them.

Unbeknownst to them, however, no one was looking for them. The tour guide assigned to bring the forty-three attendees back to the conference did notice that Allen and Day were not with the group, but she assumed they would just catch a later tram back to Palm Springs. And the conference dinner that night didn't have assigned seats, so no one noticed their absence. Even the hotel staff would incorrectly record that they had checked out of their room, despite their belongings still being there. Luck was not with them that day.

They passed the night in a small cave, hungry and freezing. Constant shivering kept them from sleep. When no search party arrived Sunday morning, they climbed toward the San Jacinto summit in order to be visible but saw no one. With no response to their yells for help, they realized they would have trouble surviving through another night of the high altitude's bitter cold. And so by early afternoon, Allen and Day started back down, heading toward lower elevation. As nightfall descended, they were exhausted, having spent all day laboring through the bouldered terrain without food or water.

On the third day, they were following a stream downhill. Things continued to look grim when they stumbled upon a campsite—the first sign of human life in three days. They were thrilled—this could finally mean food, shelter, someone to help. They called out for someone, anyone. Hearing no response, they checked around the camp. Most of the gear was wet and the radio they found had corroded, but in a yellow backpack they found a journal. One of the entries was dated May 8.

"That's today!" shouted Allen, figuring the journal keeper must be nearby. But then the couple noticed something about the date. The year was different. The entry was for May 8, 2005—exactly one year to the day earlier. Allen and Day had stumbled upon John Donovan's camp.

Almost immediately their excitement turned to despair. Even though they found no body, they could imagine only one reason for the camp to be left like that: the owner had died. It began to sink in—if someone with warm clothes, food, and supplies couldn't make it out alive, they probably didn't have much of a chance themselves.

Despite their dejection, they had to go on. The camp still had provisions, and they were going to do what they could to get out of there. Fortunately, the backpack had a small amount of food and Allen was able to use Donovan's navy blue fleece to ward off the chill. Most important were the strike-anywhere matches. Hoping to attract attention, Day used them to start a fire. They saw a distant helicopter, but the fire was too small to attract attention. The helicopter disappeared.

On Tuesday morning, they found an area covered with dried-out vines. Day was determined that they would not pass one more night out there. He added a few dozen dry logs to the vines and struck a match. Soon the whole area was on fire. Finally a helicopter appeared. After three desperate days on the mountain, at points fearing they might never make it out, Allen and Day would be going home.

⚬⚬⚬

In Donovan's final journal entry, written three days after his sixtieth birthday, he indicated he would be heading to a nearby creek. Then he wrote simply, "Goodbye and love you all."

Around 2:45 PM on June 4, 2006, nearly four weeks after Allen and Day had been saved, searchers from Riverside Mountain Rescue Unit found Donovan's body in the waters of Long Creek, wrapped in his trusty green tarp. They were amazed how far he was from the search area of the previous year. His body was near a twenty-foot waterfall, less than a hundred yards from where Allen and Day had encountered his camp. Rescuers speculated that he may have slipped from the top of the waterfall into the water below—whether accidentally or on purpose will never be known.

It is true that there are two kinds of stories of lost hikers. Luckily for Allen and Day, Donovan did not return to tell his own tale of being stuck in the mountains. If he had returned, no doubt bringing his matches and blue fleece with him, there's a fairly good chance it would be friends and loved ones telling the story of Gina Allen and Brandon Day.

Donovan sent his friend Chris Hook an email the day before he was last seen. "I hope the snow gods and mountain gods will be kind," he wrote. The gods were certainly kind. But to Day and Allen. Or maybe it was Donovan who was kind. After all, friends remember the gentle soul as one of the most generous people they'd ever met. According to Hook, "In a way, John might have saved their lives. His pack being there helped them to be found. That's how John's life went. Even in his death, he was helping people."

Today, in his honor, the John Donovan Memorial Walking Trail sits outside the Virginia hospital to which he dedicated half his life.

WILDERNESS AND THE GEOGRAPHY OF HOPE – "CODA: WILDERNESS LETTER"

By Wallace Stegner

One of the most significant features of the Pacific Crest Trail, other than its length, is that for almost its entirety it passes through federally designated wilderness or wilderness-quality lands. The wild corridor that surrounds the PCT offers travelers the unique and unparalleled experience of living in and traveling through pristine wilderness for days, weeks, and even months at a time. These wilderness experiences have come to be central to the American character and culture and of great spiritual and emotional value to genera-tions. However, with more Americans now living in cities than outside of them, and more roads in our national forests than in our national highway system, opportunities for extended and dramatic wilderness experiences are rare for most people. Nowhere along the length of the PCT is this more evi-dent than in southern California where the trail skirts the fringes of massive urban sprawl and the PCT right-of-way is under constant assault.

Here, in his famous "Coda: Wilderness Letter," written to California's Outdoor Recreation Resources Review Commission in 1962, renowned western writer Wallace Stegner describes the cultural and personal value wilderness areas have for us and the importance of protecting them. Author of The Angle of Repose, The Sound of Mountain Water, *and many other western classics, Stegner describes the historical, cultural, and spiri-tual reasons PCT hikers treasure their wilderness experiences and return again and again like pilgrims to the wild land of the PCT. Unlike the preceeding stories, each of which have a strong narrative quality, this letter articulates a philosophy of wilderness and bears slow and careful reading and rereading, to savor and absorb each idea.*

Los Altos, Calif.
December 3, 1960

David E. Pesonen
Wildland Research Center
Agricultural Experiment Station
243 Mulford Hall
University of California
Berkeley 4, Calif.

Dear Mr. Pesonen:

I believe that you are working on the wilderness portion of the Outdoor Recreation Resources Review Commission's report. If I may, I should like to urge some arguments for wilderness preservation that involve recreation, as it is ordinarily conceived, hardly at all. Hunting, fishing, hiking, mountain-climbing, camping, photography, and the enjoyment of natural scenery will all, surely, figure in your report. So will the wilderness as a genetic reserve, a scientific yardstick by which we may measure the world in its natural balance against the world in its man-made imbalance. What I want to speak for is not so much the wilderness uses, valuable as those are, but the wilderness idea, which is a resource in itself. Being an intangible and spiritual resource, it will seem mystical to the practical minded—but then anything that cannot be moved by a bulldozer is likely to seem mystical to them.

I want to speak for the wilderness idea as something that has helped form our character and that has certainly shaped our history as a people. It has no more to do with recreation than churches have to do with recreation, or than the strenuousness and optimism and expansiveness of what the historians call the "American Dream" have to do with recreation. Nevertheless, since it is only in this recreation survey that the values of wilderness are being compiled, I hope you will permit me to insert this idea between the leaves, as it were, of the recreation report.

Something will have gone out of us as a people if we ever let the remaining wilderness be destroyed; if we permit the last virgin forests to be turned into comic books and plastic cigarette cases; if we drive the few remaining members of the wild species into zoos or to extinction; if we pollute the last clear air and dirty the last clean streams and push our paved roads through the last of the silence, so that never again will Americans be free in their own country from the noise, the exhausts, the stinks of human and automotive waste. And so that never again can we have the chance to see ourselves single, separate, vertical and individual in the world, part of the environment of trees and rocks and soil, brother to the other animals, part of the natural world and competent to belong in it. Without any remaining wilderness we are committed wholly, without chance for even momentary reflection and rest, to a headlong drive into our technological termite-life, the Brave New World of a completely man-controlled environment. We need wilderness preserved—as much of it as is still left, and as many kinds—because it was the challenge against which our character as a people was formed. The reminder and the reassurance that it is still there is good for our spiritual health even if we never once in ten years set foot in it. It is good for us when we are young, because of the incomparable sanity it can bring briefly, as vacation and rest, into our insane lives. It is important to us when we are old simply because it is there—important, that is, simply as an idea.

We are a wild species, as Darwin pointed out. Nobody ever tamed or domesticated or scientifically bred us. But for at least three millennia we have been engaged in a cumulative and ambitious race to modify and gain control of our environment, and in the process we have come close to domesticating ourselves. Not many people are likely, any more, to look upon what we call "progress" as an unmixed blessing. Just as surely as it has brought us increased comfort and more material goods, it has brought us spiritual losses, and it threatens now to become the Frankenstein that will destroy us. One means of sanity is to retain a hold on the natural world, to remain, insofar as we can, good animals. Americans still have that chance, more than many peoples; for while we were demonstrating ourselves the most efficient and ruthless environment-busters in history, and slashing and burning and cutting our way through a wilderness continent, the wilderness was working on us. It remains in us as surely as Indian names remain on the land. If the abstract dream of human liberty and human dignity became, in America, something more than an abstract dream, mark it down at least partially to the fact that we were in subdued ways subdued by what we conquered.

The Connecticut Yankee, sending likely candidates from King Arthur's unjust kingdom to his Man Factory for rehabilitation, was over-optimistic, as he later admitted. These things cannot be forced, they have to grow. To make such a man, such a democrat, such a believer in human individual dignity, as Mark Twain himself, the frontier was necessary, Hannibal and the Mississippi and Virginia City, and reaching out from those the wilderness; the wilderness as opportunity and idea, the thing that has helped to make an American different from and, until we forget it in the roar of our industrial cities, more fortunate than other men. For an American, insofar as he is new and different at all, is a civilized man who has renewed himself in the wild. The American experience has been the confrontation by old peoples and cultures of a world as new as if it had just risen from the sea. That gave us our hope and our excitement, and the hope and excitement can be passed on to newer Americans, Americans who never saw any phase of the frontier. But only so long as we keep the remainder of our wild as a reserve and a promise—a sort of wilderness bank.

As a novelist, I may perhaps be forgiven for taking literature as a reflection, indirect but profoundly true, of our national consciousness. And our literature, as perhaps you are aware, is sick, embittered, losing its mind, losing its faith. Our novelists are the declared enemies of their society. There has hardly been a serious or important novel in this century that did not repudiate in part or in whole American technological culture for its commercialism, its vulgarity, and the way in which it has dirtied a clean continent and a clean dream. I do not expect that the preservation of our remaining wilderness is going to cure this condition. But the mere example that we can as a nation apply some other criteria than commercial and exploitative considerations would be heartening to many Americans, novelists or otherwise. We need to demonstrate our acceptance of the natural world, including ourselves; we need the spiritual refreshment that being natural can produce. And one of the best places for us to get that is in the wilderness where the fun houses, the bulldozers, and the pavement of our civilization are shut out.

Sherwood Anderson said it better than I can. "Is it not likely that when the country was new and men were often alone in the fields and the forest they got a sense of bigness outside themselves that has now in some way been lost . . . . Mystery whispered in the grass, played in the branches of trees overhead, was caught up and blown across the American line in clouds of dust at evening on the prairies . . . . I am old enough to remember tales that strengthen my belief in a deep semi-religious influence that was formerly at work among our people . . . . I can remember old fellows in my home town speaking feelingly of an evening spent on the big empty plains. It had taken the shrillness out of them. They had learned the trick of quiet . . . ."

We could learn it too, even yet; even our children and grandchildren could learn it. But only if we save, for just such absolutely non-recreational, impractical, and mystical uses as this, all the wild that still remains to us.

It seems to me significant that the distinct downturn in our literature from hope to bitterness took place almost at the precise time when the frontier officially came to an end, in 1890, and when the American way of life had begun to turn strongly urban and industrial. The more urban it has become, and the more frantic with technological change, the sicker and more embittered our literature, and I believe our people, have become. For myself, I grew up on the empty plains of Saskatchewan and Montana and in the mountains of Utah, and I put a very high valuation on what those places gave me. And if I had not been able periodically to renew myself in the mountains and deserts of western America I would be very nearly bughouse. Even when I can't get to the back country, the thought of the colored deserts of southern Utah, or the reassurance that there are still stretches of prairies where the world can be instantaneously perceived as disk and bowl, and where the little but intensely important human being is exposed to the five directions of the thirty-six winds, is a positive consolation. The idea alone can sustain me. But as the wilderness areas are progressively exploited or "improve[d]," as the jeeps and bulldozers of uranium prospectors scar up the deserts and the roads are cut into the alpine timberlands, and as the remnants of the unspoiled and natural world are progressively eroded, every such loss is a little death in me. In us.

I am not moved by the argument that those wilderness areas which have already been exposed to grazing or mining are already deflowered, and so might as well be "harvested." For mining I cannot say much good except that its operations are generally short-lived. The extractable wealth is taken and the shafts, the tailings, and the ruins left, and in a dry country such as the American West the wounds men make in the earth do not quickly heal. Still, they are only wounds; they aren't absolutely mortal. Better a wounded wilderness than none at all. And as for grazing, if it is strictly controlled so that it does not destroy the ground cover, damage the ecology, or compete with the wildlife it is in itself nothing that need conflict with the wilderness feeling or the validity of the wilderness experience. I have known enough range cattle to recognize them as wild animals; and the people who herd them have, in the wilderness context, the dignity of rareness; they belong on the frontier, moreover, and have a look of rightness. The invasion they make on the virgin country is a sort of invasion that is as old as Neolithic man, and they can, in moderation, even emphasize a man's feeling of belonging to the natural world. Under surveillance, they can belong; under control, they need not deface or mar. I do not believe that in wilderness areas where grazing has never been permitted, it should be permitted;

but I do not believe either that an otherwise untouched wilderness should be eliminated from the preservation plan because of limited existing uses such as grazing which are in consonance with the frontier condition and image.

Let me say something on the subject of the kinds of wilderness worth preserving. Most of those areas contemplated are in the national forests and in high mountain country. For all the usual recreational purposes, the alpine and the forest wildernesses are obviously the most important, both as genetic banks and as beauty spots. But for the spiritual renewal, the recognition of identity, the birth of awe, other kinds will serve every bit as well. Perhaps, because they are less friendly to life, more abstractly nonhuman, they will serve even better. On our Saskatchewan prairie, the nearest neighbor was four miles away, and at night we saw only two lights on all the dark rounding earth. The earth was full of animals—field mice, ground squirrels, weasels, ferrets, badgers, coyotes, burrowing owls, snakes. I knew them as my little brothers, as fellow creatures, and I have never been able to look upon animals in any other way since. The sky in that country came clear down to the ground on every side, and it was full of great weathers, and clouds, and winds, and hawks. I hope I learned something from looking a long way, from looking up, from being much alone. A prairie like that, one big enough to carry the eye clear to the sinking, rounding horizon, can be as lonely and grand and simple in its forms as the sea. It is as good a place as any for the wilderness experience to happen; the vanishing prairie is as worth preserving for the wilderness idea as the alpine forest.

So are great reaches of our western deserts, scarred somewhat by prospectors but otherwise open, beautiful, waiting, close to whatever God you want to see in them. Just as a sample, let me suggest the Robbers' Roost country in Wayne County, Utah, near the Capitol Reef National Monument. In that desert climate the dozer and jeep tracks will not soon melt back into the earth, but the country has a way of making the scars insignificant. It is a lovely and terrible wilderness, such a wilderness as Christ and the prophets went out into; harshly and beautifully colored, broken and worn until its bones are exposed, its great sky without a smudge of taint from Technocracy, and in hidden corners and pockets under its cliffs the sudden poetry of springs. Save a piece of country like that intact, and it does not matter in the slightest that only a few people every year will go into it. That is precisely its value. Roads would be a desecration, crowds would ruin it. But those who haven't the strength or youth to go into it and live can simply sit and look. They can look two hundred miles, clear into Colorado: and looking down over the cliffs and canyons of the San Rafael Swell and the Robbers' Roost they can also look as deeply into themselves as anywhere I know. And if they can't even get to the places on the Aquarius Plateau where the present roads will carry them, they can simply contemplate the idea, take pleasure in the fact that such a timeless and uncontrolled part of earth is still there.

These are some of the things wilderness can do for us. That is the reason we need to put into effect, for its preservation, some other principle than the principles of exploitation or "usefulness" or even recreation. We simply need that wild country available to us, even if we never do more than drive to its edge and look in. For it can be a means of reassuring ourselves of our sanity as creatures, a part of the geography of hope.

Very sincerely yours,
Wallace Stegner

DEEP CREEK PARADISE

By Bradley John Monsma

In southern California, more than any other section of the Pacific Crest Trail, the possibility exists of encountering trailside "wildlife" of the human kind. And hot springs, especially in desert regions, are perhaps the most notorious locations for gathering large crowds in the most isolated of areas. For these reasons, and others, the oasis of Deep Creek Hot Springs has achieved a certain mythical status. After the countless water-starved miles of the southern California PCT, for thru and section hikers, Deep Creek represents a long-awaited, desperately needed, and welcome relief from the miles of rocks, sun, and dry desert air.

However, as Brad Monsma points out, Deep Creek is sufficiently accessible to day hikers, equestrians, and semipermanent residents to create a unique and colorful bouillabaisse on a beautiful weekend afternoon. Like other popular day-hiking destinations along the PCT, these places can provide the long-distance PCT hiker with a jarring culture shock, a disturbing break in the meditative silence of the trail, or a welcome change from the seriousness of solitude. "Deep Creek Paradise" describes the diverse slice of humanity that converged on these spring-fed pools one day and reminds us all that sometimes the wildest animal on the trail might just be human.

I'm kicked back and blissed out from the warm water. My fingers and toes have long since pruned, and I'm imagining just how much like paradise this place could look to someone who has been on the trail since the Mexican border. A perfect hot soaking pool perches in the rocks above the creek just a few feet off the Pacific Crest Trail. This pool cascades into another pool, part of the flow traveling through a PVC pipe to form a hot shower that soothes stiff shoulders. The second pool, palm fringed and six feet deep, cascades into yet another pool close to river level. The flow is strong enough to keep all the pools clean and clear. Next to the so-called paternoster pools is the crab cooker, a body-sized crack where the water comes out of the rock at 112 degrees. People who manage to lie in there for a few minutes come out red as steamed lobsters. Upstream, Deep Creek tumbles down a little rapid to widen next to the springs. Little fish come and nibble at your toes if you stand still.

The best time to arrive at this perfect place is midweek on an imperfect day—a stormy one with a blizzard up above in Lake Arrowhead and blowing rain making a mess of every freeway in southern California. That keeps away most of the faint-of-heart and underprepared day-hiker riffraff.

But today is perfect—a sunny spring Saturday, not too hot. So as I watch the PCT hikers come around the bend, my heart goes out to them. I can see their crests fall, their jaws drop, their ultralight packs get a little heavier. They actually stop walking and almost check their maps to see whether they are really on the Pacific Crest Trail in a designated, official wilderness area. I have long since given myself up to the scene. But now I look around and see through their disbelieving eyes the collection of humanity funneled to the hot springs by trails from all four directions.

Dozens of people in varying states of undress wander through the springs and along the trail. The inevitable sun-weathered old guy pads along the trail toward the hikers with nothing but a t-shirt, tennies, and a can of beer. A motley crew on sandy blankets in the shade of a shrub sits drinking Bud Light and sorting through their 7-Eleven trash for leftover fast food. Across the creek, a few cholos in their sagging cut-offs smoke pot and watch a raven on the cliff. A troop of tuckered-out Boy Scouts arrives up the PCT from where Deep Creek meets the Mojave River. They commandeer the rocky knoll extending into the creek, and as the scouts glance furtively at the naturists and pray they'll be allowed to keep their shorts on, one of their leaders magically pulls a full-sized Coleman stove from his long-haul pack, sets it up on four legs, and starts cooking bacon and eggs in a skillet.

Just then six horsemen and a pack of dogs slide and skitter down the Bowen Ranch Trail. They're wearing six-shooters in holsters and spurs on their boots. One has a shotgun in a scabbard, and he's tied a bandanna over his face for the dust. Somebody says, "What the hell, are we in a movie?" But the guns are real, and suddenly there's an edge to the scene. They thunder up to the springs, tie up the horses, strip naked except for their ten-gallon hats, and jump right in. One cowboy tosses his chaps into the vacant crab cooker.

"That new leather's like a damn suit of armor," he says to no one in particular. "Nearly cut my balls off." His white-hatted amigo chuckles and starts to reply but just shakes his head instead.

The cowboys are cool and easy as they tell the other soakers about how they're training one temperamental young horse to the trail. They tell stories about horses spooked by snakes and bears and by stuff no human being can perceive. They all agree that horses are neurotic basket cases but loveable nonetheless. They talk about the history of the ranches in the desert hills to the north. I come to realize that the cowboys might be the only people here who don't mind the crowd. They're the only ones who didn't hike in hoping against hope that they'd have the place to themselves, that all of southern California would have gone to Disneyland or the beach instead. The cowboys didn't have wilderness oasis fantasies to be abused. It's just the usual stop on a long ride for them, and they take what they can get.

Tired of being upstaged, the old man of the springs—many hot springs have one—describes in detail a goddess who preened on a rock two years ago. This kindly gentleman has done everyone a favor by hiking in a length of hose and siphoning the green algae from the sides of the pools. Another guy tells how he got caught here in a snowstorm once. His clothes got wet, so he sat in the hot springs for two days until his skin started to come off and he had to be rescued by helicopter.

Meanwhile, the pack of dogs is casing the joint fast and purposefully, scaring the hell out of the few little kids and making the parents dash around to lift the littlest ones off the ground. Suddenly it gets loud. Infernal growling and barking erupts as the pack gangs up on a neohippie couple's long-haired shepherd mutt. The mutt's owners leap naked from their pool to the rescue, skating across the slippery granite and screaming at the cowboys to *do something, do something!* They get to the edge of the seething mess of dogs and then pause, thinking better of wading naked into so many snapping teeth.

The cowboys don't budge. They barely even glance at the chaos. "They're just sorting out the alpha male," they say to everyone. "It's all about the alpha male."

The dreadlocked man pauses and looks back at the cowboys, wanting to believe them about the dogs but opening his mouth like he wants to explain a more evolved notion of masculinity.

"Just hop back in and relax," says white hat. "The dogs are going to be fine once they sort out the pecking order and I'm just talking about dogs."

The woman manages to get a hand on her dog's collar but can't drag the mutt away from the pack, what with bare feet on wet granite. And now the dog seems to cower less and the pack is starting to lose interest and turn to sniffing out garbage instead. A few minutes later the couple gives up and comes back to the pool. The shepherd mutt, jumped into the pack, becomes the newest member as it goes back out on patrol.

I look back to the PCT hikers. They've been watching all this and muttering to themselves. But they've been on the trail for days, and the pools are too enticing to pass by. They find an open spot to drop their packs and their clothes. As they approach the pool, one of the cowboys welcomes them in an exaggerated cowboy drawl. "Come on in, pardners. Plenty room fer everbody."

We all scooch over and they slide slowly up to their necks into the hot water. They sigh and close their eyes as the trail miles and the local chaos disappear. Enough room for everyone.

IN SICKNESS AND IN HEALTH

By Jonathan Stahl and Amanda Tyson Stahl

As many Pacific Crest Trail hikers have experienced—especially along the hot southern reaches of the trail—it is common to battle sickness, fatigue, dehydration, and heat stroke. From coping with ordinary thirst and soreness to life-threatening medical conditions, maintaining one's physical (and mental) health is a critical concern for all backcountry travelers but especially for PCT thru hikers. Most extended trips on the PCT include experiences that test our mettle.

Although there are many Good Samaritans in this story, the Stahls also introduce one of the premiere "trail angels," Donna Saufley. Trail angels—a part of trail culture most familiar to thru hikers—populate every stretch of the PCT. But nowhere are they more abundant or, in many cases, necessary than along the southern California sections of the trail: resupplying water caches, providing rides to trailheads, offering showers and food, providing an address for mailing supplies to, and working many other kinds of trail magic. Many a PCT hiker will see their own story here in the Stahls' account of their adventures together.

IN SICKNESS (AMANDA)

It was a cold, dark morning on day 32 of our PCT thru hike. I awoke to the insistent beeping of the alarm and blinked a few times to get my bearings. It was unusual for "The Sunshine Couple" to be up this early, but we had big plans. We were going to pull a thirty-mile day to get to Agua Dulce (mile 454), where lies Hiker Heaven, run by the most famous of PCT trail angels, Donna Saufley. We crawled out of our sleeping bags and quickly packed up camp.

The southern California desert had trained us to carefully anticipate our water needs. However, by erring on the side of caution, it was easy to overestimate how much to carry. As we hit the trail that morning, we tried to drink as much as we could to lighten the load. Many hikers would just dump some water, but we were stubborn—"we filtered it, and we carried it this far, so we'd better use it" was our philosophy.

By first light, we were cruising along at a good pace. (That's just under three miles an hour for me, at only five feet tall.) Our cold, creaky limbs were warming up and we were feeling strong and well hydrated. We refused to yield to the high winds that threw sand in our eyes and tried to knock us over as we dodged heavy Coulter pinecones falling from above. By 9:30 AM we'd walked the eleven miles to the ranger station, completing the first third of our day. Perfectly positioned to achieve our thirty-mile target, we settled down to take a break and fuel up.

It was slim pickins, though. Our stove had broken 170 miles ago near Big Bear City. We'd arranged to have its replacement sent to the Saufleys', figuring we could get by with cold food in the hot desert. Unfortunately, we'd misjudged when trading some items in our last mail drop for cold foods. As a result, we were desperately hungry for the five-day section from Interstate 15 to Agua Dulce.

We scarfed down what food we had rationed for second breakfast and I filled up our water for the next leg. We threw on our packs and took off across the hot sand to head for the next water source, an RV park at the highway eight miles away. After a while, I started to feel queasy and my pace slowed. Jonathan drifted farther ahead. My mind wandered back to the ranger station, and suddenly I had a sinking feeling deep in my stomach: we did not have nearly enough water to get to the highway. For some reason, I had spaced out and filled enough water bottles for only four miles instead of eight. This was not good. I scurried to catch up with Jonathan, to tell him and apologize. We're a team and we counted on each other not to make this kind of mistake. I felt terrible and very worried.

There was nothing to do but to beeline for the RV park. My stomach grew more upset, my mind foggier. Suddenly, I was afraid I would faint, so I laid down on the trail. Very quickly all my breakfast was lost. Now the situation was downright dangerous.

Earlier that morning, climbing toward the ranger station, I'd sensed that my electrolytes were out of balance from drinking all that water. I craved salt, but we didn't have any quick fixes, so I'd waited until we stopped. But that was too late. My system was too out of whack to digest properly, and my brain wasn't functioning well when I'd counted the number of miles' worth of water we'd need.

I still had no choice but to walk. It was mostly downhill—a mixed blessing. We'd been hiking at about 5000 feet for a while and would be heading down toward 2000 feet, where it would be even hotter. Still, as my energy faded, I was glad to let my momentum carry me downhill toward water, shade, and rest.

IN HEALTH (JONATHAN)

I felt bad for Amanda. She wasn't doing well. While I'd appreciated her offer to take care of our water at the ranger station, I couldn't help but be disappointed by her serious miscalculation. I tried to ease her guilt by saying, "It's OK, I just want you to remember this the first time I mess up when we're married. It'll be my 'get out of jail free card' and maybe save me twenty dollars on flowers."

As I held back Amanda's hair, I watched what could have been a much-needed second helping of eggs shoot out over the hot sand. The poor thing had ingested so much water that morning without enough salt that when she ate her sodium-rich freeze-dried eggs her body didn't know what to do. It expelled her supply of food, water, and electrolytes, and we were low on all three. We'd underestimated our caloric needs for this section and were especially low on salty foods. We tried to replace the soups and pasta we'd ditched at I-15 with Subway sandwiches, but those could only travel so far. I was swimming in my pants after four hundred miles, and now we had to ration our food. Survival instincts intact, we'd constantly checked our watches against our time-control plan, determined to reach the Saufleys' that day.

Our only choice was to head for the RV park to rest, rehydrate, and reassess our ambitious plan. Unfortunately, Amanda weakened with each step. I was worried that she was at risk of serious heat exhaustion. I resolved to do anything possible to get her out safely. I drank sparingly, gave Amanda the last batch of Gatorade, took some of her pack weight, and tried to keep her cool by wetting her hat. It was still a few miles to the RV park, and it was slowgoing.

Fortunately, an old friend from our first week on the trail had reappeared that morning. Old's Cool and his ancient external-frame pack were destined for the Saufleys' that day too. He shared his precious water and agreed to push ahead to the RV park to get some water ready for us. I shouldered Amanda's pack so she could keep moving slowly forward. When I spotted Old's Cool up on a ridge with his cell phone, I was a little perplexed, but I kept my focus on the wobbly Amanda and on trying to hike with two packs. We caught up with him at a dirt road where, he informed us, a "taxi" would pick us up. I wondered, how would a cab find us on some forest service road in the middle of the desert? Given the circumstances, we agreed and waited in the shade of a nearby shrub. We could hardly believe what happened next.

The hum of what sounded like chainsaws reached our ears before a team of about twenty convicts clad in orange jumpsuits came into view. Their supervisor stopped to speak with Old's Cool. Instantly, the humming ceased and the supervisor hopped up to meet us at the shrub. Trained as an EMT, he asked Amanda a series of questions, stopping momentarily to radio for assistance. What's your name? What happened? When was the last time you ate? Drank? And so on.

Really, Amanda knew she just needed to get out of the sun to recover, and our ride was already on its way, but then the local fire chief arrived. Handing us each a bottle of Gatorade, he proceeded with the same series of questions. He insisted we drive down the dirt road to meet an ambulance, just to be safe. Emergency response protocol—can't argue with that. We helped Amanda into the cab of his pickup, then Old's Cool and I climbed in the back, somehow finding a place to sit amid an array of tools, a giant cooler, our three backpacks, and five hiking poles.

We drove a quarter of a mile, with Team Orange following on foot, and met the ambulance bearing a team of paramedics who were ready to put their skills into action. One moment we'd been alone in the middle of the desert and the next my exhausted and completely overwhelmed fiancée was in an ambulance, surrounded by a horde of people, mostly male, the majority of whom were convicts, being pummeled with questions: When was the last time you went to the bathroom? Are you taking any medications? Birth control? As a wilderness first responder, I understood the need to follow protocol, but I also knew we just needed to get Amanda to Hiker Heaven as soon as possible. When the paramedics realized that further medical attention wasn't necessary, the head paramedic asked, somewhat confused, "Well, then why did you call us?"

"We didn't," Amanda answered. Then the head paramedic looked at the fire chief, who looked at the work crew supervisor, and we all looked at each other in silence for a moment. We were free to go.

Meanwhile, our driver was waiting patiently alongside her white Subaru wagon. Not yet recognizing the meaning of Old's Cool's "taxi," I was baffled—this fashionable, athletic-looking, energetic "cab driver" had found her way here with Gatorades in hand. Who was she?

None other than Donna Saufley, trail angel extraordinaire. I know it wasn't intentional, but Amanda sure picked the best place to get sick. In twenty minutes we were whisked away to Hiker Heaven, where Donna had prepared the "honeymoon suite" for us. There were about thirty hikers staying at the Saufleys', camping on cots under big white tents across their lawn.

Our "bounce bucket" was easy to locate among the many other hiker packages, which were shelved alphabetically in the Saufleys' garage. A bounce bucket (and there were many of them on the shelves) is mailed by PCT hikers from one resupply to another and contains extra supplies that will be needed later on. Amanda put on her clean t-shirt and I helped her into the neatly made bed. With a cool, wet washcloth, bottle of Gatorade water, and a strategically positioned trash can, Amanda was comfortable, but I desperately needed food. I had only eaten one energy bar in the last seven hours and was eager for substantial town food.

Amanda was in no shape for a bike ride to town. Neither could she think about food or suggest what might sit well: "Something bland, maybe sweet or salty, or just whatever you think." I walked through the aisles of the store, feeling clueless but concerned, asking myself, "Is this bland enough? Would this be OK?" After an awkward mile-long ride uphill toting three bags of groceries on a rickety old bike, I returned to my fiancée feeling completely overheated and ravenously hungry myself.

"I wasn't sure what would sound good to you, so I picked up a rotisserie chicken, Kettle Chips, garlic bread, Triscuits, cinnamon buns, cold cereal, milk, bananas, ginger ale, juice, and a pickle." Amanda was surprised I hadn't eaten yet. Vacillating between the roles of self-preserving thru hiker and loving fiancé, I think I waited to eat with her as if to demonstrate my devotion or to be romantic or something. She was feeling a little better, but not at all ready to devour food as I was poised to do. What ensued was anything but romantic. Unable to wait any longer, I plopped down on the floor, stripped off my sweaty t-shirt, tore open the packaging, and lifted an entire chicken to my face.

Getting sick on a long-distance hike can be extremely unpleasant. It's also a challenge for the partner who picks up the slack. Amanda would get her turn to play caregiver up the trail in Oregon and Washington. Hiking as a couple on the PCT (and alternately volunteering to hose the vomit out of the other's shoes) showed us the true meaning of caring for one another "in sickness and in health."

WILD ECHOES: CARRION FOR CONDORS

By Charles Bergman

As you walk the Pacific Crest Trail through the western portions of the Transverse Range and north along Tejon Ranch, it is, once again, possible that you may see a California condor. Although still precariously positioned, the species has returned from the absolute brink of extinction. As a result of the most expensive species conservation project ever in the United States, by November 2010 there were 381 condors known to be living, with more than half of that total in the wild.

When Charles Bergman was introduced to the California condor in the mid-1980s, less than a dozen birds were in the wild, and conservationists were at odds about the strategic approach to their revival. In a time when mammals and bird species are disappearing at an alarming rate, this excerpt from Bergman's Wild Echoes *muses about whether the isolated achievement of condor renaissance overshadows the reality of sweeping loss and extinction. Bergman uses this case of the condor to ask much larger questions about the relationship of humankind to nature.*

I

I wasn't supposed to see what I saw. It had taken a month of patient persistence and all the subtleties of deference to get access to these condors, to be in this place at this time. It made me a witness—not to a nicely managed public-relations triumph but to a secret no one wanted to own.

Across the canyon, a condor in a pine tree was acting strange. For years, the condor has been intensely studied by the biologists I was with: Her life and her habits had been scrutinized, her nest closely watched, her mating studied, her eggs even taken to zoos to hatch, her babies raised in captivity. The most intimate moments of her life were known. But now she sat there like a stranger.

She was AC-3—"Adult Condor Three." Her mate, AC-2, sat just below her in the same pine. Of the six California condors (called in Latin *Gymnogyps californicus*) left in the wild, they were the last successfully breeding pair. They were the rarest birds in North America.

Now, in December 1985, something was wrong with AC-3. Except for very short flights, the two condors had not left this roost for over a week. That was not like this pair. Their habits were well known, since all the wild condors at this point wore radio transmitters and were followed daily. Normally, AC-3 and AC-2 foraged in the arid grasslands and on the ranches during the day and flew back to their remote roost in the mountains at night. Something was definitely unusual—maybe AC-3 was very sick. [...]

Condors are the biggest birds in North America, amazingly big. And black. In flight, with their wings nearly 10 feet tip-to-tip, they have sometimes been mistaken for small planes. [...] The story of the California condor in the twentieth century has been a story of death and loss happening right before our eyes, as we watch helplessly. Estimates of the condor population in the past vary widely and, since the bird loves to fly over huge ranges, are necessarily very rough. The best estimates nevertheless trace a steady, ineluctable decline. Major loss seemed to come between 1880 and 1920, caused largely by shooting and egg collecting. Before then, the bird soared in skies as far north as Washington and even British Columbia—Lewis and Clark reported condors on their journey down the Columbia River. [...] Between 1920 and 1950, the condor's range had shrunk to southern California [...] by 1975, the number had dropped to forty-five. The population declined suddenly to about twenty in 1980, when a major effort was galvanized to save them through the formation of the Condor Research Center.

Still, matters worsened. In 1984, despite a staff of twelve full-time biologists, the Condor Research Center knew of only fifteen condors in the wild, with five breeding pairs. But in some ways, the future for the species looked brighter than it had for decades, since a captive flock of eighteen condors had been created, amid intense controversy, in two zoos—the Los Angeles Zoo and the San Diego Wild Animal Park.

Then came a disastrous winter. By March 1985, biologists realized that six of the wild condors were missing. In the space of one winter, 40 percent of the wild population had vanished, and only one condor carcass had been found to suggest why (high levels of zinc and lead in its blood). Worse, in this latest group of losses, four of the last five pairs of breeding condors either died or were broken up, leaving only AC-3 and AC-2.

Of the nine condors remaining in the wild, three more were captured and placed in the zoos. [...] The controversy was whether we should leave the six [remaining] in the wild, try to protect them from whatever was killing them, and try to preserve habitat for future condors if the species were ever restored or whether we should capture all the remaining birds, put them in the zoos, and pin all hope for the species on a program of captive breeding. [...] Why— after millions of dollars, after half a century of conservation efforts, after at that time five years of desperate biological triage for the species—why had we been reduced to removing the condors from the wild? [...] It is a question of cultural authority over endangered species, a question of power and impotence.

[...] The project finally broke in a paroxysm of finality and futility—the decision to "bring the birds in." This decision was not a giving up. It seemed, and still does seem, the last and best hope for the condors. Yet, despite the optimism that was attempted in press conferences and news releases, having to capture the condors was anything but a triumph. It was impossible not to feel, especially as I looked at AC-3, that something had happened we could not control.

II

Emotional responses to the vulture, as to other animals, are so strong that we are blind to their arbitrariness. And this is what ultimately victimizes the condor, the wolf, the sparrow, and other animals: our attitudes, which we mistake for reality. What we don't see—and what is very hard to see—is that we choose the facts we believe. I feel tyrannized by beliefs I don't understand, can't determine the origins of, or, worst of all, can't even see as they shape my world. [...] The loathing of vultures stinks of deep cultural roots, so ingrained that our fears seem instinctive.

III

On Easter Sunday, 1987, the last of the California condors in the wild was captured and transferred to a zoo [...] this seemed to bring to a close a long conflict, a scandal really, over what to do with the condors. [...] The ostensible battle was whether or not some of the condors should be left in the wild. On the one hand, conservation groups such as Friends of the Earth and the National Audubon Society wanted as many condors as possible in the wild. For a long time, the U.S. Fish and Wildlife Service supported leaving a contingent of condors in the wild while building a captive flock. The main argument for this position was that having condors in the wild made it easier to protect habitat, and in the long run, good habitat was crucial for the survival of the species in the wild.

On the other hand, the Los Angeles Zoo, the San Diego Wild Animal Park, the California Fish and Game Commission, and several of the biologists on the project (though not all of them) favored capturing all the remaining condors and putting all the hope for the species, at least given the immediate crisis, in a captive-breeding program. Then, if and when captive breeding succeeded, young condors raised in the zoos could be released into the wild and trained to be free-flying.

In one camp were the ecologists, preservationists and traditionalists. In the other camp was a new breed of biologists, ecologically rooted but manipulative and willing to intervene in natural processes.

Of all the people I met who favored keeping condors in the wild, Jesse Grantham was the one I got to know best. [...] Immensely dedicated, Jesse organized his life around the unpredictable schedules of the condor chasing after the birds all day and remaining on call for any emergency. One person on the project called him an "old-fashioned notebook naturalist." When a condor died not long before I met him, it was Jesse who went looking for it in the wilds and found it. And in an almost personal way, he was extremely worried about AC-3, trying to decide whether to risk going after her to see what was wrong, knowing full well that she might die from the stress of the handling.

One time, when we were out in Jesse's pickup, hauling around stillborn calves from a local dairy (he put them out for the condors, so the birds could have "clean," or lead-free, carcasses to feed on), he made clear what was at stake for him with the California condor. It was much more than a single species. He was fighting for wilderness and for a way of life that included more wilderness. [...] Here is the imaginative foundation of the fight to save the condor by leaving it in the wild, by preserving its habitat, by keeping its prehistoric traditions unbroken. It is really a romantic attempt to let the future catch up with the past.

IV

Somewhere along the line our dreams for the condor got tangled up in power-lines and windmills, lead bullets in deer and cyanide baits for coyotes, potshots from guns and collisions with airplanes—a gruesome and disparate list of the ways condors had been dying in the wild no matter how we tried to protect them [...] some new logic would be required to save them. Noel Snyder, more than anyone, articulated and campaigned for a new approach to saving the condors. [...]

Noel's frayed brown sofa, in his living room in Ojai, California, was famous: Condor biologists called it the "Coma Couch." For eight months Noel had lived on that couch—eating there, sleeping there, working there. The preceding March, when the six condors had turned up missing, presumed dead, Noel had begun arguing vociferously to capture all the remaining condors. [...]

The plan Noel developed for the condors was innovative, unorthodox, and obviously controversial—it cost him his job with the U.S. Fish and Wildlife Service. Giving up on the wild population, he proposed a three-part plan: First, catch all the condors and put them into the two zoos. Second, breed them in captivity (which at that time had never been successfully done with condors). Third—and this was by far the most unusual and interesting aspect of the plan—release the condors produced in captivity at some indeterminate later date, and train them in the wild so that they would not fly out of the remote mountains in the Transverse Range north of Los Angeles.

In Noel's view, the condors' current foraging habitat in the ranchlands around the San Joaquin Valley was the principal problem. He took the plight of AC-3, a bird he knew intimately from years of watching her in the field, as further confirmation that the condors had to be removed from that area and prevented from returning to it in the future. It was killing them, and there was nothing anyone could do to stop the birds from dying as long as they remained where they were so visible, so accessible, so vulnerable. Noel called it "terrible habitat." [...]

To help an endangered species, you can try either cutting down on deaths or improving birthrates. Like many of the most endangered species, condors are slow breeders. It takes six or seven years for the birds to reach sexual maturity; then they lay one egg per nest, and are thought to breed only every other year. [...]

The conventional wisdom said that condors never lay a replacement egg [if one is lost], but forty days later, these two condors did lay a second egg. This not only proved that condors "double-clutch," as it's called, but also enabled Noel to get permission to pull condor eggs, take them to the zoo to hatch, and stimulate the nesting condors to lay additional eggs. [...]

When the baby condor hatched on April 29, 1988, in San Diego Wild Animal Park, it was the first condor produced by captive breeding. Named Molloko, it was additional vindication for biologists like Noel, as well as 6.75 ounces of hope for the condor species. Mandan, the program's second chick, hatched in April 1989, bringing the population of condors to twenty-nine. [...]

Noel encouraged me to meet with Mike [Wallace], then fresh from years of experiments in Peru, where he had been releasing Andean condors into the wild. On the basis of his work there, as well as what he knew of experiments with griffon vultures in Europe, he was utterly convinced that he could not only release California condors into the wild successfully but also train them to do exactly what he wanted. [...] Mike will use what he laughingly calls "carcass management" to teach them to fly, eat, and breed completely in that area. Using birds that have never before been wild, he'll teach them a new tradition in the safety of a remote wilderness. [...]

Opponents like Jesse Grantham are left someplace between a guffaw and a howl at the prospect of trained condors. Condors are birds of flight, they say. That's what the 10-foot wingspan is all about—the birds think nothing of flying 100 miles at the drop of a hat. Not only would trained condors [...] be a desecration of the birds' dignity—one step away from feeding them Kibbles and Bits on [late night talk shows]—but it's close to biological hubris to believe we can totally control such a bird.

V

We should ask ourselves, why we are willing to allow biologists to tell us what a condor is, plan its future, control its fate. It is hard not to suspect that there is something convenient for us in this arrangement, something useful to us in having the condors in the zoos, something all right in the failure of the condors in the wild. [...]

This is taking us closer to the secret of the condor. Its extinction is not a local problem, the result of shooting or lead poisoning or even habitat loss. Nor is the epidemic of extinction in our time a local problem. It is a necessary consequence of our way of seeing nature and relating to it. The fact that we define extinction largely in biological terms, instead of, say, social or psychological terms, is simply an expression of the way we see nature—an expression of what caused the problem in the first place. Biologists may have some stunning successes with endangered species, and they may even save the condor. I hope so. They have enabled the brown pelican to make an exhilarating comeback and have helped the peregrine nest in tall buildings of our cities. But these are isolated achievements in a landscape of much more sweeping loss and extinction—thousands of plants and animals in danger. During the twentieth century, mammals and birds have disappeared at the average rate of about one species per year.

Biologists may be able to document the problem, but surely we are not so naïve as to think they can solve it. They cannot solve it because the scientific way of understanding nature has helped cause the problem. [...] Underneath, it was about science as power. [...]

What has happened in the particular case of the condor is a symbol of what is happening more broadly with other endangered species. By trying to control animals through "bio-power," we create failures while we create successes. The focus on a single species, the emphasis on identifying problems, on generating solutions, and on gaining control over nature—these are the forms of power expressed in our current approach. [...] The problem of endangered species is only superficially a biological problem. Endangered species are the inevitable expression of our power over nature.

VI

The biologists decided [...] to try to catch AC-3. They had to learn what was wrong. [...] For almost a month she had not left Bittercreek Gorge. She was so weak that when [they] finally captured her, they just walked up and grabbed her.

Their worst fears were confirmed by tests. The high levels of lead in her system, present for at least two months, had slowly debilitated her. The lead had poisoned her system. She could eat but not digest. (Lead paralyzes the peristalsis, and the gut freezes up.) AC-3 was starved, scrawny, dying. Her crop was in fact engorged. There had been so much damage to her nerves that she was not able to swallow any of the meat in her crop. [...]

AC-3 was taken to the San Diego Wild Animal Park, and veterinarians treated her for lead poisoning. They laid her out on a white antiseptic table, stuck plastic tubes in her to feed her intravenously, and pumped her system repeatedly, trying desperately and futilely to clean her out. Fifteen days after her capture, on January 18, 1986, AC-3 died.

VII

The closest I have ever come to heaven was the time I flew with condors. [...]
The pilot was Buck Woods, a young biologist who specialized in radiotelemetry
work from planes.

[...] By late afternoon, the two condors [AC-8 and AC-9] decided to
take off. They were so big that they needed a cliff, good winds, and a running start. With their wings flapping for balance, the ungainly pair lumbered
down an open slope, making toward the cliff, and then lifted themselves
into the air currents of the mountains. The warm air of afternoon carried
the condors into an easy, dreamy glide, so different from their cumbersome
movements on the ground.

In the air, the condors had another culture, built on winds and air and
wings. Next to us, AC-9 cruised on giant wings, body immobile, steady and
strong. The feathers at the tips of his wings blew and fluttered as he glided
through the air. His head swiveled, the way a modern dancer isolates and moves
a single body part. I looked out of the plane window, watching his red head
rotate while he flew, looking below, looking sideways.

And looking straight at me.

There's nothing like being transfixed in the gaze of a spectacular wild animal. Always it's a shock to me—the sudden recognition of strangeness. In the
condor's stare, I felt a disorienting self-consciousness that came with losing my
role for a precious moment: I was no longer sure whether I was the seer or the
seen. I got a fleeting sense of what I must look like to the condor, both of us
made visible in the same light of day. [...]

AC-8 and AC-9 spun together in lovely pirouettes above their roost. The
sun burned red along the horizon, and the condors hovered just above the canyon. The late rays of light splashed off their broad wings. Emblems of the species, polished and brilliant and unforgettable, the two condors hung just above
the dark abysses below.

AGUA DULCE TO BAKERSFIELD...
THE HARD WAY

By Dave Claugus

As the Pacific Crest Trail crosses the Mojave Desert, one cannot help but contemplate one's own death. Dotted with names like Death Valley and Deadmans Gulch, and with a frontier history that still seems to live and breathe in the present, the very land itself seems fixated on death and dying.

Many PCT hikers know well the hardships of this region—long miles without water, sunburn, heat stroke, and others. However, nothing compares to the dread a backcountry hiker feels the moment a serious injury occurs. In contrast to the Stahls' story, "In Sickness and in Health," Dave Claugus's reinforces the risk of solo hiking, even in an age of cell phones. (A risk further reinforced in Jim Rea's "The Rescue of Over the Hill Jim" and Carolyn Eddy's story in the Oregon/Washington volume.) In this real-life survival story, he captures the emotions and determination many hikers have felt who have had to seek rescue in the wilderness.

Claugus also introduces us to a threat to the arid ecosystem of the Tehachapis—the irresponsible and illegal presence of off-road vehicles. Endemic in many stretches of this fragile landscape, ORVs have at best rutted and obfuscated portions of the PCT, at worst obliterated the trail.

I left Agua Dulce and the gracious hospitality of the Saufleys feeling reenergized and optimistic about the final 110-mile leg of my journey. After sharing a few moments with long-distance solo trekker Andy Skurka, who passed me on the trail on his way to completing the Great Western Loop, I quickly walked to Lake Hughes some thirty miles away, where I picked up a resupply package.

While at Lake Hughes, I decided to stay the night at a place called the Rock Inn, which turned out to be a curiosity straight out of the Old West.

Aptly named, the Rock Inn is built entirely of river rock. All of the structural walls are stone. Upstairs there are a few small rooms for rent, with a bathroom down the hall. Downstairs is a large saloon and restaurant, with a long walk-up bar and numerous round tables perfect for playing cards. The owner is a brassy and buxom woman in her mid forties, who could easily answer a casting call to play Miss Kitty in *Gunsmoke*. The majority of the other patrons were bikers (new millennium cowboys?), who would stop in for a snack, a beer, and to flirt with Miss Kitty before roaring off down the town's main street. Resisting the temptation to order a shot of whiskey, I instead ordered dinner. Before long I was listening to the in-house entertainment, an acoustic medley of country-and-western as well as blues tunes. The music added immeasurably to a nice meal. I slept well that night.

The next day I pushed hard, walking about twenty-seven miles, stopping just short of where the trail crosses the Antelope Valley and the Mojave Desert. I woke up early the next morning in anxious anticipation of the famed desert crossing, where water is nonexistent and the snakes are numerous.

In one of the great ironies of the PCT, to cross the Mojave Desert you actually walk alongside and often directly over the Los Angeles Aqueduct, as this is one of the few public easements in the area. The feeling of walking across the desert mile after hot, thirsty mile, knowing you are just a few feet from an endless but unobtainable stream of clear, cold, fresh water is nothing short of surreal. I worked hard to focus my thoughts on anything but the aqueduct and in the end managed just fine. For all my anticipation, the desert crossing turned out to be just another long trail without water.

I camped that night at a dry Cottonwood Creek, with jug water supplied by some of the many anonymous trail angels who provide much needed support for PCT hikers in southern California. After a quick dinner, I settled into my bag and, while listening to a local radio station, drifted off to sleep knowing that I had just twenty-two miles to the end of my hike.

The first ten miles of the next day included about 2000 feet of elevation gain but were uneventful. Then came the motorcycle trails. As I got into the Tehachapis, I found it increasingly difficult to stay on-trail because there were motorcycle paths everywhere, obscuring the PCT. Repeatedly, I found myself off-trail, which meant time and energy expended to find my way back to the correct route.

About 2:00 PM, I again found myself off-trail. I walked up a steep slope of about fifteen feet to see if I could spot the trail from a higher vantage point. No luck. As I was walking down the slope, everything changed in an instant. Probably because I was tired, distracted, and frustrated by the repeated task of finding the correct trail, I lost my concentration just enough to slip and fall. As I fell, I heard a snap as loud as if you were breaking a branch across your knee, and I immediately knew that I had broken a bone in my foot or leg. (As it turned out, I broke three metatarsal bones in my foot and both the tibia and fibula bones of my right leg.)

Instantly, I knew my hiking trip was over and my survival trip had begun. I checked to see if I had a compound fracture which, fortunately, was not the case. I tried to put weight on my right foot, with excruciating pain as the result. I thought I would pass out if I pursued this option. I also tried my cell phone with no luck—no service. Then I checked to verify how much water I had remaining (forty ounces) and how much food was left in my supplies (two thousand calories). Knowing I was off-trail, alone, and that the nearest hiker was at least a day behind me, I decided that my best course of action would be to try and find the PCT and, in the process, maybe find a place where I did have cell phone reception. How to do this? Scooting on my butt or crawling on all fours seemed like my only options.

So I opened my pack, got out my foam sleeping pad, and tore part of it into two sections about six by twelve inches each. I folded those over on themselves and, using first-aid tape, secured them to my knees as pads for crawling. Then I retrieved a pair of extra socks and wore them as gloves for my hands. Finally, I cinched up my pack and started crawling. I crawled with determination, knowing that if I allowed doubt to slip into my mind, I would be a goner for sure. While I was hoping it wouldn't come to it, I was prepared to crawl the entire six miles to the nearest paved road, where there would be help. This might have taken me two to three days, but I repeatedly told myself that I would and could do it.

After about a grueling hour and a half, and just a half mile of progress, I tried dialing 911 on my cell phone again, again with no luck. Then I thought about trying another number: I called 411 and got through to the operator! She asked what number I wanted. I replied, "911." Her response was, and I quote, "I am sorry sir. I can't connect you to that number." Before I could argue, we got cut off. Go figure.

Next, I tried a friend in Sacramento and to my joyful surprise got through. I quickly told him I was in real trouble, but before I could say another word the call ended. I was crestfallen. I tried again and fortunately got through. And fifteen seconds later we were cut off again. This time I'd been able to communicate some additional information. This process of calling, getting out just small bits of information, and then getting cut off repeated itself five or six times before I knew my friend had what he needed in order to call for help. Finally, I turned off my cell phone to save the battery.

At this point I still hadn't found the true PCT and, for simplicity, I'd told my friend I was on the trail. So I kept crawling, trying to find it, and to my great relief I finally did, but only after another mile of excruciating progress. I also found that I had better cell phone reception. I called my friend again, and together we determined that the rescue helicopter, which by this time had been searching for hours, was looking for me on the PCT east of Tehachapi-Willow Springs Road—I was west of the road instead. My friend, who by now was driving hell-bent for leather to Bakersfield to provide whatever help he could, called the police again and got them redirected.

About a half hour later, I heard the sheriff's helicopter for the first time. It missed me. More disappointment. Just fifteen minutes later, though, it did locate me and landed nearby, to my grateful relief. The final two hundred yards of my hike was on the back of a very strong deputy sheriff who just wouldn't let me crawl to the helicopter, despite the difficulty of carrying me uphill to the aircraft.

It was getting dark as I was loaded onto a stretcher—the medevac team started an IV, pumped me with pain killers, and flew me to a hospital in Bakersfield. I was struck by the irony that I had always planned to return to Sacramento via Bakersfield—just not in a helicopter. At the hospital I was fit with a temporary cast and released around midnight.

Looking back on this experience, I was initially very disappointed— disappointed that I had not completed my trip under my own power. Now, with some reflection, I am focused on the 552 miles I *did* walk rather than the 6 miles I didn't. I am focused on my determination to survive my injuries despite the difficulties. And I am focused on the help and support my friends and family gave me during the hike, my rescue, and my subsequent convalescence. I am a fortunate man. And I will be out hiking the PCT again—this time using trekking poles!

THE LAND OF LITTLE RAIN

By Mary Hunter Austin

Many different sections of the southern Pacific Crest Trail, near the Tehachapi Mountains and the Mojave Desert, will bring to the hiker's mind the vivid descriptions of this "Land of Little Rain," captured here by Mary Austin. From the stark ridgelines of this region, hikers can look to the east, across vast stretches of sprawling desert, basin, and range. In the valleys and stretches of trail at lower elevation, PCT hikers will encounter much of what Austin describes here. A resident of Owens Valley in the early 1900s, Austin was an inveterate desert traveler and a successful writer, capturing the unique beauty and wild diversity of the California desert in such works as The Land of Little Rain, The Country of Lost Borders, *and* California: The Land of the Sun, *among others.*

East away from the Sierras, south from Panamint and Amargosa, east and south many an uncounted mile, is the Country of Lost Borders.

Ute, Paiute, Mojave, and Shoshone inhabit its frontiers, and as far into the heart of it as a man dare go. Not the law, but the land sets the limit. Desert is the name it wears upon the maps, but the Indian's is the better word. Desert is a loose term to indicate land that supports no man; whether the land can be bitted and broken to that purpose is not proven. Void of life it never is, however dry the air and villainous the soil.

This is the nature of that country. There are hills, rounded, blunt, burned, squeezed up out of chaos, chrome and vermilion painted, aspiring to the snow-line. Between the hills lie high level-looking plains full of intolerable sun glare,

SOURCE: Excerpted from *The Land of Little Rain*, by Mary Austin (University of New Mexico Press, 1974 [1903]).

or narrow valleys drowned in a blue haze. The hill surface is streaked with ash drift and black, unweathered lava flows. After rains water accumulates in the hollows of small closed valleys, and, evaporating, leaves hard dry levels of pure desertness that get the local name of dry lakes. Where the mountains are steep and the rains heavy, the pool is never quite dry, but dark and bitter, rimmed about with the efflorescence of alkaline deposits. A thin crust of it lies along the marsh over the vegetating area, which has neither beauty nor freshness. In the broad wastes open to the wind the sand drifts in hummocks about the stubby shrubs, and between them the soil shows saline traces. The sculpture of the hills here is more wind than water work, though the quick storms do sometimes scar them past many a year's redeeming.

Since this is a hill country one expects to find springs, but not to depend upon them; for when found they are often brackish and unwholesome, or maddening, slow dribbles in a thirsty soil. Here are the long heavy winds and breathless calms on the tilted mesas where dust devils dance, whirling up into a wide, pale sky. Here you have no rain when all the earth cries for it, or quick downpours called cloud-bursts for violence. A land of lost rivers, with little in it to love; yet a land that once visited must be come back to inevitably. If it were not so there would be little told of it.

This is the country of three seasons. From June on to November it lies hot, still, and unbearable, sick with violent unrelieving storms; then on until April, chill, quiescent, drinking its scant rain and scanter snows; from April to the hot season again, blossoming, radiant, and seductive. These months are only approximate; later or earlier the rain-laden wind may drift up the water gate of the Colorado from the Gulf, and the land sets its seasons by the rain.

The desert floras shame us with their cheerful adaptations to the seasonal limitations. Their whole duty is to flower and fruit, and they do it hardly, or with tropical luxuriance, as the rain admits. It is recorded in the report of the Death Valley expedition that after a year of abundant rains, on the Colorado desert was found a specimen of Amaranthus ten feet high. A year later the same species in the same place matured in the drought at four inches. One hopes the land may breed like qualities in her human offspring, not tritely to "try," but to do. Seldom does the desert herb attain the full stature of the type. Extreme aridity and extreme altitude have the same dwarfing effect, so that we find in the high Sierras and in Death Valley related species in miniature that reach a comely growth in mean temperatures. Very fertile are the desert plants in expedients to prevent evaporation, turning their foliage edge-wise toward the sun, growing silky hairs, exuding viscid gum. The wind, which has a long sweep, harries and helps them. It rolls up dunes about the stocky stems, encompassing and protective, and above the dunes, which may be, as with the mesquite, three times as high as a man, the blossoming twigs flourish and bear fruit.

There are many areas in the desert where drinkable water lies within a few feet of the surface, indicated by the mesquite and the bunch grass (*Sporobolus airoides*). It is this nearness of unimagined help that makes the tragedy of desert deaths. To underestimate one's thirst, to pass a given landmark to the right or left, to find a dry spring where one looked for running water—there is no help for any of these things.

Along springs and sunken watercourses one is surprised to find such water-loving plants as grow widely in moist ground, but the true desert breeds its own kind, each in its particular habitat. The angle of the slope, the frontage of a hill, the structure of the soil determines the plant. South-looking hills are nearly bare, and the lower tree-line higher here by a thousand feet. Cañons running east and west will have one wall naked and one clothed. Around dry lakes and marshes the herbage preserves a set and orderly arrangement. Most species have well-defined areas of growth, the best index the voiceless land can give the traveler of his whereabouts.

If you have any doubt about it, know that the desert begins with the creosote. This immortal shrub spreads up to the lower timberline, odorous and medicinal as you might guess from the name, wandlike, with shining fretted foliage. Its vivid green is grateful to the eye in a wilderness of gray and greenish white shrubs. In the spring it exudes a resinous gum which the Indians of those parts know how to use with pulverized rock for cementing arrow points to shafts. Trust Indians not to miss any virtues of the plant world!

Nothing the desert produces expresses it better than the unhappy growth of the tree yuccas. Tormented, thin forests of it stalk drearily in the high mesas, particularly in that triangular slip that fans out eastward from the meeting of the Sierras and coastwise hills where the first swings across the southern end of the San Joaquin Valley. The yucca bristles with bayonet-pointed leaves, dull green, growing shaggy with age, tipped with panicles of fetid, greenish bloom. After death, which is slow, the ghostly hollow network of its woody skeleton, with hardly power to rot, makes the moonlight fearful. Before the yucca has come to flower, while yet its bloom is a creamy cone-shaped bud of the size of a small cabbage, full of sugary sap, the Indians twist it deftly out of its fence of daggers and roast it for their own delectation.

So it is that in those parts where man inhabits one sees young plants of *Yucca arborensis* infrequently. Other yuccas, cacti, low herbs, a thousand sorts, one finds journeying east from the coastwise hills. There is neither poverty of soil nor species to account for the sparseness of desert growth, but simply that each plant requires more room. So much earth must be preempted to extract so much moisture. The real struggle for existence, the real brain of the plant, is underground; above there is room for a rounded perfect growth. In Death Valley, reputed the very core of desolation, are nearly two hundred identified species.

Above the lower tree-line, which is also the snowline, mapped out abruptly by the sun, one finds spreading growth of pinon, juniper, branched nearly to the ground, lilac and sage, and scattering white pines.

There is no special preponderance of self-fertilized or wind-fertilized plants, but everywhere the demand for and evidence of insect life. Now where there are seeds and insects there will be birds and small mammals and where these are, will come the slinking, sharp-toothed kind that prey on them. Go as far as you dare in the heart of a lonely land, you cannot go so far that life and death are not before you. Painted lizards slip in and out of rock crevices, and pant on the white hot sands. Birds, hummingbirds even, nest in the cactus scrub; woodpeckers befriend the demoniac yuccas; out of the stark, treeless waste rings the music of the night-singing mockingbird. If it be summer and the sun well down, there will be a burrowing owl to call. Strange, furry, tricksy things dart across the open places, or sit motionless in the conning towers of the creosote. The poet may have "named all the birds without a gun," but not the fairy-footed, ground-inhabiting, furtive, small folk of the rainless regions. They are too many and too swift; how many you would not believe without seeing the footprint tracings in the sand. They are nearly all night workers, finding the days too hot and white. Nothing so large as a man can move unspied upon in that country, and they know well how the land deals with strangers. There are hints to be had here of the way in which a land forces new habits on its dwellers. The quick increase of sun at the end of spring sometimes overtakes birds in their nesting and effects a reversal of the ordinary manner of incubation. It becomes necessary to keep eggs cool rather than warm. One hot, stifling spring in the Little Antelope I had occasion to pass and re-pass frequently the nest of a pair of meadowlarks, located unhappily in the shelter of a very slender weed. I never caught them sitting except near night, but at mid-day they stood, or drooped above it, half fainting with pitifully parted bills, between their treasure and the sun. Sometimes both of them together with wings spread and half lifted continued a spot of shade in a temperature that constrained me at last in a fellow feeling to spare them a bit of canvas for permanent shelter. There was a fence in that country shutting in a cattle range, and along its fifteen miles of posts one could be sure of finding a bird or two in every strip of shadow; sometimes the sparrow and the hawk, with wings trailed and beaks parted, drooping in the white truce of noon.

If one is inclined to wonder at first how so many dwellers came to be in the loneliest land that ever came out of God's hands, what they do there and why stay, one does not wonder so much after having lived there. None other than this long brown land lays such a hold on the affections. The rainbow hills, the tender bluish mists, the luminous radiance of the spring, have the lotus charm. They trick the sense of time, so that once inhabiting there you always mean to go away without quite realizing that you have not done it. Men who have lived there, miners and cattlemen, will tell you this, not so fluently, but emphatically, cursing the land and going back to it. For one thing there is the divinest, cleanest air to be breathed anywhere in God's world. Some day the world will understand that, and the little oases on the windy tops of hills will harbor for healing its ailing, house-weary broods. There is promise there of great wealth in ores and earths, which is no wealth by reason of being so far removed from water and workable conditions, but men are bewitched by it and tempted to try the impossible.

You should hear Salty Williams tell how he used to drive eighteen and twenty-mule teams from the borax marsh to Mojave, ninety miles, with the trail wagon full of water barrels. Hot days the mules would go so mad for drink that the clank of the water bucket set them into an uproar of hideous, maimed noises, and a tangle of harness chains, while Salty would sit on the high seat with the sun glare heavy in his eyes, dealing out curses of pacification in a level, uninterested voice until the clamor fell off from sheer exhaustion. But when he lost his swamper, smitten without warning at the noon halt, Salty quit his job; he said it was "too durn hot." The swamper he buried by the way with stones upon him to keep the coyotes from digging him up, and seven years later I read the penciled lines on the pine head-board, still bright and unweathered.

But before that, driving up on the Mojave stage, I met Salty again crossing Indian Wells, his face from the high seat, tanned and ruddy as a harvest moon, looming through the golden dust above his eighteen mules. The land had called him.

The palpable sense of mystery in the desert air breeds fables, chiefly of lost treasure. Somewhere within its stark borders, if one believes report, is a hill strewn with nuggets; one seamed with virgin silver; an old clayey water-bed where Indians scooped up earth to make cooking pots and shaped them reeking with grains of pure gold. Old miners drifting about the desert edges, weathered into the semblance of the tawny hills, will tell you tales like these convincingly. After a little sojourn in that land you will believe them on their own account. It is a question whether it is not better to be bitten by the little horned snake of the desert that goes sidewise and strikes without coiling, than by the tradition of a lost mine.

And yet—and yet—is it not perhaps to satisfy expectation that one falls into the tragic key in writing of desertness? The more you wish of it the more you get, and in the mean time lose much of pleasantness. It is possible to live with great zest, to have red blood and delicate joys, to pass and re-pass about one's daily performance an area that would make an Atlantic seaboard State, and that with no peril, and, according to our way of thought, no particular difficulty. At any rate, it was not people who went into the desert merely to write it up who invented the fabled Hassaympa, of whose waters, if any drink, they can no more see fact as naked fact, but all radiant with the color of romance. I, who must have drunk of it in my twice seven years' wanderings, am assured that it is worth while.

For all the toll the desert takes of a man it gives compensations, deep breaths, deep sleep, and the communion of the stars. It is hard to escape the sense of mastery as the stars move in the wide clear heavens to risings and settings unobscured. They look large and near and palpitant; as if they moved on some stately service not needful to declare. Wheeling to their stations in the sky, they make the poor world-fret of no account. Of no account you who lie out there watching, nor the lean coyote that stands off in the scrub from you and howls and howls.

TALES OF DESERT SYMBIOSIS

By Mike Cipra and Caryn Davidson

The mountains, I become part of it
The herbs, the fir tree, I become part of it.
The morning mists, the clouds, the gathering waters,
I become part of it.
—Navajo chant

Sometimes a particular plant or animal comes to symbolize our kinship with the natural world. From their first exposure to the Joshua tree, Mike Cipra and Caryn Davidson found themselves repeatedly pulled back to the world of the Yucca brevifolia, *an icon of determination and survival. Perhaps it is fitting that the lure of the Joshua tree led both authors into careers dedicated to explaining and protecting this area of the Mojave, through which the Pacific Crest Trail dances and where these still, statuesque forms stand as trailside companions. This is a wonderful story of interdependence—a lesson many PCT hikers learn, a reminder that our own survival is not possible in the absence of a vibrant natural world. The Joshua tree and yucca moth, the desert and the trail—we become part of all that we encounter.*

The Joshua tree first appears briefly along the PCT just east of Big Bear (with the uplands of Joshua Tree National Park visible to the east). But it is not until the PCT crosses the Mojave in Sections E and F that the Joshua tree dominates the desert landscape.

EPIGRAPH SOURCE: *Earth Prayers*, ed. Elizabeth Roberts and Elias Amidon (HarperCollins, 1991), 50.

On a PCT hike to Big Bear this spring, we watched the land transform into something it was not supposed to be. Joshua trees grew in robust bunches beneath pinyon pines and rose out of recently burned scrub forest like spiky green phoenixes. We were at nearly 7000 feet, rarefied air for these sentinels of the Mojave Desert. The elevation ceiling of *Yucca brevifolia* is considered to be a thousand feet lower than where we ate our lunch, surrounded by these perfectly weird and beautiful plants.

Walking the PCT is an invitation to reflect on how poorly the natural world conforms to our definitions. Changes in elevation and topography create transitions in ecological communities, and these changes over the space and time of a PCT journey challenge us to continually reexamine and appreciate the unpredictable earth—the blue-bellied fence lizards that have never seen a fence, the red-tailed hawks with tail feathers that are less rufous than sun-bleached, and yes, the Joshua trees that are technically not trees at all and, moreover, that are not supposed to be here.

We're all refugees from another world up here, including the hikers that share this intersection of dirt and sky, all of us becoming something we never knew we could become. And—this is an important difference from the last two billion years or so of the DNA-defined critters—we're taking the planet along on our particular journey.

MIKE

I was seventeen years old—an angry, awkward kid. Pretty creepy around girls. A constant tide of hormones made me want to crawl out of my own skin. On a sunny day in May, I ditched school and drove a beat-up 1965 Ford from inner-city Los Angeles to the Mojave Desert, emerging from the smog of the LA basin to clear skies and withering heat. I had a battery-operated cassette player strapped in the shotgun seat, pumping this awesome new album by U2 called *The Joshua Tree*.

My near worship of that album was only part of why I wanted to see a Joshua tree so damn bad. Honestly, I wanted to see another living thing that looked as awkward as I felt. I wanted to see branches sprawling in every direction and to caress those sharp daggers that were its leaves.

Inside Joshua Tree National Monument, I parked the car and walked into a whole forest of *Yucca brevifolia*, more than a million of those awkward-looking plants. It was not a religious experience. I was just a lonely human being on Earth, surrounded by trees that looked like people but kept blessedly silent. I found a path in the desert, and I walked for miles.

Mormon pioneers came up with the name we use for this member of the agave family, because they saw the prophet Joshua in the anthropomorphic form of the plant, reaching his hands toward God. I've never believed in anything as grand as what the prophet Joshua saw, but I do believe that my experiences in the desert wilderness led me to a path working in conservation. What else could lead a dopey urban kid to become a park ranger at Joshua Tree National Park? What drives me today to strap on a backpack and walk hundreds of miles on the Pacific Crest Trail?

For an answer, I look to the Joshua tree, a species that has a symbiotic relationship with a particular insect that is crucial to the survival of both species. Joshua trees rely on the female pronuba, or yucca moth, for pollination. As far as scientists can determine, no other animal visiting Joshua tree flowers is able to transfer the pollen from one flower to another. In fact, the female yucca moth has evolved special organs to collect the pollen and distribute it onto the surface of the flower. She lays her eggs in the flowers' ovaries, and when the larvae hatch they feed on the Joshua tree seeds. Without the moth's pollination, the Joshua tree could not reproduce, nor could the moth, whose larvae would have no seeds to eat.

Symbiosis is nature's feel-good story. It gives us hope, as we walk upon this earth, that there is a way for us to live in balance with other living things.

CARYN

I saw my first Joshua trees when I was sixteen. I noticed them through the passenger-side window of my boyfriend's blue, surfer-chic VW bus, and I soon got a closer look when we broke down along the highway on our way to Arizona. While he reattached a valve cover with a length of coat-hanger wire, I wandered and took a mood reading of the landscape. Its unexpected openness made me slightly ill at ease; its unfamiliar vegetation was disorienting. But I was seduced and felt drawn into its idiosyncratic beauty.

Eighteen years later I moved to the Mojave Desert and began working at Joshua Tree National Monument. That improbable development allowed me to become far more intimate with the landscape that I had first glimpsed as a teenager; and it has engendered a visceral relationship that continues to sustain me.

Like a Möbius strip of causes and effects, the Joshua tree expresses the complex interplay of the desert's harsh conditions: Less than ten inches of rain per year, often half that amount. One-hundred and seven degrees in the depths of summer. Twenty-seven degrees at midwinter. Few plants can tolerate the bipolar point spread of the Mojave Desert's temperature range. But without the desert's extreme temperatures, the Joshua tree's meristems, or growing tips, would not undergo the damage required to produce a flower. Without flowers, Joshua trees would be incapable of attracting the female yucca moth, whose singular agenda—finding food for its larvae—ensures that the flowers' pollen is distributed so that, after fertilization, the fruit appears. The sacrificial fruit nurture the larvae, and although many more seeds are produced than are eaten by the emerging moths, the vast majority of those seeds are eaten by hungry desert animals.

The improbability of a Joshua tree seed falling on the ground, germinating, and surviving into treehood is enormous. In fact, it is estimated that around half of the young Joshua trees in the national park owe their existence to "nurse plants." In this not-so-symbiotic relationship, seeds that have fortuitously landed in a perennial plant, such as a blackbrush, receive protection from foraging rabbits, ground squirrels, mule deer, and wood rats. Once the young tree is established, at around four years old, its leaf blades are fibrous and tough enough to withstand the assault of the herbivores. The Joshua tree grows up through the nurse plant and kills it.

And adolescence does not always preclude animals from gnawing on the Joshua trees. In drought years, one can see widespread evidence of animal desperation: blunt leaf blades have been chewed off at their base; pseudobark is stripped away from trunks and branches; and holes have been burrowed to gain access into the Joshua tree's roots.

In the continuous quest for food, termites bore into the soft wood of dead Joshua trees, while opportunistic yucca night lizards—North America's smallest reptile—devour the termites. In the unending concatenation of appetites, night snakes eat the lizards, hawks swoop down on the snakes, and many are fed. It has been said that nature is a conjugation of the verb *to eat*, in both the passive and active voices.

☙❧

The Joshua tree doesn't merely tolerate the Mojave Desert's seeming inhospitality—it has thrived in this harsh place. It depends on the intense mood swings of this vast ecosystem. But take it from two former teenagers who now live in the desert and walk in its mountains: those Mojave mood swings are changing. Climate change is driving desert temperatures up, and some researchers are predicting that the additional few degrees of stress will cause the Joshua tree as a species to disappear from great swaths of its southern range. How this may affect the ecological web connected to those forests of Joshua trees is anyone's guess.

So do we continue to consume without sentiment or regret, as nature sometimes teaches us? Or do we attempt to live in a symbiotic balance with the world, as nature also teaches us?

It is initially painful for us as organisms to consume less. But as anyone who has walked the PCT knows, it is also very freeing to make do with less, to distill our possessions to a level of supreme efficiency, and to do all this while connecting with the natural world. There is no "silver bullet" to addressing climate change, but reducing our consumption is a great start. And so is walking the earth, for that matter.

And when you find yourself walking on the PCT, take a moment in the cold of morning or the heat of noon to stop among the Joshua trees. Maybe you will be lucky enough to see a Joshua tree in bloom, its massive cluster of lilylike flowers looking like an absurd growth of popcorn perched on a branch of sharp green leaves. Maybe you will be able to look inside the wet bloom and see the wings of the yucca moth glowing with pollen.

There is an awkward hope in the natural world, improbable sources of strength that sustain us on the trail, beauty that haunts us importantly throughout our lives. Sometimes these moments suggest new ways of interacting with other creatures. And sometimes, when we witness the world undressing itself, that experience has enough power to alter the fundamental path of our lives. It is not naïve to believe we can change. This is simply what walking on the earth teaches us.

CLIMBING A RIDGE IN WIND

By Linda "Blue Butterfly" Bakkar

When preparing for a walk along the Pacific Crest Trail, we typically anticipate the challenges of rain, snow, or blistering sun, consider the possibility of encounters with wild animals, and ready ourselves for the requisite physical exertion. But rarely do we expect to be assaulted by a withering, fatiguing wind. We're not talking about a gentle cooling breeze or a warming morning zephyr. We mean the angry blast created by the rapidly warming air along the desert, east in southern California, that pulls the mad rush of cooler air from the west. "Convective mixing" meteorologists call it.

The tempest is at its most intense when forced into the relatively narrow openings offered by mountain passes. There is a reason why wind farms have sprung up along the San Gorgonio and Tehachapi Passes. The inevitable unequal heating and cooling creates a daily atmospheric maelstrom.

Linda Bakkar describes her battle with the exhausting gale in the semiarid mountains that form the "Sierran Tail," the high country well south of Walker Pass.

The southern California portion of the Pacific Crest Trail is mostly desert land, though it is not flat. The trail climbs and descends over and around strings of hills and ridges, which are covered with a variety of bushes and cacti—and in the springtime, they are sprinkled with gardens of tiny, brilliantly colored flowers. Water is scarce. Shade is a welcome treat when it can be found.

In the late spring of 2008, I had hiked more than six hundred miles from the border with Mexico. I was attempting to thru hike the PCT. On this particular day, I reached the road to Willow Springs, near the slopes of Pinyon Mountain, and the wind was fierce. Occasional stands of Joshua trees grew in this area, and colonies of evergreens lined the tops of the higher hills. But I was in the open, and I was in for a challenge.

The wind had been blowing since the day before. Clouds were hovering over the Sierras to the north, and some were breaking away to spread out and race across the sky. At times, they blocked the sun but were then quickly pushed on by the turbulent air. Since this part of the trail had a reputation for being hot and dry, I was surprised to feel the coolness of the increasing wind.

The wind, oh the WIND! It was cold too. Though I was mostly in the open, I could see the trees on the ridgetops thrashing with the force of the wind, and the sound of it was so loud that I had to shout to be heard by my hiking partner.

I came to a water cache, where gallon jugs of precious water were tied together with a blue nylon rope, in the shade of a stand of Joshua trees. I drank a full twenty ounces and then filled all my bottles for that day and the next—there would be no water for the next fifteen miles. I silently thanked the trail angels who made this water cache available. I shouldered my pack, heavy with four liters, and turned to look up at the next section of the trail.

The rugged mountain loomed in front of me—with cliffs, rocky ledges, and gritty slides. Trees at the ridgeline were bending and swishing in the wind, and the noise frightened me a little. If it was this bad down here, how would it be way up there? I had to do it, though.

I started up the trail with my usual steady pace—step with the right foot, pole plant with the left arm, step with the left foot, pole plant with the right arm—and music entered my mind to keep the beat of my steps. But it didn't work this time. A gust of wind slammed me toward the hillside, and I had to reach out with my poles at an angle against the slope to regain my balance. I began again, but the wind pushed at me from the front, and I struggled against it.

When it subsided, I realized the trail actually made a very gentle ascent as it switchbacked upward. But the wind drove at me, and I had to use extreme effort to move into it. Then a rogue gust hit me from the uphill side, and I had to brace myself to keep from pitching out over the bank.

I finally made it to the end of a switchback, continued around the corner, and turned back the other way to work my way uphill. Now the wind knocked me forward, pushing me from the back, pushing my raised foot farther forward than I had intended, and making me struggle just to keep from running. When I got to a place behind a tree, I had some relief. But in one or two steps more, I was out in the open again and fair game for the wind. It was a battle I fought, a battle to gain ground and not get pushed off or down. "What am I doing out here?" I wondered. "This is dangerous!" I prayed. And I kept going.

When the wind diminished, between gusts I moved as fast as I safely could to get more trail behind me before I had to brace again. The sparse trees provided a moment of relief, but I couldn't just stand there using a tree as a shield. I had to keep going.

As I struggled, I found myself groaning and grunting with each step. I looked to see if anyone else was near enough to hear, but I was alone on that part of the ridge—so I just let the sounds come out as they would, because maybe it would help.

At last I made it around the top of the ridge and found a slope covered with trees—and they took the force of the wind, while I walked more easily. I was exhausted. My feet hurt, my knees hurt, my ears hurt...everything seemed to hurt. But I was grateful I had the stamina to climb that ridge and that I had the opportunity to experience and meet such a challenge.

I found a flat spot for camping, and though it was early I decided to stay the night. The trees were battling the winds for me, deescalating them, and what was left was powerless as it flung against me in little wisps. I loved the trees for their protection.

Lying down to sleep, I used ear plugs to cut the noise of the thrashing branches and howling winds. Then, in the morning, all was still. A few birds chirped as the sun rose, but the wind had died. I packed to head north, on trail that was new to me. A new day had begun.

THE MANY FACES OF TRAIL MAGIC

By Barney "Scout" Mann

It usually does not take many trail miles before backpackers begin dreaming about food—invariably food they are unable to carry or prepare on the trail. That certainly explains the temptation to indulge in trail-town excess—the family-size pizza for just one person, the second order of a burger and fries, or the large stack of pancakes with the omelet chaser.

Other stories in these volumes introduce the concept of trail angels and trail magic, but none make trail magic the complete focus, as Barney "Scout" Mann does here. So imagine, after endless days of rehydrated meals on the trail, the attraction of a buffet complete with pasta, salad, vegetables, and fresh fruit. It is an instant and welcome oasis in one of the bleakest landscapes along the Pacific Crest Trail. Now that truly is magic.

TRAIL MAGIC *(noun)*: An act of unexpected good will toward hikers.

If this was free association and you heard the words *trail magic* on a psychiatrist's couch, you'd think *outdoors, majestic scenery, magic.* Your next thought might be *Mount Whitney* or the name of that secret lake you've told no one about. But in the long-distance hiking world, perhaps the world's most arduous psychiatrist's couch, these two words have a specific meaning. That soda or beer from a car camper, that ride to town when you haven't stuck out your thumb, that trailside cooler left with a note, the homes opened to hikers nearby the trail—whether it's elaborate or simple, planned or unplanned, all are *trail magic.*

SOURCE: A version of this story was published in the magazine of the Pacific Crest Trail Association, *The Communicator* 21, no. 1 (February 2009).

What follows is told in six viewpoints, one act, recounting a planned trail-side meal in the middle of nowhere, June 6, 2007, 625.9 miles north of the Mexican border on the Pacific Crest Trail.

THE PLANNER: BARNEY "SCOUT" MANN

It's day thirty-eight of my 155-day thru hike. A year ago Dan Gizzo asked me, "Where can I help you guys? I have a jeep. I'll help you out anywhere." Dan and I had been adult Boy Scout leaders together. My wife, Frodo, and I conferred, so I told him, "Meet us north of the Mojave Desert, at Road SC47. Cook us a homemade dinner. There may be more than the two of us."

It's spare high desert where Road SC47 intersects the Pacific Crest Trail, a moonscape where astronauts might have honed their survival skills. It's all hard-baked shades of tan, dotted with Joshua trees and scattered, dirt truck trails that might not see a vehicle a week. It's 15 miles into a 20-mile waterless stretch, and that's 20 waterless miles only if you count the man-made water caches. Otherwise, it's 35.5 waterless miles.

Days before Dan's arrival, we put out the word to other hikers: "Trail magic, mile 625.9, Italian dinner, 2:00 to 5:00 PM." Days before, we call Dan twice: "Plan on two to fifteen." Then, "Plan on two to twenty."

The original idea, that Dan provide us a little trail-magic dinner in the desert, has grown faster than a blister on the Hat Creek Rim. He's bringing a two-vehicle caravan packed to bursting with a four-course, four-star Italian dinner. That morning, Frodo and I start hiking sixteen miles away. It doesn't matter. Gusting winds make us grab each other for support. It doesn't matter. Trail magic is on the horizon.

At 1:15 PM., at Road SC47, a hundred yards below the trail, it's like a refugee camp. A score of hikers are huddled under patches of shade and a windbreak shelter. I see worry in Frodo's eyes. Dan's always early. I stifle doubts.

At 2:00 PM, a cry: "Two cars on the road!" From a black Jeep and silver Hummer, food and goods come pouring. Dan and his brother Joe get to work and open what's been dubbed the "Trailside Gizzo Bistro." For the next three hours, we eat, we exclaim, "Oh, you must try a cherry tomato and a grape in one bite" and "Thank you!" We eat, play football, and all swear to love Hummers (at least for a while). Then at 5:15 PM, everything pours back in the opposite direction. Everything. Hikers head out. The site looks like it did that morning. Like Brigadoon, Gizzo Bistro shined, faded, and was no more. How do I say thanks? I can't. Dan, you created a miracle. Trail magic.

THE MAGICIAN: DAN GIZZO

It's four hours into the six-hour drive from San Diego and we're on Highway 14. From Palmdale through the town of Mojave it's a windblown, dusty highway. We're headed north, not sure what's in store. Two four-wheel-drive vehicles, cooking gear, food for twenty, and a map with a large circle around SC47 and the Pacific Crest Trail. We're running late.

Leaving the womb of smooth pavement, we hurl boldly onto the first of six dirt roads. We hit the first bumps. Laughter. The next series sends gear flying. A shovel hits my head. Then we're lost. It takes six miles to get back on track. Finally, seven miles later, we enter that scrawled circle on the map. We crest Road SC47 just before the PCT, and I see figures crawling out from scraggly brush. It's like an apocalyptic science-fiction movie, with dusty, bundled forms emerging. Then one stands taller than the rest, arms waving wildly. It's my old friend Scout.

With many helping hands, we set up a kitchen and buffet table in minutes. Pasta and sauce are cooking; salad, veggies, a huge fruit bowl are set out; and, of course, there are two coolers of soda and beer. Scout said we might serve two to twenty. We're feeding twenty-four! All kinds, all ages, all walks of life. Smiles, laughter, and so many saying thank you. Then there's that wonderful silence that comes when hungry people begin to eat. The boys discover my football and the scene takes on a beach barbeque feel. A hiker named Out There asks, "Can I buy your hat?" I brought my shade hat on a whim. Out There lost his. I give it to him. What made me grab it this morning? Later, at some point, I finally stop trying to deflect all the gratitude. I smile. I absorb it. In the end, I ask one thing. Please be nice to Hummers. Then, the goodbyes. It's hard. My friends are going up the trail. Even though a warm bed and wonderful family await me, I still want to go with them. Scout and Frodo, thank you for letting me be part of this. Trail magic.

THE RECIPIENT: RYLEY "HOOVER" BREIDDAL

After a 4:45 AM start, we've only covered 14 miles and have 10 more miles to go. We overtake a woman hiker. She's going to skip the trail magic. "I don't want a *party* on the PCT. I don't want to see it." All morning, my worry has been the reverse. What if I don't see it? What if I arrive too late? In 600 miles, Gaby and I have never done a 24-mile day, much less 24 miles by 2:00 PM. What if there's no food left?

But we arrive just as hikers line up at the buffet. Real food. It's overwhelming. I feel euphoric and my primal pleasure center fires off like the Fourth of

July: SALT. FAT. HAPPY. Thank you! We're in the middle of nowhere and all this is happening. There are so many thru hikers, so many I've never even met before. Then it all packs up. Gone in a seeming instant. Everybody leaves. With no more miles left in our feet, Gaby and I bed down alone for the night. Trail magic.

The Trail Magician's Wife: Monica Gizzo

It's 5:15 AM. "It won't fit," I say. My sleep-rimmed eyes flit from Dan's stacked supplies to the Jeep and Hummer. It's the same thought I had last night when I measured Dan's four gallons of homemade marinara sauce against our Tupperware supply. Now I watch Dan's brother Joe as he piles boxes in willy-nilly, while Dan carefully places each one, piecing together a jigsaw puzzle only he sees. Dan did so much research that he added a tow chain, shovel, and wood blocks to his gear in case a tire got stuck in the sand. What will the day be like for him?

Magically, it all fits. They drive off, adventure-bound, and my day begins. With a still-new baby, I've just gone back to work. I'm a psychologist, my work is with children with autism, but today our nanny is off, and my charges are my own, Catherine, age two, and Sophia, now five months old. Midmorning, mid–phone call, Dan leaves cell phone range abruptly. What's happening to him now? It's nightfall by the time I hear from Dan again, and the girls are already long since asleep when Dan returns. We unload and trundle off to our warm bed. Dan can't stop talking. He pulsates with enthusiasm as the day's stories unfold. "And then," he continues, "I gave Out There my hat." With a bemused smile, I think, thank you hikers. Trail magic.

Trail Journal Readers:
Shelley Mann-Lev and Eliana Ward-Lev

Over the course of the summer Scout has posted online tales of his hike. Scout's sister and eleven-year-old niece avidly watch for new posts in their Santa Fe home. This is Continental Divide Trail country, and it's now four days after the first scraps of food were loaded into the Jeep and Hummer. Every time a new Internet posting comes, Shelley and Eliana read it out loud. "Eliana, come quick. Two more!" Their faces glow in the flickering light of a million pixels from the computer screen, and the two take on the roles of the far-off hikers as they read. "Eliana, I'm Scout and you're Frodo."

With a voice an octave higher than Scout's baritone, Shelley gives life to Scout's words: "Dan's resupply has grown faster than a blister on the Hat Creek

Rim." Eliana winces. "Yuucck. Uncle Barney hasn't posted more blister pictures, has he?" Then Eliana reads as Frodo: "I didn't sleep well at all last night. It was cold and windy, and I kept worrying about what Dan's trail magic would be like in the middle of a windstorm." Both think they would like to be there. Both are happy to be at home. Both think, Thank you, Scout, for keeping this trail journal. It must be hard to hike those miles and yet steal away time to write. Trail magic.

A Still Small Voice: A Merriam's Kangaroo Rat
A week later, near Road SC47 and the PCT, six paces from where Ryley and Gaby sleep, tiny whiskers poke out from a burrow. It's well past midnight when a Merriam's kangaroo rat darts into the open. It's seven days since her shallow burrow network was largely destroyed. This half acre is her home. She's solitary, territorial. It takes a half acre, 22,000 square feet, to support one three-ounce kangaroo rat.

In the two years since she was born, she hasn't taken a drink. She likely never will. Like all twenty-two species of North American kangaroo rats, she neither sweats nor pants. It's a luxury Darwin dictates she can't afford in the desert. Her body metabolizes water directly from a diet of seeds—boxthorn, saltbush, juniper, bladder sage. And she's cute. Yes, *cute* and *rat* in the same sentence. She looks like a mini kangaroo imagined by a child: rounded, soft, and furry with long hind legs that tuck under a long, tufted, white-tipped tail.

In a single leap she can travel nine feet. When startled she pops two feet straight in the air. And most everything out here likes her—likes her for prey. The high desert is a serious place. When she reaches the outer leg of her gathering foray, she can't believe what she finds. Spilled trail mix—bits of nuts and salted sunflower seeds. Overwhelming! Euphoria! Her primal pleasure center fires off: Thank you. Distracted, she doesn't see the coyote break from cover. Liquid sinew and fur, a streak of desert lightning. On instinct she "pops" and then leaps to her burrow's nearest backdoor. "Where is it? Where is . . ."

Trail magic.

SOUTHERN SIERRA
RANGE OF LIGHT

COVERING SECTION G–SECTION H

Walker Pass—Mount Whitney
John Muir Trail—Tuolumne Meadows

THE BEGINNINGS OF THE
JOHN MUIR TRAIL

By Theodore S. Solomons

Similar to early visionaries like Catherine Montgomery (see Barney Mann's story in the Oregon/Washington volume) and Clinton Clarke, Theodore Solomons is credited with conceptualizing a "crest-parallel trail" through the High Sierra. This was a possibility he pursued on three extended high-country trips in the 1890s. With the founding of the Sierra Club and the publishing of John Muir's The Mountains of California *in 1894, this final decade of the nineteenth century proved to be one of feverish activity in Sierra mountaineering. Here Solomons recounts his early scouting trips and introduces some of the individuals who were later key in completing the work he had begun (such as Joseph LeConte and Walter Starr).*

Notably, Solomons named the spectacular Evolution Valley and the surrounding high peaks—Darwin, Haeckel, Wallace, Fiske, Spencer, and Huxley (all evolutionists of his era)—and developed a remarkably accurate map, which he presented to the Sierra Club in 1896. It was not until 1915 that the California legislature allocated funds to build the Sierra Nevada trail that would become known as the John Muir Trail. The 211-mile John Muir Trail runs from Yosemite Valley to Mount Whitney, mostly on the same tread as the Pacific Crest Trail. Thus, Solomons stands as one of the earliest forefathers of the PCT, and his story is an appropriate way to begin this section on the Range of Light.

The idea of a crest-parallel trail through the High Sierra came to me one day while herding my uncle's cattle in an immense unfenced alfalfa field near Fresno. It was in 1884 and I was fourteen.

Source: Excerpted from "The Beginnings of the John Muir Trail," by Theodore S. Solomons, *Sierra Club Bulletin* 25, no. 1 (February 1940): 28–40.

The Holsteins were quietly feeding, and I sat on my unsaddled bronco facing the east and gazing in utter fascination at the most beautiful and the most mysterious sight I had ever seen. It was May. The rain-washed air of the San Joaquin plain was crystal clear. I have thought since of an earlier May when John Muir waded out into that valley in a sea of flowers and first beheld his Sierra. I must have felt that day in my cruder, boyish way something of the awe and reverence that filled the mature man when he looked upon those zones of light and color—the bloom-flooded plain, the old-gold of the foothills, the deep blue of the forest, the purpled gray of rock, the flashing teeth of the Sierra crest.

I could see myself in the immensity of that uplifted world, moving along just below the white, crawling from one end to the other of that horizon of high enchantment. It seemed a very heaven on earth for a wanderer. And heaven on earth it was—and will be until our new race is very old. I made up my mind that somehow soon I would make that journey.

I found wings for a first skirting flight when I was eighteen and took a long vacation trip from the lower Fresno mountains to Lake Tahoe. There, and in its approaches in Calaveras and Alpine counties, I got my first feel of High Sierra under foot. This initial journey through a mildly contoured, well-mapped region yielded only the personal result of whetting the urge to a full-length crest-wise journey. It took four years of working and saving and some six months of preparation before I was both able and ready for the plunge.

[…] Sidney Peixotto […] had agreed to become a co-explorer with me; and our plan was no less than the complete subjugation in a single season of the entire High Sierra of California. In deference to any delays or difficulties we might conceivably encounter we proposed, however, to take plenty of time to do it during that season of 1892. We were to run into the mountains in early May and emerge when the job was thoroughly done.

The preparatory work included a search for every scrap of information, verbal and graphic, including the county maps. It all proved pitifully meager. In desperation I raided the Surveyor-General's office, and almost swooned with delight when they handed out plat after plat of official land surveys. Apparently the southern High Sierra was not only explored but meticulously surveyed, with section corner stakes set into gorge depths and frowning cliff faces—pitons, perhaps, driven by sledge-equipped eagles! And meticulously platted, with an artistry that rendered every sepia-wash canyon and ridge in bold relief.

I carefully copied on crackling tracing paper every township plat as far south as the Kern River. A singular fact was common to all of them—a paucity of place names, the plats abounding in such vague legends as "High Rock Ridge," "Deep Valley," "Confluents [sic] of San Joaquin River." My spirits rose. There were still trails to be made, scenery to be described, peaks and streams and lakes to be named!

It seems incredible that no one told us, not even the Surveyor-General's staff, who must have been humiliatedly aware of it, that these gorgeous specimens of the draughtsman's art were pure fabrications, the products of an imagination unsullied by the slightest acquaintance with the Sierra Nevada. We discovered it in the field—bitterly.

On May 17, 1892, with a new spring wagon and two small mules which we christened Shasta and Whitney, we started for Donner Lake, were soon bogged in snow, and shipped to Truckee first the wagon and, a bit later, ourselves—an ignominious beginning for explorers. There was a brief respite from snow around Tahoe. After that we were in it and out of it, tracing a staggering course, with much cooling of heels while snow banks melted. We finally reached Yosemite in late June.

There we relaxed. After all, our main enemy, the snow, was going fast, and we had the rest of the summer to explore the southern High Sierra! So we took a month of pure joy in Yosemite before we met young Joe LeConte and made a kind of practice trip with him to Ritter, a foretaste of climbing and a full savoring of alpine grandeur. [...] We started [again] on August 9th. [...] Whitney and I found much in common, many adventures and mighty slim pickings toward the end. But we brought back several boxes of glass [photographic] plates and scads of data of all sorts. Best of all, a start had really been made toward determining the route of the future John Muir Trail.

Court reporting had financed mules, camera, flour and bacon. But I now turned to newspaper work; and the next summer I had a chance to cover the Columbian Exposition in Chicago, and I sacrificed the Sierra for that professional opportunity. But the following year I organized a new onslaught, abetted by Leigh Bierce, son of the controversial Ambrose Bierce.

Meantime the Sierra Club had come into being and I made the acquaintance of John Muir, who now gave me what he remembered of the lay of the high streams and the crests they drained. He had bestowed no place names and made no diagrams, yet I gained substantially from several pilgrimages I made during the next year or so to his home in quest of mountain knowledge.

With Bierce in 1894 I made the blunder, as in 1892, of beginning too far north—in the Grand Canyon of the Tuolumne this time. When we started out the precious month of July was two-thirds gone. But I knew the place to be superb and that it needed photographing badly. At that time a practical camera outfit, in both bulk and weight, was about twenty times the encumbrance it is now, and the descent of the Canyon was a clothes-tearing, mad enough scramble without such a handicap.

Bierce and I made the descent without accident to the plates or otherwise. Our chief difficulty was getting back to Yosemite. The law of diminishing returns worked well for us in the matter of our food supply—too well, for we fasted nearly three days. But the utensils and the forty-pound camera equipment got no lighter on the five thousand foot climb out of Pate Valley. In an older butcher shop in Yosemite I feverishly developed the plates. And, that done, again I turned to the high mountain route, and with a pack horse and two jacks we took the shortest way to the place on the South Fork of the San Joaquin where I had left off two years before.

[. . .] I had found that from the Tuolumne southward at least to the headwaters of the Bear-Piute divide it was entirely feasible to lead a pack animal as close to the crest as one would ordinarily care to camp. Indeed, the course that had been pursued was, with little deviation, precisely the present route of the John Muir Trail. But from the head of Bear Creek it was, then as now, the Piute Basin that was the sticker.

That problem we were about to tackle—rather naively, considering that September was drawing to a close, when a heavy snow storm scared us half to death, so that we shot our animals "to save them from a worse fate," abandoned our outfit, including the precious exposed plates, and went floundering out of the mountains. I often wondered why I had not had the sense to wait out that storm; for rarely, anywhere, does a first snow stay.

This misadventure left me with an emphatic preference for old snow rather than new; so it was bright and early next year that Ernest Bonner and I resumed the quest where it had been interrupted. We headed for Bear Creek and found the remains of the abandoned camp.

The big camera in its case seemed perfect. But when I grasped the strap and withdrew it, it fell apart into many pretty little pieces of wood. The glue had dissolved.

On Bear and Mono Creek, I made several knapsack trips out of which many pictures, topography sketches and place names were born. The reconnaissance was pretty thorough and yielded the conclusion that the zigzag forming the Bear-Piute divide was practically impassable for us. Nor does it appear to have improved since, for the Muir Trail avoids it and crosses Selden Pass.

Bonner and I got back to our summits by ascending the South Fork, avoiding the basin of Piute Creek altogether and exploring the next one, which turned out to be the true head of the San Joaquin River, though it now bears the name Evolution Creek. [...]

[...] As I photographed and sketched I felt that here was a fraternity of Titans that in their naming should bear in common an august significance. And I could think of none more fitting to confer upon it than the great evolutionists, so at-one in their devotion to the sublime in Nature.

From several heights I could see that at the head of the basin was an easily accessible gap or pass to the highest Middle Fork streams of Kings River. In a dream that night I even *saw the trail*.

Returning to the South Fork Canyon and ascending it, we found the sheepmen were right and the Whitney Survey wrong—the river reached no higher than the southern ridge of Goddard, miles from the crest. We climbed the mountain then set out to follow the Goddard divide to the gap (now the Muir Pass) on which I had pinned my hopes. But snow, rain and hail drove us, soaking, down.

We reached lower Goddard Creek the next day, and, the following, that flower park called Simpson Meadow on the Middle Fork. Then we fought our way down the canyon into Tehipite Valley, visited Tehipite Dome, made a cut-off to the Tunemah Trail, and on to the great South Fork Canyon. [...]

I had now completed a kind of reconnaissance of the unexplored High Sierra. It fell short by perhaps ninety-five percent of the original preposterous scheme of a complete exploration. But I had at least followed down the range from Yosemite to the Kings River Canyon, and that is what I had made up my mind to do. The vast Alpine complex called the southern High Sierra remained much as it was—terra incognita; and I had gained a whole-hearted respect for the job! But the ground was broken and a skirmish line traced from which in subsequent years J. N. LeConte and others of the exploring group of the next two decades continued the battle against the unknown.

I assembled the data and worked out in detail the results of the series of expeditions and made them into an elaborate report [which included the following:]

a map of the region, and an album of 139 views of the principal scenery encountered. *[...]* Under a special head at the end of the report

I described a continuous route through the High Sierra from Yosemite
to Kings River Canyon over which animals may be led. *[…]*

On the same day LeConte presented a new map which embodied the topo-
graphic results of all my exploration as well as of his own and others.

I made two trips in 1896. […] One was with Walter A. Starr and Allan L.
Chickering, who accompanied me on a three week mopping up trip over part
of the ground I had covered in previous years.

I attempted some improvements in the northern part of the route during
the following summer—that of 1897. [. . .] A humiliating experience awaited
me, prelude to my last high mountain journey in the Sierra for thirty-five years.
I had an appointment of many months' standing to lead a party of the United
States Geological Survey into the upper Merced-San Joaquin High Sierra; and
as, of course, they would be mounted it was plain that I should be mounted,
too, if I expected to keep hoofs off my heels. My pack mule, whom had [been]
dubbed Mule-o, was a young and lovable animal, but he had never been rid-
den. I conducted Mule-o into the Crocker field opposite the house, got a saddle
on him without difficulty, though he turned and nibbled at the stirrup rather
thoughtfully. And then I mounted—and immediately dismounted. . . . Mule-o
really attended to that.

The stage-station porch had been vacant when my sleek little friend and I
began our séance. I had wanted it to be just that way. But this was like a fire or
a murder. By magic, Crocker's porch became peopled with stable hands, stage
drivers, tourists and the sympathetic Crocker family. Unseemly laughter rang.
[…] I rode Mule-o finally; but besides the dubious honors of the encounter I
carried away—in my person—several parts of the rail fence which Mule-o had
used to rub off his back a very large and persistent horse-fly. He made a model
riding mule, and much impressed the geologists, whose mounts, as perhaps I
may impart after forty years, were nothing to brag about.

I hoped that by interesting the Geological Survey in our California Alps as
an economic asset they might speed up the survey of the High Sierra. This little
inspection tour was helpful, for the next year Marshall had the Lyell Quad-
rangle on his plan table. […]

[To summarize,] the series of expeditions opened the way for travel parallel
to the crest; and by roughly orienting the drainage systems and establishing a
series of landmarks they furnished a considerable body of data which facilitated
the subsequent and much more extensive work of continuing and perfecting the
route. The John Muir Trail of today was the final result.

WILDERNESS BOUNDARY

By Walker Abel

Much of the Pacific Crest Trail runs through formally protected wilderness areas and extensive expanses of quality wildlands, making the PCT one of the wildest of our nation's long scenic trails. In 1964 the Wilderness Preservation System was established with the following words: "In order to assure that an increasing population, accompanied by expanding settlement and growing mechanization, does not occupy and modify all areas within the United States and its possessions, leaving no lands designated for preservation and protection in their natural condition, it is hereby declared to be the policy of the Congress to secure for the American people of present and future generations the benefits of an enduring resource of wilderness."

The Wilderness Act goes on to define wilderness as "an area where the earth and its community of life are untrammeled by man, where man himself is a visitor who does not remain," further noting that wilderness areas contain "ecological, geological, or other features of scientific, educational, scenic, or historical value" for all Americans. In the following piece, Walker Abel, an instructor for the Sierra Institute, one of our nation's premiere outdoor-education institutions, reflects on the vital lessons we learn about ourselves and our place in the world when we take the time to cross the "wilderness boundary."

A professor of mine used to make a repeated theme of the "wilderness boundary," always distinguishing between the physical boundary, marked by a Forest Service sign, and the elusive psychological boundary marked, we generally assumed, by the sudden growth of hair on the back or the irresistible urge to crouch amidst the sagebrush, tilt the chin toward the stars, and howl. He himself was something of a shape-shifter, adopting one persona at the chalkboard in the classroom and another altogether when the wind was blowing along the night ridge. Of course, when you're a professor of humanistic and transpersonal psychology in northern California in the 1970s, you're not worth much to your students unless you dare to dart in and out of the shadows on the fringe.

Some years after this tutelage, I came to also teach at a university and to lead groups of college students on extended field trips into the wilderness. From the very start and continuing now through twenty-two years of this work, I've adopted many of my former professor's themes, including this emphasis on the wilderness boundary. I don't think I can claim through the years to have birthed a bunch of wolf pups, but I do like to think that many of my students have discovered something within themselves that was always there but that was waiting for certain conditions before it could show itself.

I'm talking about an ease and comfort in the wilderness, a sense of having returned home. Trails such as the Pacific Crest are pathways into a latent and inherent side of ourselves that welcomes us when we activate it again. To the extent that we evolved in unbroken close contact with the earth, it stands to reason that when we return to that contact, we recognize it as familiar and fall into its mood as we would with an old tune of music we used to love dearly but hadn't heard in decades.

We might consider the Domeland Wilderness in the southern Sierra. This is an area of 130,000 acres within Sequoia National Forest. The Pacific Crest Trail passes through the northeast corner of the wilderness. When I first brought groups to this wilderness, and in particular to Rockhouse Basin along the South Fork of the Kern River, we could drive to within a mile of the river. At road's end, there was a locked metal gate and a Forest Service sign announcing one's entry into the wilderness. That was the physical boundary—we would unload our packs from the van, step over the threshold, and begin our journey.

Before 1964, when Congress privileged this area with federal wilderness status, this gate and boundary did not exist. A person could drive clear to the river and then up and down along the willow and sagebrush terraces on the banks. Certainly even at that time, some boundary was crossed. One has gone to the "mountains," one has gone to the "woods," one has gone to the "river." You left your house and drove over diminishing roads to a camp under ponderosa pines with the sounds of the soughing Kern River all about you.

But for Robert Greenway, the professor I mentioned at the outset, the depth of the wilderness experience involves more than just getting there. And how you get there may affect that depth. This car access had consequences, which my group and I discovered quickly: quantities of broken glass, scattered cans, assorted trash. Over the years, like good minimal-impact campers and volunteer PCT trail crews, we've carried quite a bit of this debris out. One year we found close to two dozen empty cans of an herbicide, which we strung on a line and then tied to a long pole, carrying the dead cans on our shoulders like carcasses.

After 1964, when the boundary and gate went up, the regular deposit of car trash ended. Thirty years later, in 1994, the wilderness boundary changed again. In that year the California Desert Protection Act added 36,000 acres to the wilderness, and now when we wanted to hike in to Rockhouse Basin, our vehicles encountered a gate and boundary about four miles farther to the east. This of course made the hike in (and out) a little more difficult. Now it was five miles to the river instead of one. The boundary had intensified. The threshold was more challenging to cross, the guardians more ferocious.

Yet it has never been Greenway's or my contention that difficulty of access in itself creates a deep wilderness experience. In my university groups, it is common that several participants have never backpacked before. Therefore I tend to pick locations that are fairly easy to reach but that aren't overly popular. Still, what makes our wilderness areas what they are is that you have to walk in (or ride a horse). That one limit—no cars—instantly means the majority of Americans won't bother to make the effort, and so the area is preserved in more or less its "untrammeled" state. This can be seen up and down the entirety of the PCT's wilderness-quality corridor. Even when it passes through lands without wilderness designation, the pedestrian character of the PCT has preserved its wilderness quality.

In the case of the Kern River, despite the expanded wilderness boundary, the trail there remains fairly easy. It follows the old road and is almost entirely downhill. From the high point in pinyon pine forest, an enticing view presents itself of the river below, with its green corridor of bankside willows and, on its flats, large ponderosa pines. Though the full length and breadth of Rockhouse Basin is not yet visible, still students can see a hint of where we are going and can feel the allure of a welcoming base camp. The river valley is the only apparent flat land in a great expanse rolling away to the west of steep ridges and exposed granitic domes. Partway down the trail, the green fragrant pinyons give way to standing charred skeletons where the forest burned some years ago. Though they have their own beauty, the dead trees tend to silence the students, most of whom have never been through a hot burn site. Their minds perhaps full of the chatter and music of the passenger van we traveled in, or of the recent town where we bought supplies, the students begin to quiet. Now the weight of the pack, the rhythm of the steps, the feel of wind and sun, the tone of these leafless trees all work together to accentuate that we are leaving one world to enter another.

For all PCT backpackers, leaving the car is a significant moment. From the first step, what the walking in does is create a separation from our common, human-centered world. Though humans are part of the world, and the whole world is one totality, still we can say that at a relative level there is a boundary between the modern human world of pavement, buildings, technology and the more ancient world of rivers, mountains, trees. And perhaps we can also say that as we move from the human world into the wild one, then we also can change, like a chameleon, adapting in some fashion to our new environment. That at least is a premise in my courses, and it is what Greenway meant by crossing the "psychological" wilderness boundary.

Many things contribute to this chameleon change, having to do with such things as a more immediate and intimate relationship to water, air, sun, space, fire, rain, animals, birds, breathing, and so on, but I want to single out one overriding quality of the change that interests me most. I'm talking about feeling ourselves part of something bigger than just the human realm. It is both a humbling experience and yet also one that is profoundly affirming of the self. Mary Oliver writes in her poem "The Buddha's Last Instruction" about sitting open and attentive to the sunrise and feeling the first light upon her, the "ocean of yellow waves," and realizing in that moment that "clearly I'm not needed / yet I feel myself turning / into something of inexplicable value." That's exactly the paradox—a diminishing of grandiosity when one is subsumed into a bigger context and yet simultaneously is validated in feeling part of that very context.

Students always talk of feeling small within the palpable size of the wilderness. It would take a good part of the day to walk from one end of Rockhouse Basin to the other and back again, with the resin of sagebrush coating your shins and knees. You can sit by the river and feel that the water comes from countless snowfields far away, in the rock and thin windy air of the high mountains. Downstream, the long journey is to San Francisco Bay, Golden Gate, and the Pacific Ocean. More immediately, bear are often seen, as well as deer, jackrabbit, and beaver. In addition, rattlesnakes are common, which along with cold and difficult weather, can make clear that we adapt to the world rather than the world to us. Gradually, under these cumulative influences, a mind shaped by wilderness may replace a mind shaped by city life.

Buddhist teachings say that the heart of perfect wisdom and compassion is always within us; we merely have to let the obstructions fall away. I like to think that the same is true of wilderness mind—it wanders lithe within us on untrammeled paws even as we shop the frenetic mall or pound coffee in the stress of the office. A lament of any nature lover is how easy it is in those city or dominantly human environments to forget the reality of wind and rain and the big cycles of the stars and seasons. And worse, with time and repetition, it's easy to take those human environments as the norm.

But maybe it's also easy to remember. The poet William Everson once said, "I have a certain naïve faith in nature, a faith that if you can live in the immemorial presence of its abiding forms a kind of holiness rubs off on you." It is a common aphorism on my programs, and within PCT trail culture, that "Nature is the teacher." I am quite convinced that the main influence in crossing the psychological wilderness boundary is simply the wilderness itself. I'm sure this is why so many of us return, again and again, season after season, to the PCT, the high country, and the simple crossing of the physical wilderness boundary.

And yet we raise obstructions against that influence. As Greenway has often pointed out in his writings, it is easy to carry our culture out with us across the physical wilderness boundary. In other words, we can carry the mall with us, we can carry the office. The trick, I think, is to wear those obstructions down. As in some meditation instructions, where the recommendation is to leave distracting thoughts and feelings alone and to come back quietly to the breath, if we have the intention in the wilderness to leave cultural thought patterns alone and just come back again and again to the present moment, it seems our perspective begins to shift and we feel ourselves as not exclusively confined to the human realm but also as part of the big cycles of nature.

Of course, meditation sounds like the easiest thing in the world until you try it and encounter the terrible demons of boredom and restless thoughts—in the same way, to truly cross the psychological wilderness boundary is not necessarily easy. Ironically, I find that one way to wear the obstructions down can be to stay in a base camp rather than moving every day. While I certainly think there is a place for thru hiking, and I have great admiration for those who undertake major journeys such as hiking the length of the PCT, I want to put in a word for inaction. A fixation on mileage and making time can almost be blinders to what is around us and within us. Furthermore, it is not impossible that all the required daily tasks of breaking camp, hiking, map reading, and setting up camp at the end of the day can all serve as distractions from the moment.

With longer periods of base camping, one retains a sense of leisure. It is in these unstructured leisure moments that I believe the "holiness" rubs off on us.

Students, for example, on a free afternoon, swim or wade across the Kern River and find a shallow cave with a few simple pictographs on the walls and feel something of time and silence and old ways. Or they sit together under the trees and find occasional lapses in the conversation and laughter, and those lapses are easy and spacious as the day itself. The day is going nowhere in particular. No effort is needed to make things right. Something is safe and untouched and has never been the least bit damaged, and they can rest inside it. I'm really talking about a small leak, a little crack in the wall of the self, and into this opening drips a steady, almost unnoticed dose of wind and changing light and odors of earth and leaf. The slow leak, however, happens even as we sleep and is cumulative. It's like invisible hands quietly stuffing the world into our permeable shells, until it's the world inside and out. Then we might understand the Taoist, who says, "Diving into the river, there is no splash."

Often this leak is so subtle in its gradation of change that one hardly notices. It is often upon return to conventional lives that students most notice what has happened. For some, the jarring return to the city environment highlights the contrast between the wilderness and the urban mind. They may look around, like Chief Sealth, for a "quiet thicket" and ask, what have we done to this earth? They may remember the easy camaraderie and the low-stress quality of group interactions in the wilderness and contrast it to the pace and pressures they now see in the world around them, and they may ask, what have we done to ourselves? For many, the leak may reverse itself, and the sagebrush and jackrabbits of Rockhouse Basin will begin to drain out the other way. Then they may ask, what's happening to me? They might begin to feel like scarecrows, a being no longer full of the wild world but now stuffed with something less real.

Fortunately, if nature has been the teacher, it has left them with the lesson of welcome—they know they can walk back across that boundary again. The Pacific Crest Trail and other such pathways do not cease to exist when we leave. It is even possible from afar to feel their continued presence in the world, to suddenly pause a moment while reading the paper and draw solace and strength in the image of a light snow falling right now on the sagebrush of Rockhouse Basin. Or, in getting water from a sleek chrome tap, to feel this is the same earth as the cascading Sierra rivulets where I dip my cupped hands to drink. For very advanced practitioners, getting into the bathtub, there is no splash.

HOMECOMING

By Charlotte E. Mauk

From its earliest origins, the Sierra Club has been associated with explor-ing and protecting the high crest of the Sierra Nevada. For over fifty years the club's "High Trips" took hikers and horseback riders in groups as large as two hundred, supplied with strings of pack horses and led by seasoned guides, into the high country for recreation, education, and conserva-tion. These were not just hiking trips. In the early years, John Muir's The Mountains of California *and Joseph LeConte's* Ramblings in the Sierra *were both recommended readings, while Muir, C. Hart Merriam, and others gave lectures in the field. Although predating the Pacific Crest Trail itself, these High Trips introduced generations of Americans to the High Sierra and, as prominent environmentalist David Brower, first executive director of the Sierra Club, observed, were "the best source of the conserva-tion warrior."*

After years of promoting improved access to the mountain regions as one of its core tenants, in the early 1950s the Sierra Club formally changed its statement of purpose to emphasize the importance of preservation. The High Trips were increasingly replaced by smaller outings, out of a concern for the impact of backcountry recreation. Charlotte Mauk was among those who began to challenge the philosophy of "the more visitors to the Sierras the better."

In this excerpt, however, PCT hikers drawn back to the high country will identify with Mauk's feelings on her return to the southern Sierra on one of the High Trips of 1946, and they will enjoy reading about this early history of High Sierra tripping.

SOURCE: Excerpted from "Homecoming, 1946," by Charlotte Mauk, *Sierra Club Bulletin* 32 (1947): 19–30.

"Just when does a High Trip actually begin?"

I found myself pondering the question as we doggedly put one foot ahead of the other up the long, dry trail. [...] A few days earlier I might have stated readily enough, "Oh, when all the High Trippers gather at the road end for the first dinner in camp."

[...] That night, at Horseshoe Meadow, warm campfire light glowed on the shafts and branches of trees which stood above the circled campers, and sparks danced in rising showers when wood was thrown into the flames. The firelight found lesser echoes in flames still playing in the pit fires in the star-roofed kitchen, or in dying flickers in the stoves, or even in tiny billy-can fires by scattered bedsites. [...] Maybe High Trip begins, for some people, with the first real campfire. [...]

On our high route we were hot and dry—but not that hot. When our course began to swing northward, we could get views across the Kern to the Kaweahs and the tumbled country near Mineral King, and our parched throats were suddenly not quite so dry. We were not yet in the high, cool atmosphere of the mountains we knew, but we had at least glimpsed the kind of country that was familiar to us—and we were moving north. Presently some rugged, serrated crests came into view, timber slopes before us dropped down to green little valleys, and we worked down through beds of lupine to a camp on Rock Creek.

It was at this campsite that I found yet another possible answer to my question. Our camp at Horseshoe Meadow, although nearly as high as this, had looked out to a single rocky eminence and some round and gentle wooded hills; here, though, the horizon was high and jagged, made up of broken spiry crests rising above the highest straggling timber and topping the steep cliffs of irregular granite blocks. The eye was compelled upward. This was actually *in* the mountains, not just a stopover on the way to them. The real beginning of a High Trip may well be the first morning we wake up in a camp—near timberline—from which we can reach truly alpine meadows, explore cliffs and clefts and spires, or climb a major peak.

Even this answer did not satisfy me, though. Neither on this morning nor at any other time had I sensed a moment of demarcation, after which I could tell myself, "Well, the High Trip has really got under way, now." I only knew, with a deep conviction independent of explanation or logic, that I had experienced a home coming. This camp was new to me, yet here, under sheltering trees beside a lush meadow, with austerely beautiful peaks rising beyond, was a familiar high-mountain reality I had been seeking through the haze and heat and dust of those first days.

What it was I had been seeking—and now had found—I could not say. The happiness of a mountain day is not a thing, and cannot be analyzed into so many distinct parts. It is a nonmaterial entity to be experienced and cherished by all the senses, but not to be questioned. Perhaps a part of the charm of mountains is that the very joy of existence is in itself sufficient answer to almost any question. It is enough to recognize, without trying to catalog, the brilliance of the sunshine; the clear blue vault and the answering blueness caught in shadowed clefts; the fragrance that the sun draws from a pine tree; the silver glint on willows dancing in the wind; the crystal smoothness of a streamlet curving through a meadow; those rugged, thrusting crags against the sky; the tender, graceful pattern of tiny plants against a boulder; the sound of wind in branches overhead, from gentle whisper to a surflike roar; the rough and satisfying feel of sun-warmed granite.

One of the finest things about a High Trip is the opportunity for solitude. Not the dubious isolation that one achieves in a city by locking himself into a room which is still surrounded by people and activity, but a release from mechanized compulsion, an opportunity to feel at one with a natural world. To seek solitude in the company of [...] other human beings may seem paradoxical; yet wilderness has a way of absorbing people, imperceptibly. [...] So long as they leave behind them no artifacts nor structures, no disruption of the balanced interplay of indigenous lives, no scars upon the forests and meadows, they can come and go with no damage to the natural scene. Their voices are swallowed by the vastness, their footsteps are not reechoed. [...]

Out of the solitude may grow a sharper perception of the quiet life about us, a deeper appreciation of its features, a fuller understanding of the world's wild beauty. Alone, or with a sympathetic companion, the wanderer in the mountains is receptive to what amounts to religious experience. It may be the culmination of a lengthy crescendo, as the final dazzling brightness of a blazing sunset; the ultimate step onto a summit and the scanning of a horizon which has become ever wider as ridge after intervening ridge dropped below it; the long-awaited breaking of a magnificent thunderstorm which has grown through hours of swelling clouds and brooding purple-gray shadows. Or it may be but a fleeting moment of revelation, as a glimpse of exquisite grace and rhythm in a wind-stirred columbine, the mysterious poignant sweetness of the song of a hermit thrush, the irised flash of flying spray above a pool.

These things, perhaps unanalyzed but surely recorded, make up man's deepest memory of mountain experience. He may never mention to another his own inmost feelings, nor even admit to himself that there is something poetic about his personal response to surpassing beauty. He may scarcely recognize its absorption into his spirit. But the unrecognized recall of a myriad of strangely moving moments of awareness blends into the nostalgia which is evoked by a photograph or a painting, a word picture, or the vivid memory of some mountain scene.

[But] it is the superficial memory, the less significant incident, which a camper is likely to recount when he tries to tell someone else about a High Trip. It probably is the only kind of incident he could describe; inner reactions— or the personal connotations of the simple beauty of grass, rock, trees, flowing water, life persisting in unexpected places—are too private. The big things are always surfaced over, in memory as well as in communication, with little things—those little things that are noticed first, perhaps forgotten soonest, but of most importance in lending color and texture to the pattern of High Trip days. It is the little things that amaze, confound, or amuse the newcomer; the little things whose recall delights the returning old-timer. [...]

With the end of the trip only a day's walk away, little surges of regret must have directed each camper's last-day thoughts to a review of what the two or four or six weeks had brought to him. What must the images have been that superimposed themselves on the grand pattern of cliffs, forests, meadows, streamside trail, rugged colorful peaks, rushing falls and rapids, tranquil lakes, and final rock pass? What inner perceptions intensified the beauty of delicate flowers, moss-softened stones, the glisten of pine needles or their patterned shadow on granite, nodding graceful grasses or the tiny rill chuckling beside them, the countless minutiae which become more precious with each day of mountain experience? It is of these images and these perceptions that a fabric is woven to clothe the framework of remembered itineraries. For each individual the images are—and must be—distinct and personal, yet there are enough common threads to relate all the tapestries and to enrich them with shared interest.

The answer was clear at last. High Trip begins, for any individual, at the moment he first discovers that he is at home in the mountains, and after that it never has to begin again, for it never really ends. There may be breaks and interruption—sometimes for many years—but for that person High Trip goes on as long as his spirit can seek and find mountain wilderness.

HIGH ODYSSEY:
THE WHITNEY CONQUEST

By Orland "Bart" Bartholomew and Eugene A. Rose

While not actually on the Pacific Crest Trail (it is the southern terminus of the John Muir Trail which separates from the PCT nine miles earlier), few resist the Siren call of Mount Whitney, the highest peak in the contiguous United States at 14,495 feet. Identified in 1864 by the California Geological Survey team, it was named for the team's leader, Josiah Whitney. Although summiting Mount Whitney can be treacherous, there are a number of nontechnical routes to the top, including the trail that takes off from the PCT. As a result, a 1956 article in the Saturday Evening Post *reported that "an amazing assortment of people make it to the top.... History records that one man walked barefoot, another pushed a wheelbarrow, and someone tried to ride a bicycle. Some climbers bundle up in heavy coats, some wear bathing suits, and some wear nothing at all. One man went to the top done up in a fashionable business suit with a fedora and a bow tie and carried his blankets and food in a suitcase." But no story trumps that of Orland "Bart" Bartholomew, who spent the winter of 1929 following the Sierras from south to north. He did so using rake-handle poles, ice creepers (boot spikes), and custom-made hickory skis that were shorter and wider than the sport skis of the period. In mid-January, he made his intrepid assault on Mount Whitney.*

A strong wind was blowing, and as Bartholomew emerged from the trees he could see great snow banners sweeping off the upper peaks.

SOURCE: Excerpted from *High Odyssey: The First Solo Winter Assault of Mt. Whitney and the Muir Trail Area*, by Eugene A. Rose. Copyright © 1974 by Howell-North Books. By permission of the Pentrex Media Group.

New snow made the skiing difficult because his heavy pack pushed the skis deep into the powder, slowing his progress to less than five miles that day. But he continued the next morning along the high shelf of the Kern River Canyon and joined the snow-covered John Muir Trail at midafternoon. Nearby on an exposed southern slope he found an excellent campsite free of snow and comfortably close to a good supply of firewood.

Bart rose early the next day, January 9. His assault on Mt. Whitney began inauspiciously enough. A hard wind was whipping his little tent ominously despite the shelter afforded by the campsite. The wind tore at his breakfast fire, whirling up billows of smoke and erratic flames. It was, he thought, an inconvenience to have his meal thus disturbed; little did he realize the wind that day would endanger his life.

While he loaded his pack and made himself ready he could see part of the great mountain. He planned to continue up Whitney Creek and prepare a base camp just above timberline from which to make his try at Whitney's summit. He estimated the distance to be less than four miles with a rise of about 800 vertical feet.

As he set out, he knew the day would be a tough one, for the wind was swirling blankets of snow across the mountainside. Though the sky was clear, he found himself enveloped from time to time in a horizontal "snowstorm" which closed off his level vision at only a few feet. He donned goggles to keep the stinging particles from his eyes.

But as Bart climbed, his view became wider and at each rest stop more of the surrounding landscape lay revealed. At his back was the giant Kern Canyon, running straight and true, north to south. Towering above the gorge, its rugged flanks poking high into the sky, was the Great Western Divide. On his right stood the giant form of Mt. Hitchcock and beyond it the rolling, featureless country he had recently crossed. Directly in front was the huge bulk slanting ever upward, Whitney the challenging—never before topped by man in winter.

The wind became stronger, buffeting him at every step, forcing him to focus all his attention on the task of climbing. At times his heavy pack—which had been an anchor or a drag—became a great sail in the wind. He strained forward, each upward movement seeming to require maximum effort.

A little gully appeared and Bart stepped gratefully down into its partial protection from the wind. There he rested and had an early lunch, abbreviated to crackers, chipped beef and dried fruit to save time. He was dismayed at his lack of progress in the morning but donning a fur-lined parka from his pack, he headed again into the fury of the wind.

The sky had become slightly overcast and he hoped it might signal a lessening in the force of the blow. It was not to be: the wind became stronger. But with his goal in mind he strove on, gaining only inches at times against the invisible force. Leaning, straining, he zigzagged slowly up and around ridges, seeking some momentary respite from the gale. Occasionally he rested, braced against solidly planted ski poles. Then he would go on, slowly, slowly making his way into the white hell.

The wind grew worse. The heavy canvas parka flapped violently while snow, pine needles and sand from exposed points of decomposed granite blasted him. The temperature dropped and the wind continued to gain speed, screaming about him in terrifying fury. Twice he was overturned by the wind and sent tumbling across the frozen surface. Sometimes great corkscrews of whipped snow would envelop him, cutting off the feeble sunlight.

Progress then became impossible: he couldn't ski, couldn't see—even standing took great effort. Never in his high mountaineering had Bart experienced such an alpine hurricane. And yet he pushed on, knowing by now that survival depended on finding some shelter where he could rest the night, for daylight was dimming by the minute. The temperature was falling but the wind continued its relentless battering.

He strained every muscle against gravity and fatigue as he moved on, hoping, praying, for some sanctuary, however slight, which would get him through the night alive. Shelter was imperative, but there was no protection here on the side of the great mountain.

Desperately he peered into the darkening surroundings: above an empty vastness, barren, gray; below the same bleakness. Then, through whipping snow, he saw a large tree braced against a boulder some seven feet high and ten feet long, big enough to afford a windbreak. This would be his campsite.

He peeled off the pack, stepped out of the skis and forced them into a crack in the rock lest they be blown away. His little tent became a flapping monster when taken from the pack, but he managed at last to get it tied to a sturdy branch of the tree and to a fallen log nearby.

Attempts to start a fire were even more frustrating. His matches would be blown out before their feeble flame could ignite the twigs he had laid as kindling; then even the twigs were blown away. Time after time he failed, but he knew that without fire for warmth and cooking he would not survive the night. In desperation, he took his frying pan and a handful of twigs into the tent, put the twigs in the pan and scratched a match. Slowly the flames flickered up through the tiny pieces of fuel and he added more twigs. Ignoring the smoke that seemed to fill the tent, Bart warmed his hands at the rising flame, and when the blaze reached toward the canvas of the tent he tipped the contents of the pan into the firepit just outside. The wind whipped the flames into a fury of sparks and in a sickening moment they were gone.

But a fire was a necessity; so Bart rigged a strip of canvas from his pack as a windbreak and again kindled a fire in the frying pan. This time the flames held, flashing upward through the larger sticks he had prepared. Patiently he added more wood as around and over the windbreak the wind whipped the flames through the sticks with the force of a blast furnace. Bart crouched upwind from the firepit to give the blaze a little more protection. Finally, when he felt the fire was stable he went to his pack and took out the large pot in which he would melt snow for tea. In that moment another monstrous blow came out of the night and once again the fire was whipped to oblivion. Bart crawled into the tent, wrapped himself in his down robe and slept as the night roared away outside.

The drama started in the darkness before dawn. In the high camp on Whitney's western slope, Bart awoke to find clear skies and cold air outside his little tent. The battering storm that had ravaged the mountain a day earlier had vanished. He crept upon the dark, icy stage and fixed a quick breakfast. By the gleam of the campfire he put together a light pack and made ready for the next act of his winter-long odyssey. This was January 10, 1929, the early prologue for another classic encounter between man and mountain.

Bart mounted the skis and moved out just as dawn's light outlined the gigantic form of the mountain above. The first hour went smoothly and he had climbed the lower approach to a maze of chutes that raked the west face of the giant peak. Here he was forced to remove his skis and replace them with ice creepers, which were more suited to the steep, frozen slopes. With the aid of these simple and inexpensive crampons, he climbed well up into the chutes— dragging his skis by a rope tied to his waist. He estimated that he had climbed over a thousand vertical feet when he encountered a pinnacled ridge, coated with ice and snow, intersecting the chute and barring his way to the top. Doggedly he picked his way around the point with great difficulty and managed to clear the barrier.

Then he was moving higher again, looking skyward for the next obstacle. The chute ended under an insurmountable wall which forced him to move over a broken ridge and into a parallel gully. Soon he ran into another barrier, and several times the process of crossing from one gully to another was repeated. While he had the satisfaction of moving upward, he concluded he was lost in a labyrinth of gullies with no idea where the summit lay.

A great feeling of frustration came over Bart. He peered into the basin below, trying to find the speck which marked his camp and thus establish a reference point. He knew his original plan of veering to the north for the summit was being destroyed, but his frustration was tempered with determination. He had often become confused about direction in a heavily forested area, he recalled, but had never thought it would happen here on an open and exposed mountainside!

He glanced up at a new overhanging wall covered with the blue opalescent, high-mountain ice and finally decided to turn southward towards nearby Mt. Muir. Carefully inching his way across another ridge, he entered a larger chute that again led upwards. His enthusiasm was renewed and he progressed easily, again on the skis which allowed him to stay on the frozen surface. The ascent in this broad chute went well at first but slowed as the slope steepened. Once his skis dislodged a large mound of frozen snow which fell far down the hill, disappearing from sight and sound. Realizing that a fall on his part would follow a similar route, he carefully unfastened the skis and replaced them with the sharp ice creepers.

By midmorning he made his first rest stop, pausing long enough to study the maps carefully. Bart estimated his position as somewhere along the 13,000-foot contour, about 1500 feet below the summit. Here the snow was thinner, undoubtedly whipped away by high winds. Yet he moved on up the chute, climbing at an agonizingly slow pace. With each upward step the route became more difficult and occasionally he had to thrust the tail of a ski into the snow—using it as a ladder rung to gain another foot or two. While such antics were helpful, Bart knew they were extremely hazardous, and any slip could be fatal.

By mid-afternoon, with the sun already headed down the western sky, Bart stumbled upon the ice-glazed Whitney trail at an elevation of 13,600 feet.

"Six hundred feet in five hours," he gasped in disgust; he couldn't believe his snail-like progress. But with his goal in sight he moved quickly along the rocky though gentle trail. Now a new adversary—time—had signaled its challenge and he hurried on towards the crude stone cabin atop the peak. He wrote:

> *Though the scramble northward along the crest of the ridge required less sustained effort, there was still much treacherous country to cross. The footing might be at one moment on a narrow ledge of ice-covered granite, the next on a wind-glazed drift. Impatient as I was to reach the summit, it seemed all obstacles known to mountaineers had been amassed to thwart progress. By the time Whitney's broad shoulder had been reached the sun was alarmingly low.*

He moved swiftly up along the rim of the mountain, his ski equipment flung across one shoulder.

In another hour he was there. The summit was under his feet, and above him there was nothing—only the blue-black winter sky.

Bart hurried to the rock cairn marking the actual summit, and as he dropped his pack a feeling of euphoria overcame his weariness. Stumbling to the lip of the sheer eastern wall, he peered down into the valley miles below with all its Lilliputian objects. Instead of the thrill of excitement or triumph there was a feeling of anxiety, an inclination to bolt back down the mountainside. He noted later in his diary:

> *… but even thus fortified, how small the thrill of victory! Rather one is lost in the awe of forces and factors about him: the infinite solitude, the savage terrain, the weird dissonance of the wind. And the danger of being trapped on the mountain by darkness.*

Then he remembered: he hadn't eaten since breakfast, nearly nine hours earlier. He went to his bag for some biscuits and dried fruit. For a moment he rested, ever mindful of the sinking sun in the western sky. Already the long shadows were about, carrying the icy cold that numbed his hands and fingers.

Bart repacked his gear and headed down the trail. He hurried along; thoughts of trying to find his way through the maze of gullies and chutes at night urged him on. Soon he was running back down the trail to a spot near the 14,000-foot level where he remounted his skis.

Now the adversary was descent and the enemy was darkness. With all efforts concentrated on speed, Bart reached the 12,600-foot level just as the sun set behind the distant Kaweahs. Here at the head of one of many long chutes he removed the skis once more and tied them together as an improvised toboggan. With his heels hooked over the tails of the skis, he leaned forward, grasped the bindings and set off straight down the chute, praying that he had selected an unbroken gully.

He found himself propelled downward and gaining alarming speed. The walls of the chute became a blur as he schussed by. Realizing the great risk, he tried to turn off the fall line by turning the skis abruptly to the side. The maneuver sent him catapulting across the ridge and into the next chute, where he came to a grinding halt.

Miraculously, he was uninjured. To complete the descent less perilously, he put on the ice creepers and again mounted the makeshift sled. By digging the creepers' points into the frozen snow he made a slower, controlled run. The new chute turned out to be the right one, unbroken and leading to the lower slopes. He arrived back at camp an hour after dark, thankful for his safety. The casualties were his injured pride, frayed nerves and two pair of trousers which had frozen and cracked during the impromptu descent.

FORESTER

By Suzanne "Tailwinds" Finney

Fear, challenge, courage, and success are themes that characterize virtually any extended hike in the High Sierra. Wading across swollen streams, crossing snow-packed passes, and being exposed to severe weather conditions above tree line can be terrifying. The anticipation that accompanies the approach to well-known challenges can be both exhilarating and debilitating. You read and reread every descriptive word in the guidebook and absorb the nuance of every comment made by those "survivors" you encounter. Although you fight the creeping sense of fear, it begins to gain control. Your muscles go rigid, your balance falters, and your strength seeps away. You become your most raw, exposed, humble self.

Not far north of Mount Whitney is Forester Pass, which at 13,180 feet is the highest point along the Pacific Crest Trail. The trail from the south has been blasted from the barren rock face and can be made treacherous by snow and ice. The north side often has abundant snow. Suzanne Finney returns us to a more contemporary time with her account of crossing Forester with the support of her hiking partner, "Blue Butterfly." In this story she captures that sense of extreme personal challenge and vulnerability that many PCT hikers have felt while climbing its high passes. But there is nothing like the sense of euphoria that comes with suppressing your fear enough to successfully cross the pass, navigate the raging river, or survive the early-season snowstorm.

"There's no snow on Forester."

Yesterday we had received this good word from some young southbound hikers. They told me just what I was hoping to hear. It seemed unlikely that we could be that lucky, but, after all, they had just come over the pass. As we broke camp and started hiking, I was hopeful despite a faint tightening in my stomach.

The morning hike took us through a basin surrounded by peaks. Snowfields many hundreds of yards wide obscured the trail, sun cups frozen in place. I doubted that the pass would be clear of snow judging from our present circumstances. It occurred to me that "there's no snow on Forester" might really mean "I'm such a wilderness stud that snow doesn't bother me." Which is way different than there being no snow at all.

Once we entered the basin, snow slumped into arrays of sun cups that looked like rows of waxy, dripping candles. At first the snowfields were easily navigable. But as we kept climbing, they became more frequent and the trail became impossible to follow. There was much debate in our group about which tiny notch in the seemingly impenetrable wall of rock ahead was Forester Pass.

My thoughts alternated between vague worries and apprehension: Would I be able to handle the altitude? If I slipped on the snow, could I stop myself from falling down the mountainside? Quietly, I just followed the group. The ice ax I carried was no comfort. My experience sliding downhill headfirst on my back near Mount Baden-Powell had reinforced my fear that I was just a passenger on my pack. However, I kept my fears in check, as I did not want to waste any energy I needed to get over the pass. This pass represented a point of success or failure for me—if I could accomplish Forester then I could handle anything.

So I deferred to the experience of Blue Butterfly, who was almost giddy with excitement. She relished this type of challenge and clearly enjoyed the snow travel as well as the routefinding.

Finally we got close enough to the vertical wall of rock to see the switchbacks that had been blasted or chiseled into the side of the wall. They appeared to be clear of snow near the top, although the base of the mountain seemed completely snow covered. One vertical chute near the top was fairly narrow but very, very steep.

Blue Butterfly stayed with me, and her joyous spirit infused me with a sense of fun. I recalled that on the porch at Kennedy Meadows, sharing a cheeseburger with Squatch, a thru hiker, he had related his own experience hiking over Forester. When he reached the top of the pass, he said, hundreds of blue butterflies appeared out of nowhere and flew over his head through the pass. He called it a "magic moment." I wished for a similar magic moment for our Blue Butterfly.

As we started up the steep switchbacks, heartened by how wide the trail was, I did not feel the panicky fear of heights that I had been dreading. This climb would have terrified me six months ago, but experience on the trail helped temper my fear. As I looked back over the territory we had covered, I saw the large snowfields and barren ground that dotted the basin behind us. Ahead, the trail switchbacked precipitously up the vertical wall. Blue Butterfly stopped to photograph the delicate and hardy blue tubelike flowers that grew in the cracks of rock. As I labored uphill, taking short breaths, Blue Butterfly taught me pressure breathing and the rest step—both useful techniques to get me to the top. With each step my exhilaration increased—I was doing it! I was making it to the top! My initial apprehension turned to a comforting certainty that I would make it without mishap or drama.

Then we came to the vertical snow chute.

Snow and my fleeting sense of comfort cascaded steeply from the top of the pass across the trail and continued down at an angle that guaranteed a very long fall, were one to slip. There was no way around it, either above or below. We were close to the top of the pass now, and the walls appeared nearly vertical. I sneaked one small peek down the chute and was sorry that I did. My vision narrowed. It took all my self-control to deal with the immediate problem, which was to take that first step onto the snow and ice.

Hikers who had gone before us had made steps across the chute, but these had not penetrated far into the snow. Shade kept this chute from softening up much. On some level, I understood that the focus and concentration to take this step-by-step would keep my fear from turning into panic.

If I slipped, it was a long, long way down, with a sudden stop at the end. Blue Butterfly called it a good chance for some ice ax training, and out came the ice axes. My heart was in my throat as I imagined the consequences of a slip and fall. The steep slope of snow was not far across, but the icy footprints looked pretty sketchy to me. Blue Butterfly told me to follow in her footsteps and to place my ice ax in the snow on the vertical wall. I faced the wall, twisted between the forward-facing footsteps and the wall of snow to my right.

"Place your ice ax in the hole, like this." *Thwack.* Blue Butterfly's ice ax went in about two inches and would go no further. I followed suit. *Thwack.* The handle of the ax made a nice lever that moved easily from side to side. I couldn't imagine how this was going to save me if I slipped.

I progressed like this, methodically placing the ice ax in a hole, stepping into Blue Butterfly's footsteps. She was exceedingly patient with me, as was Tahoe

Mike, who was undoubtedly rolling his eyes at my hesitancy and fear. We progressed like this: step, ice ax, step, ice ax, step. Or was it step, step, ice ax, step, step, ice ax? I can't remember. I only remember the numb fear and gratitude that I was being coached over this section.

Tahoe Mike, ever the consummate counterphobic, offered to take my picture if I cared to pose. I did not care to pose. I cared only for getting across this slippery slope. I wanted desperately to be safely across. Finally, I could see that we had it made, and with my feet back on solid ground, I flew up the last couple of switchbacks to the clear-of-snow pass, where a sign marked the top: Forester Pass, 13,180 feet. Made it! Now all that was left was the descent on the other side.

"No snow on Forester?" Oh, now I get it . . . no snow *on* Forester. All the snow was on the ascent and the descent.

The entire north side of the pass was covered with snow, with a frozen lake at the bottom. Rather than following the obscured trail, previous hikers had cut across the slope to the southwest. Below, there was a rib of rocks and boulders, and below that the trail descended into a valley. Downward-facing footsteps led the way down the snow slope. No choice but to go for it.

I looked at my watch. Already 3:30 PM, so we obviously weren't going to make it to Bullfrog Junction tonight. Our new goal became the campsites at Bubbs Creek.

The rib was not the official trail, so it was a matter of finding the best route to climb down the rocks. Luckily, the rocks were snow-free, but they were still a both-hands-and-feet exercise. Finally we regained the trail, which now had intermittent snowfields covering it. I continued on, with a mixture of pride and dread.

Blue Butterfly assured me that were I to slip and fall I would not be going anywhere because the snow was sticky. But I was still haunted by the turtle episode on Baden-Powell. A couple of times I froze on the snow, afraid of slipping to my death. I envisioned a long cartwheeling plunge down the snow into the icy lake, never to be retrieved. No matter the reality and scope of the danger, my mind had created this fear and I had a full-time job controlling my imagination and my thoughts.

Blue Butterfly tried everything to keep me moving. She made little platforms for my feet. That worked for a few steps. My feet slid. My shoes had no grip. I was awkward and nervous. Then we tried glissading. We didn't get much speed on the sun cups. Finally she taught me to plunge step and I relaxed a bit—this seemed to be something I could do.

I was no longer paralyzed by fright but I was still very slow. We would descend along the trail, then come around a bend, and there would be more snowfields to cross. Whenever I thought it was over, there was always more. But Blue Butterfly patiently stayed back, lending me her skill and experience to help me navigate safely through this dangerous terrain.

As we descended, the snowfields eventually disappeared, trees reappeared, and the hike became easier and faster. Before dark we arrived at Bubbs Creek. At 6:30 PM we decided to camp, exhausted. All of us had underestimated the difficulty in making miles in this section. The combination of high altitude, routefinding, snow travel, and rock climbing took its toll. We wearily chose camp spots and pitched our tents, with little energy for conversation.

Our home for the night offered a pink- and amber-tinged view of the rock walls and mountains we had just come through. I set up my tent between Blue Butterfly's and the creek so I could hear the soothing rush of water all night. I fell asleep quickly, happy to have Forester behind me and grateful for Blue Butterfly's closeness, understanding, and patience. This happiness was combined with confidence and excitement...but also apprehension about what challenges Glen Pass would have to offer tomorrow.

THE MYSTERY OF THE APPLE PIE

By Gary Funk

For those who have thru hiked the Pacific Crest Trail, or section hiked it for a number of years, one of its most amazing features comes not from the trail itself but from the human culture that has grown around it. Hikers commonly see each other year after year and meet serendipitously in small rural diners, at trailheads, and at backcountry campsites. Trail angels, and addicts who return season after season, lend a hand to travelers in need, only to meet that person's mother, best friend, or hiking partner at some other distant place and time. In this humorous tale, Gary Funk captures this timeless and spaceless quality of PCT culture. A relatively fresh apple pie stashed in a trail register would indeed be difficult to resist, and who would ever suspect that you might be held accountable for taking a piece a quarter century later?

The LeConte Canyon area of the PCT, where this story takes place, is heavily traveled and visited. Here one can find solitude and silence, but the PCT hiker is just as likely to find hiking mates, rousing evening conversation, and folks to share food with. In addition to swapping updates on trail conditions, hikers share stories, many of which, like this one, are carried along the way and passed along from one PCT hiker to another, from the backcountry to the city and beyond.

It was the summer of 1977, and I had just graduated from college. I had no immediate plans, so I filled up the gas tank of my 1962 blue Ford Econoline van and headed off to the Sierras to meet up with my friends Mark and Marty—the San Diego Truckers. They had started hiking on the Pacific Crest

Trail a few months earlier and were somewhere in the southern Sierra. Despite being a drought year, the month of May managed to dump enough snow to be considered the worst May in a hundred years (or at least so they say).

Guessing they would be a few days behind schedule, I estimated that they would soon be hiking through LeConte Canyon, where the Bishop Pass Trail connects with the PCT. So I decided to surprise them at the ranger station near Little Pete Meadow. From the road's end, I strapped on my snowshoes and made my way toward Bishop Pass, with the goal of climbing over it that day. My pack felt very heavy. Maybe it was the extra food I was bringing in, or maybe my mind had distorted the memory of how much work this could be.

The hours passed by as I made my ascent up Bishop Pass only to reach complete exhaustion on top. The pass was completely clouded over and I decided I'd had enough, so I set up my tent right then and there. The clouds swirled and the wind howled, but I didn't care as I fell asleep. In the morning I felt rejuvenated. The sky cleared as I descended from the 11,780-foot pass and reached the junction with the Pacific Crest Trail.

Knowing firsthand what it's like when a calorie-starved body (fed on dehydrated food) craves fresh food, I had packed in pork chops, lettuce, fruit, and a few extra goodies. The kicker was a fresh Dutch apple pie from Schat's Bakery in Bishop. I stored the food in a snowbank on the side of the LeConte Ranger Station and began my wait for my friends. I camped right on the trail, figuring I would see them coming by.

I knew connecting up with them would be a gamble because there are so many things that can slow you down in bad weather. I checked the nearby trail register—I knew that if they had already come by they would have signed in. I didn't find their names. In fact, I didn't see any entries from the last several days. So I had a strong feeling my friends would be by soon.

Evening came and there was still no sign of them, or anyone else hiking on the trail. With the sky being overcast sky and pines towering overhead, there was little to see in the night sky, so to bed I went. The morning arrived and looked a lot like the day before. Moisture on the shrubs and the damp trail deterred me from day hiking, so I hung around camp waiting. After a few hours of contemplating life and watching the dark-eyed juncos jumping from branch to branch and bush to bush, I became bored.

Hours slowly passed with nothing happening and no one in sight. A complete day passed, just like the one before, with no one hiking by. I could only watch those birds jump around for so long, so I decided to head out. I left a note on the trail register telling Mark and Marty that I'd packed the food in the snowbank by the ranger station. I was about to head back over Bishop Pass when I noticed that the pie would fit quite nicely under the cover of the trail register. I imagined what it would be like if I had been hiking along for a couple of months, saw a trail register, and opened it up thinking I would sign in...only to find a freshly baked apple pie. It would be a gift from heaven. "Why not?" I thought. So, I put the pie under the cover and headed out. While climbing up the trail, I considered what might happen if someone else came by first. But realistically I could only envision one outcome.

Many days passed before I finally connected up with Mark and Marty at the South Fork of the San Joaquin River and began hiking with them for a few weeks. I was worried about keeping up with them—they were in great shape, having been hiking for about two months now. My worries didn't last long after finding out that sometimes they took a four-hour lunch break.

"Hey, what did you think of the pork chops?" I asked.

"Great, just great, Gary. We built a fire and found an old grill and roasted them up. A little salt and pepper, and they were real tasty."

"And the lettuce?"

"It's hard to explain what it's like to taste something so fresh when you've been out so long. So crispy, like a garden salad at a fine restaurant."

"Annnnd?"

"And what?"

"The pie, what about the pie?"

"What pie?"

"The apple pie I left at the register!"

"There wasn't any apple pie at the register."

"Yes there was—I brought in a Dutch apple pie from Schat's Bakery."

"Get out of here! You wouldn't have brought a pie over the pass."

"No, really. I did."

"Sure, Gary. Sure you did. You must have been hallucinating on your three-day solo out there."

And so began the mystery of the apple pie—and the harassment I received for the next twenty-five years whenever the subject came up.

Three years after the disappearing apple pie, in 1980, while taking a break from graduate school, I decided to day hike up from Humber Park in the San Jacinto Mountains. As I drove away at the end of the day, dusk had begun to settle in and the road grew foggy. I saw a hiker walking. He had a certain look to him. I knew that PCT hiker look, so I stopped. His name was Gary, same as mine, and sure enough he was hiking the PCT.

"This time from north to south," Gary said.

"You must have hiked it before?"

"Yes, I hiked it for the first time from south to north in 1977."

"Really? Did you know the San Diego Truckers?"

"Yes! I met Mark and Marty for the first time in LeConte Canyon. They were eating some pork chops by a fire."

"No way! You can't be serious." This was too amazing. "I packed those pork chops in for them."

"You're kidding! They told me a friend of theirs had packed them in. So, you were the guy."

"Hey, there was an apple pie too. You don't know what happened to it, do you?"

"Well, you know, actually I might. I think the Kelty Kids ate it. There were three of them and they were just ahead of me."

Wow, a clue to the mystery of the apple pie after all this time. I wished him luck and headed down the road, feeling like I had been transported back in time, in some surrealistic dream.

More years passed. I graduated, got married, got a job. In the mid-1980s, Mark, Marty, my brother, and I reconnected and started making annual backpacking trips. We relived past adventures and, inevitably, the subject of the pie would come up. I'd be reminded how I made up the story and had been hallucinating at LeConte Canyon. I would insist that the Kelty Kids ate the pie, but I could gain no ground.

Then in 2002, a full twenty-five years after the mythic pie incident, I was sitting at my desk reading e-mails about normal work issues when I saw this message: "Looking for Mark and Marty." Transported back in time, I opened the message. It was from someone named Carl, one of the Kelty Kids. "I saw your name and address in a PCT register," he wrote, "and am trying to find Mark and Marty for a reunion." Below his note was this PS:

In one of our more desperate moments, we did something to Mark and Marty that was so rude and unthinkable that I still feel bad about it today, 25 years later. When we trudged through the snow to arrive at the junction to Bishop Pass Trail, whaddaya know? There's a fresh apple pie in the trail registry box. A single slice had been taken and it looked mighty good. We, of course, were famished as usual and no one else was around to claim the pie. Not wanting it to go to waste, we decided to have a bite or two and leave the rest to its rightful owners in case they showed up sometime. Before we knew it, the three of us had devoured the entire pie. We just could not stop.

I couldn't believe I was reading this! At long last, the mystery of the apple pie was solved. Mark and Marty could harass me no longer. I wondered what it must have felt like when the Kelty Kids discovered that pie—deprived taste buds starved for sweet sugar, with each bite the craving surging stronger. I harbored no ill feelings toward them—the pie would have been irresistible. I did wonder, though, where did that first piece go, before they got there?

Two days later I received another e-mail, this one with the subject line "Blast from the past." It was from the PCT hiker Gary, whom I'd briefly met back in 1980 alongside Highway 243. He had been in contact with Carl about the reunion, and I scrolled through their exchange, which had all been forwarded along with Gary's note to me. My eye caught this line that Gary had written to Carl: "Remember the pie at the Bishop Pass Trail Junction? That tasted great!"

Wait a minute. Gary had told me that the Kelty Kids had eaten the pie. He never mentioned any participation on his part. I e-mailed him back.

"Hey, you never told me you ate any of the pie."

"Oh, did I fail to mention that part?"

I laughed out loud—the infamous mystery of the apple pie had finally been solved. And to Gary's credit, he only ate one piece! The story came full circle at the next PCT Kickoff, when Carl kindly bought an apple pie for Mark and Marty, to redeem all those involved. A fitting gesture. But I bet it didn't taste as good as the one I'd left at the trail register.

THE GHOST OF MUIR PASS

By Suzanne Roberts

For nearly 160 miles, the John Muir Trail (JMT) and the Pacific Crest Trail follow the same footpath through some of the most dramatic scenery in the Sierra Nevada, including Muir Pass. Although the region abounds with the landmarks named after men, it has had its share of female travelers and explorers too. Indeed, the demographics of backcountry travelers have changed much since John Muir's time, when backpacking and peak bagging were almost exclusively male endeavors. Suzanne Roberts, in her whimsical style, touches on some of the perceptions about women in the mountains and introduces an intrepid but mystical silver-haired spirit, more representative of the strong-woman archetype one finds on the PCT. Today, many women like Roberts, Amanda Carter, and Anicca Cox (see their stories in the Oregon/Washington volume) are taking to the trail and enjoying their rightful place alongside men in our rugged and beautiful wilderness areas.

Tom says camping in the Muir Hut is illegal, but we have met other hikers who have done it, so we decide to break the rules. As Edward Abbey says, "Live dangerous." Even Erika, our self-appointed commander of the trip, agrees. Muir, we think, would be happy to have us as guests for the night in a hut dedicated to him. According to Tom, it is 10.3 miles to the pass, with a 4000-foot elevation gain. Tom also says we will "assault Goddard Divide" and "search out Muir Pass." Tom is the author of our guidebook. Because we closely follow his *Guide to the John Muir Trail*, we feel an intimate bond with him: First we called him by his last name, Winnett. As time passed, he became Thomas. Now he is simply Tom.

"Sounds like we're going to war," Erika says, "to search out and assault." Dionne and I laugh, since we have secretly started calling Erika the Commander because she is so bossy.

"So male," I say.

"The women will seek out and conquer," Dionne laughs and raises her cup of hot Tang. Erika and I meet her cup with ours. We drink hot Tang and eat dried fruit for breakfast because we have run out of oatmeal and granola.

We have a long hike ahead of us, but we sit around for a while, joking about war metaphors, ourselves, the language of men. Finally, I say, "Well, we should probably get going." We get our things together, put on our "heinous loads," as we now call our backpacks, and start up toward the pass.

Our rocky trail climbs through a canyon of granite. Chaparral and Indian paintbrush cling to the rocky walls. Two male hikers pass us. After a while, two women come down the trail. One is wearing frosted pink lipstick. The other has frizzy hair and is out of breath. "Where are you going?" The one with the lipstick asks.

"Muir Pass," I say, before Erika has a chance to tell her that we are hiking all the way to Yosemite. Though other hikers—some hiking the PCT and not just the JMT—and rangers have responded to Erika's boasting with "Today?" and "Wow, that's a long way to go before dark," she keeps on bragging.

"It sure is snowy," Frizzy Hair says. "We were there yesterday. Surely, you aren't going all that way today?" She puts her hands on her hips.

"Sure we are," Dionne says. "We're going to sleep in the hut." Erika glances sideways at Dionne. Erika may have agreed to break the rules this once, but she surely doesn't want to broadcast it.

"In that drafty little thing?" Hair asks.

"It's a dank hole," Lipstick adds.

"We heard from a couple of guys—other JMT hikers—that it's fine for sleeping," I say.

"What's a JMT hiker?" Lipstick asks.

"Someone who is hiking the whole John Muir Trail," I answer.

"How far is that?"

"It's 211 miles, but we have to hike a little farther to get food and stuff. We're hiking 230 miles." Now I'm the one who's bragging.

"What for?" Hair asks. I don't answer her. Partly because if I tried to explain, she wouldn't understand. Partly because I am not so sure myself. Hair doesn't pursue the question. Instead, she says, "Well, you wouldn't catch me sleeping in that little hut for a hundred bucks."

Lipstick adds, "I wouldn't for a thousand. People have died in there, you know. Campers were killed by lightning. Wait till you see it. It's a pit."

"Well, we'll decide when we get there," I say.

"Who are you with?" Lipstick asks. Dionne, Erika, and I look at each other. We aren't sure how to answer.

Finally I say, "We're together." I point to Erika and Dionne.

"So you girls are alone?"

"Alone?" Dionne asks. I know what this woman is getting at, but I won't give it to her.

"We're not alone. We're with each other," I say.

"You must have a gun?" Frizzy Hair asks.

"No," we all say.

"You're brave," both women say, "a credit to your sex." They hurry off down the trail toward their husbands. The women whisper. I can only make out the word *crazy.*

We continue on. I can't imagine carrying a gun. If I had one, I wouldn't know what to do with it. These women cannot imagine being "alone," yet today I feel much safer than I did when we were with Jim or Jesse, our male hiking partners who have already quit. Hair and Lipstick can't imagine that three women, or *girls* as they called us, would be wandering around out here "alone." I wonder if these women have their facts straight about the hut. Though I feel safe enough with my two girlfriends, I don't necessarily want to sleep in a place where people have died.

We are on the edge of the forest. The damp earth is broken by an emerging snow plant. The red plant erupts from the soil like a miniature volcano.

"Look at this you guys," I call to Dionne and Erika. "It's a snow plant."

"Trippy," says Dionne. "It looks like something from outer space. How come it has no leaves?"

"It isn't green because it doesn't photosynthesize. The plant doesn't make its own food," I explain. I tell Erika and Dionne that this red plant is usually the first flower of spring. It breaks through soil and pine needles shortly after the snow melts.

A hiker approaches. His t-shirt is ripped, and gray hair peeks out from under a blue bandana on his head. He asks us, "Whatcha lookin' at?"

"A snow plant." I point to the crimson plant.

"Funny little things. Phallic as hell, if you ask me." He laughs. Men find their penises in the most unlikely places.

"Where ya headed?" He asks.

"Muir Pass," Erika says.

"You girls won't make it up there tonight...No way."

"It's not much farther, is it?" Dionne asks.

"No, but it's covered with snow. And it's late." He looks at his wrist, though he isn't wearing a watch. "No. You girls definitely won't make it up there tonight."

I want to tell him that we have hiked much farther in a day, that we have come more than a hundred miles, that we went through puberty a long time ago and are no longer girls. I want to tell him that the snow plant's red, convoluted folds look like a vagina. Instead, we thank him for his advice and keep hiking.

"What do you think?" Dionne asks. "About what that man said?"

"I think he doesn't know us," I answer.

"It isn't that far. What's a little snow?" says Erika.

"Yeah. He doesn't know that these women are out to conquer," Dionne laughs.

The trail crawls up the rocky ridge, passing the last of the trees. Stunted whitebark pines hunch over like gnomes. Blue sky hangs over us, and the land stretches white across the horizon. We walk through the first snow patches. Farther ahead, there is only snow. I begin to wonder.

The trail passes Helen Lake, which is named for one of John Muir's daughters. I wonder what Muir thought of women in the wilderness. Muir says that the outdoors is the "natural place for men," but what about women? I wonder if Helen and her sister Wanda went traipsing around the wilderness.

We follow dirty footprints through the snowscape. The snow has melted into ripples, gray and white pockets. The slushy snow moves under our boots like sugar. I carefully place my walking stick and step. We move up the hill, our shadows follow behind, stretching gray. Water trickles under snow. I try not to look into the deep holes where snow has melted away from granite, worn thin. Some of these minicrevasses are so deep they appear bottomless and large enough to swallow a foot, a leg, a hiker. I know that a misstep can mean a sprained ankle, a broken leg. I dig my walking stick into the snow, choose steps with caution, try not to posthole.

An older woman is standing off the trail, looking at a map. We say hello. Erika and Dionne keep hiking. I ask the woman where she's going.

"Overland," she replies and points toward the surrounding mountains. Silver braids hang from underneath a floppy hat. She wears glacier glasses, pale yellow wind gear, and a small orange backpack. Two ski poles stick into the snow next to her.

"What about the trail?" I ask.

"No trail...I have my map. And my compass." She pats her pocket. "I prefer to go cross-country."

"Where are you going?"

"Overland," she says again. She folds up her map and puts it in her pocket. She grabs her ski poles and starts walking. I look up the trail. Erika and Dionne are almost to the top. I turn back toward the woman, and she is gone. She couldn't have made it over the ridge. I stand and stare. I want to disappear into the late afternoon sun, to go alone overland without a trail, as she has, without fear. I hike to the top of the pass, looking around for the woman. I can find no rational explanation for her disappearance. In my imagination, she is the ghost of Muir Pass. Perhaps she was struck by lightning one night in the hut, and now she prowls overland, across granite, snowy peaks, and sky. Not such a bad fate, I suppose. I continue to the top where Erika and Dionne are waiting.

We leave our packs on the rocks and walk through the splintered wooden door of the hut. The granite walls are stained a sooty gray from illegal fires. Lipstick and Frizzy Hair are not too far off—the hut is certainly dark and drafty, gothic. I imagine the ghost of Muir Pass returning from her foray overland—ruddy cheeked, windblown, a little travel stained. She would lean against a ski pole next to the box of crumpled paper that sits in the corner, rake through the scraps that litter the floor, reading messages from hikers: "Flying high on Muir Pass," "Skiing powder down to Wanda Lake today," "Joey and Dave are here." She knows people feel the need to leave some sort of mark behind. She has seen names on mountain ledgers, the carvings in aspen trees, crumpled scraps of paper in a stone hut. She sees these for what they are—tiny messages of hope.

I go sit outside against this stone hut and look out over the lake basins, rocks, and snow. Not a tree is in sight. I take out my journal and sketch the view. Yellow and pink reflect in Wanda Lake below, mirroring sky. The mountains change color—tan to yellow, pink to black. The sky is on fire. The warmth of the day has left the granite rocks.

Watching the day slip behind the mountains feels like prayer. When my mother is asked why she doesn't go to church, she always says, "You don't need four walls to pray." My prayer is one of thanks for this place, for the body that got me here.

I finish my drawing and write, "In the Range of Light." I sit for a moment. The wind twists through the canyon, sweeps over the divide, rustles through my hair. I add the word "Home." I rip the page from my journal, go into the hut, and leave my message with the rest for the lady ghost of Muir Pass.

THE SEARCH FOR WALTER STARR

By Norman Clyde

When Norman Clyde joins the search party to find his friend and fellow mountain climber, Walter A. Starr Jr., they focus their search on the Ritter Range. This area, just west of the Pacific Crest Trail and south of the Yosemite Park boundary, is defined by two high mountains, Mount Ritter and Banner Peak, and a series of jagged peaks known as the Minarets. The Minarets, which become a central player in this mystery, form an arête, a thin ridge of rock left when two glaciers erode parallel U-shaped valleys. Not insignificantly, the tallest of the Minarets is named for Norman Clyde.

It is no coincidence that after the rest of the search party returns to civilization, Clyde remains behind to search for the lost climber and eventually succeeds in finding his body. A revered climber in his own time, Clyde was known for his enduring stamina, often carrying an eighty-pound pack complete with books to read, as well as for his keen mountaineering and climbing skill. During a "vacation" in Glacier National Park, Clyde scaled thirty-six peaks in as many consecutive days, including eleven firsts. By the age of fifty in 1935, Clyde was the veteran of more than six hundred mountain ascents. The tale he recounts—of searching for and tracking the clues left by Walter Starr—has become the stuff of legend and truly demonstrates his unparalleled skill and determination.

Almost undoubtedly Walter Starr had met with mishap somewhere in this group of mountains, the Ritter Range, and was either somewhere on them or in the country lying between them and his camp. If killed or seriously

SOURCE: Excerpted from "The Quest for Walter Starr, Jr.," Norman Clyde Papers, Bancroft Library, University of California, Berkeley. Additional thanks to Mary Millman for her assistance and support.

injured he was probably in the mountains, but if he were only crippled he might have attempted to reach camp, and being unable to do so, would be in the lower country. A man with a sprained ankle or broken leg may spend days going a short distance. The plan of the campaign was based on these facts. Those without special mountaineering experience were to comb the area lying between his camp and the base of the Ritter Range. The mountaineers were to search the peaks and spires, a difficult, arduous, and somewhat hazardous undertaking.

Early the next morning four climbing parties were on their way. Three excellent young climbers, Jules Eichorn, together with Glen Dawson and Richard Jones proceeded to search one portion of the Minarets, especially the second-highest—Michael's Minaret—while Oliver Kehrlein of Oakland and I were to direct our efforts to another section of the great spires, focusing upon the highest of them, known as Clyde's Minaret.

Past a number of groves of mountain hemlocks, and through gradually rising alpine meadows we filed along to the glaciated bluffs immediately below the Minarets. Along these cliffs Kehrlein and I proceeded, carefully inspecting every foot of the way until we were abreast of the highest of the Minarets. Aside from a few footprints which might have been those of a party other than the one for whom we were searching, we discovered nothing. Unfortunately we did not know the pattern of the soles of the basketball shoes generally worn by the missing man when rock climbing.

Leaving the bluffs, we crossed a small but rather steeply pitching glacier to the base of Clyde's Minaret and continued up its precipitous north face. More tracks were observed in the decomposed granite on the ledges, but these also were in all likelihood those of another party. Upon reaching the jagged top of the great spire, the signature of Walter Starr was not in the register in the cairn. However, we knew that he did not always sign his name on the top of a mountain and furthermore there was no pencil in the register can and he might have failed to bring one with him. No evidence of his having been there was discovered.

As we looked out over the mountains an inky mass of clouds was seen advancing from the southwest and another from the northeast. As the top of a pinnacle more than 12,000 feet above the sea is not the most desirable place to encounter an electric storm, we left the summit before we had searched it to our entire satisfaction. On our way down we zigzagged back and forth, minutely observing every square yard for clues, but none were found.

As it was now late afternoon we were obliged to return. While doing so we paused and reconnoitered on the margin of Upper Iceberg Lake, lying on

Minaret Pass a short distance northeast of Clyde's Minaret at an elevation of some 10,000 feet. We thought Starr might have passed this lake on his way to the mountain. While looking about, I noticed a strip of handkerchief with blood marks on it.

"Someone has lost his footing and cut his finger on a sharp rock as he came up the steep slope to the north of the pass," I thought as I stowed it away in my rucksack.

Upon our return to camp we found that the large party had come upon no certain evidence of any kind in the lower country. During the day an aeroplane carrying Francis P. Farquhar, President of the Sierra Club, as observer, had circled the peaks of the Ritter Range several times, evidently without result.

Walter A. Starr, Sr., and his son Allan had climbed Banner Peak and searched the North Glacier in descending, but found no record on the summit. Two, however, who had climbed Mt. Ritter, discovered that Starr had written a note in the register on its summit. Among several statements was one to the effect that he had his ice axe with him. The latter having been found at his camp was proof of his safe return from Mt. Ritter. The other Minaret party which had climbed Michael's Minaret from the west, saw a line of ducks. The markers crossed the upper end of a chute and led to "The Portal" on the north side of Michael's Minaret. There were also several footprints and a portion of a cigarette, which was said to be the brand usually smoked by the missing man. Eichorn and Dawson had climbed from "The Portal" to the summit of the Minaret but found no evidence of Starr having been there, and were forced to make a hurried descent by the same storm that drove me from Clyde's Minaret. By its brown marking the fragment of the handkerchief which I had brought in was identified as similar to those generally carried by Starr.

Haunted by the ducks on the northeast face of Clyde's Minaret, Kehrlein and I returned on the following morning to Upper Iceberg Lake. Swinging around to the slope east of it, we selected a vantage point from which the entire northeast face could be readily surveyed with binoculars. An object about a third of the way up the mountain puzzled me. The fact that it was brown indicated that it might be a khaki-clad person, but as the light falling upon it seemed to be diffused through it rather than reflected from it, this inference seemed to be precluded.

Having come to the decision that this face of the peak should be thoroughly investigated, we proceeded to climb it. In about half an hour we reached the long ledge. After examining several ducks, I carefully removed the rocks of one of them. Beneath was a tuft of grass the color of which had not faded in the least. This was certain proof that the ducks had been made very recently. As we began to advance up the peak we presently came upon more ducks. Then there was a gap. Evidently the climber was in the habit of putting markers only when he thought that there might be special occasion for them on his return. A little later we reached the object which had aroused our curiosity. It was a bed of oxalis, or miners lettuce, a few feet in length on a ledge, with a profusion of brown seed vessels; both the color and the diffusion of light were therefore explained.

The ducks appeared to lead into a large alcove-like recess in a chute or couloir, with almost vertical walls of perhaps a hundred feet above it. Then they were lost again. Working my way upward along narrow shelves, I succeeded in getting within a few yards of the rim of the wall, but the remainder being very hazardous, I desisted from the attempt to scale it. While traversing to the right along the ledges toward the rib of rock separating this couloir from another adjoining it to the north, I again came upon ducks. There was one on the very crest of the rib and others in the next chute. I called down to Kehrlein. In a few minutes he joined me.

Together we proceeded up the couloir. Although the line of ducks was not continuous, they were sufficient to indicate clearly the path of the climber. As we neared the head of the couloir, an approaching mass of dense black cloud, warned us that we had better get off the precipitous face. The rocks were difficult enough to scale when dry, and furthermore, a storm striking the pinnacle would be likely to precipitate loose stones down upon us. (Starr's name was found the following year by Jules Eichorn on the summit of the Minaret, faintly marked on a piece of cardboard. Starr's diary subsequently proved that the ducks we followed marked his route.)

At round table that evening, after an animated debate, it was decided that further search would almost undoubtedly prove futile, and it would be best to give up. To find a person in such a maze of pinnacles, only a few of which had been scaled, was like finding a needle in a haystack, it was thought. Not yet ready to abandon the quest, however, I declined to accompany the remainder of the party.

On the following morning I set forth on my lone quest. There is another Minaret—Leonard's—climbed but once prior to that year, which it seemed possible that Starr might have attempted to scale. It might be well, therefore, to ascend this and incidentally to ascertain whether the missing man had gone north of Michael's Notch. In a word, my plan was to be one of gradual elimination. As now there was no further hope of finding Starr alive, there was no special occasion for hurry. [...]

As human muscles have a habit of eventually clamoring for rest, after climbing and searching for an average of at least ten hours daily for five days, I thought it might be well to accede to their demand by spending a day in camp. On the following day, the twenty-first of August, I decided to settle, if possible, the matter of Clyde's Minaret. Returning to the northeast face, I again followed the line of ducks up its precipitous front. They ceased entirely at the head of the couloir up which Kehrlein and I had followed them on the previous climb. Continuing to the summit, I inspected cairn and rocks very carefully without finding any certain evidence. Barring the possibility of his having been forced back by a storm, however, I felt convinced that Starr had been there. [...]

Early in the morning of the twenty-fifth I again traversed the alpine meadows, again clambered up on the glaciated bluffs and then continued up along a slanting ledge ending in a short chimney, out of the upper end of which I climbed onto Michael's Notch. From it an easy descent brought me to the west base of the Minarets. I then went southward about a mile to the west side of Michael's Minaret and continued around its southwestern shoulder. Noting a shelf running along the precipitous—almost sheer—west face, I decided to follow it for some distance and then climb above it in order to get a vantage point suitable for using my binoculars.

While reconnoitering, I came to the conclusion that higher up probably a ledge would be found leading around this shoulder and into the upper portion of a deep chute to "The Portal," from which the final spire of the Minaret is usually scaled. While I advanced upward the climbing became rather delicate, as the holds grew progressively smaller. They were firm and sharp angled, however, and there was no occasion to worry about loose rocks—the face was too steep for rocks to find lodgement.

As anticipated, a ledge did lead into the couloir. After going some distance up the latter, I examined the northwestern face of the spire. Evidently it was scalable, but the ledges tended to slope downward at a precarious angle, and there was a predominance of rounded corners. Knowing Starr's reliance on rubber-soled shoes, I made a mental comment to the effect that this reliance was perhaps a little too great. After climbing it for some distance I suddenly made the decision;

"This can be climbed, but I'm not going to do it."

Having returned to the couloir, I continued up it to the notch ("The Portal") at its head. The ascent of perhaps five hundred feet from it to the narrow, blade-like summit of the spire involved a good deal of aerial and some rather hazardous climbing. Seated on the topmost rock, several feet in diameter, for upwards of a half hour, I swept the Minaret with my binoculars. Gathering clouds then warned me that I had better be gone.

As I carefully and deliberately made my way down toward the notch, I scanned and re-scanned the northwestern face. Much of it was concealed by irregularities. Suddenly a fly droned past, then another, and another.

"The quest is nearing an end," I reflected.

Upon reaching "The Portal" I began to follow a ledge running in a northwesterly direction. When I had gone along it but a few yards, turning about, I looked upward and across the chute to the northwestern face. There, lying on a ledge not more than fifty yards distant, were the earthly remains of Walter A. Starr, Jr. He had obviously fallen, perhaps several hundred feet, to instantaneous death. The quest had been long, arduous, and hazardous, but the mystery of the vanishing Walter Starr, Jr., was at last solved. The life of the daring and young climber had come to a sudden and tragic end.

A few days later a party of four was again scaling Michael's Minaret. We followed the route which Starr had marked with ducks while making his climb three weeks before. Several hundred feet below the remains, two stopped, but Jules Eichorn and I continued up the perilous face. We interred the body of Walter A. Starr, Jr., on the narrow ledge where he lay, while his father looked up from below. Such an aerie would have been chosen as his final resting place by this departed lover of the mountains.

THE BEAR AT LYELL FORK CREEK

By Krystal Rogers

Ursus americanus, or the American black bear, long ago discovered a taste for human food, which was often sufficient to overcome its fear of humans. As every Pacific Crest Trail hiker in the Yosemite area knows, this region, perhaps more than any other, is famous for its dangerously habituated black bears. In the early years of the park, bears were fed constantly, until the detrimental impact on their health, eating habits, and foraging behaviors became apparent, not to mention the increasing number of problematic encounters between bears and people. Even after people stopped feeding bears on purpose, bears along certain sections of the PCT have feasted on improperly stored food and have become quite savvy at solving whatever defenses backpackers implement (aside from the bear canister). Stories abound of bears climbing trees to get at bear bags, breaking into cars at trailheads, and even walking into tents in the middle of the day to find a snack.

Although Krystal Rogers and her hiking partner Glenn try hard to do the right thing, and rely on past successful experiences, this story is a reminder that the bears of the Sierras are "smarter than the average bear" (Yogi Bear included). The particular stretch of trail described here is near Donohue Pass, but any PCT hiker passing the Yosemite Valley, Tuolumne Meadows, and on through the John Muir Wilderness will be familiar with the precautions required to travel safely with food still in hand and gear intact.

Glenn and I left Tuolumne Meadows with bellies full of our last round of ice cream and candy bars, after a mellow three-day detour hike with my good high school friend Jen. We'd had a great hike to Yosemite Valley via

Sunset Lakes, Clouds Rest, and Half Dome. After repacking, saying our fare-wells, and going back to the lodge one last time for ice cream, we got a late start hiking, to say the least. By the time the lodge's shuttle dropped us off about half a mile from the PCT trailhead, the sun was high in the sky and afternoon was in full swing. We had resupplied with all kinds of crackers, cereal, fresh carrots, apples, trail mix, tuna, peanut butter and jelly, and other dehydrated trail food. We figured we could afford to carry the extra weight of the more luxurious foods, since this would be a short six-day stretch.

We only made it about eight miles in from Tuolumne Meadows. This was a crowded area, and we passed dozens of tents along winding Lyell Fork Creek as we looked for our own spot. We found a lovely, established site at the base of the climb up to 11,000-foot Donohue Pass—secluded but still close enough to "civilization" that the local bears frequented the area nightly. We were prepared, with our mountains of food packed to the brim in our two bear canisters.

After finishing our gourmet macaroni and cheese dinner with freshly steamed broccoli, we strategically repacked our canisters, tucking granola bars and various ziplock bags of food into every crevice and crack. We needed to make room for *all* the smellables: toothbrushes, toothpaste, lip balm, lighters, first-aid cream. As it started to get dark, it became clear that not everything would fit once we included fuel, pots and pans, and the precious but bulky crackers and cereal. Even if we did grind the crackers into the crumbly pile they were destined to become in a day or two, it would never all fit.

We remembered that we were in Yosemite. We had read all the signs at the ranger stations showing the sad and frustrated cartoons of hikers struggling to hang their food, struggling to get it down when they'd hung it out of their reach, or finding a slobbery, crumbly, mess of a bag when they woke in the morning. And yet we'd hung our food every night for two weeks from Sonora Pass to Tuolumne with no problems. We felt like counterbalance pros. But Yosemite black bears have remembered skills that other bears don't.

We knew this. It was also apparent that there was no way we were going to fit everything into our measly little bear canisters. What else could we do but hang a bear bag? We searched the forest over for the theoretically perfect bear-hang branch described in the guidebook: "15 feet off the ground, 4 feet away from the trunk (or was it 5?), 5 feet down from the branch," and so on. But, that perfect branch, on that perfect tree, never lives near any campsite I've camped in. So it was no surprise that we didn't quite find the perfect tree. But we did find a pretty good one, not too far from our sleeping site. We proceeded to hang two bear bags, using the only close-to-acceptable bear-bag method in Yosemite: the counter balance. Like a team of amateur acrobats, we threw the rope over the branch, attached the first bag to the end, pulled it up as high as it would go, and then tied the second bag to the other end and pushed it up to an even level with the first bag.

"Good job," we thought, congratulating ourselves. We were tired, full, and ready for bed.

"Are you sure that's high enough?" I muttered, not really wanting to change the bags, knowing this was the best we could do without wandering around all night in search of the perfect but nonexistent branch.

"Do you see anything better?" Glenn said, not a little frustrated.

We decided the bags, though not hung perfectly, were close enough. "A bear's not gonna get that. Let's go to bed." Glenn concluded.

The next thing I remember is waking up, not to scratching sounds, but to the sound of Glenn rustling out of the tent and crunching over leaves into the darkness toward the trees. "Get outta here bear!" he yelled in his deepest, most manly voice. "Hey bear, *get* outta here!"

It took me a few minutes to recognize what was happening and to realize that Glenn was in the dark, by himself, yelling at a Yosemite black bear in the middle of the night. "I guess I better go out there" I thought, shaking a little. I heard Glenn yelling, "Krystal, come here, and bring some rocks!"

By the time I hobbled out of the tent and found my way over to the tree with some rocks from the campfire ring, squinting in the darkness all the while, the bear had taken a bite out of every package of crackers until he found the treasure: the tasty, sugary, fruity granola cereal carefully packaged in its very own baggie. The food stuff sack was shredded in half and dangling like a piñata, its contents scattered on the ground, and the bag (with fuel, pots, and pans) was a couple of inches off the ground.

Glenn and I started throwing rocks (me a little hesitantly) and yelling more, trying to sound intimidating, while we watched the bear lick and crunch and munch the entire bag of cereal. We needed to defend our food, and we wanted to do our part to help the bear have a negative experience so that maybe he would stop trying to steal human food. We kept pelting him with rocks and yelling, but as Glenn pointed his headlamp to look at the bear, I swear I could see him weighing the situation in his mind and consciously deciding that eating the cereal was worth getting pelted by a few rocks. It wasn't until after he had finished eating the entire bag that he seemed to even notice the barrage of tiny rocks we were sending his way. After licking his lips, he nonchalantly and slowly began to saunter his way back up the hill and into the woods with a huff.

"That's right bear, you just keep walkin', and don't come back," I said, trying to be brave.

This was no baby bear—he was a veteran, huge, a papa, a Yosemite black bear. He must've been so excited when he found that some stupid hikers had hung food in a tree. "What, do they think we can't climb trees?" he must have wondered. It probably took him less than a minute to get that bag down, so it's good that Glenn acted fast. The bear would've eaten everything else too if we hadn't gone out there in time.

I'm glad I wasn't alone.

Although we considered ourselves experienced backpackers, who took bear and food protection seriously, we now take our place in the pages and pages of stories about stupid hikers whose food got eaten by a Yosemite black bear. Our shredded bag should go into the bear bag hall of fame in the ranger station among the other tattered messes adorning the walls.

"Sorry Mr. Bear!" I thought as we rummaged through the mess, dividing trash from food still fit to eat. "Hopefully you won't get any more hiker food any time soon—you know it's for your own good."

Fortunately, that was the only time a bear got our food on the entire five-week trip, but it was definitely not the only bear story. As a matter of fact, a week later, while at Vermillion Valley Resort, taking a zero day and after having picked up our resupply box, the resident black bear came calling. All of our food was secured in our bear canisters, but anyone who's been to VVR knows about the hiker barrel there: a huge fifty-gallon drum full of food that hikers leave for others when they realize they sent themselves way more food than they can ever eat on the trail.

The barrel is usually properly secured with a steel-fastened lid, but someone didn't close it properly that night. A group of us hikers were camped outside the main lodge, not far from the hiker barrel area. We heard a huge crash in the middle of the night and a bunch of rustling. Dogs barked and the rustling stopped, but a few minutes later it started again. I heard the unmistakable sound of a bear munching and rummaging in the barrel, and I just lay there, a little terrified for about five minutes, before finally saying, "Glenn, I think there's a bear in the hiker barrel. What should we do?"

"Not my problem." He mumbled back, unphased and half asleep. "Do *you* want to go throw rocks this time?"

I WAS THERE

By Andrew Becker

Informal and formal trail registers dot the Pacific Crest Trail, serving much the same function as Andrew Becker observes of summit registers in the High Sierra—bulletin boards, public forums, and personal ads. These peak and trail registers are a part of mountaineering and backpacking culture that, as time has passed, have left an interesting, somewhat random, and quirky written record of trail life.

Becker explores both the tradition and history of peak registers through the Range of Light, from Black Kaweah and Mount Brewer in the Great Western Divide to Mount Dana and Lyell in the north. Becker notes the connection between Black Kaweah and Walter Starr Jr., the same Walter Starr who was the subject of Norman Clyde's epic search, detailed earlier in this section.

As conveyed in "Blazes in the Sky" in the Oregon/Washington volume of the Trailside Reader, *perhaps peak registers are also examples of human nature and our desire to make our temporary presence more permanent and our achievements more public. It has been said that everything we write, from the most carefully crafted story to the hastily scribbled words on a bathroom wall, serve the same purpose—that of simply saying, "I was there."*

With the sun falling fast behind me, I look up at Black Kaweah and weigh my options. I'd taken on this remote and treacherous peak as part of my search for the historic summit registers climbers have left scattered throughout the Sierra Nevada, informal archives in the great conversation

SOURCE: A longer version of this story was published as "I Was Here" in *Sierra* 93, no. 4 (July–August 2008).

between climbers living, dead, and yet to be born. Only a few hundred people have visited this 13,765-foot peak since the first alpinist clambered to the top almost ninety years ago. Among them was Walter Starr Jr., who summited shortly after the first ascent. Arriving without pencil or pen, he improvised by signing his name in his own blood. That signature, encased for decades in an aluminum box on Black Kaweah's peak in Sequoia National Park, is one of the Sierra climber's treasures.

But my hopes of topping out sink with the sun, and instead of following in Starr's footsteps, I begin a badly planned retreat in the rapidly gathering darkness.

Sierra peak bagging, as recorded in summit registers, began in 1864. On July 2, as Confederate forces advanced toward Washington, DC, William Brewer, the Yale University-educated field leader of the California Geological Survey, and Charles Hoffman, the team's German-born topographer, scaled a 13,570-foot peak eleven miles northeast of Kaweah in what is today Kings Canyon National Park. Two days later, under cloudy skies and in freezing temperatures, Brewer and surveyor James Gardiner returned to the summit of what has since come to be known as Mount Brewer.

"We planted the American flag on the top, and left a paper in a bottle with our names, the height, etc.," Brewer later wrote in his journal. "It is not at all probable that any man was ever on the top before, or that anyone will be again—for a long time at least."

Exactly 143 years after the first ascent, and several weeks before my Kaweah climb, I'd heaved myself onto that same granite ridge on a blazing afternoon under an impossibly blue sky. After catching my breath, I anxiously looked for the summit register, finding it inside a custom-made cast-aluminum box. Thousands of people had visited the top before me, but this register only recorded the past four years. It included political rants, testimony from a very recently reformed smoker, and a note from a party of three who claimed to be Brewer's descendants. Over the years, scrawled in old registers now stored back in civilization, some climbers' entries aspired to poetry; others oozed with vulgarity. Their observations ran from effusive to terse ("Decided to celebrate my 38th birthday here—should have stuck to handball"), to stark confessions of stark nudity, as one woman reported. A subsequent visitor verified her clothes-free status, adding parenthetically, "crazy woman."

The note left behind by Brewer and company soon became a tradition for climbers. In the summer of 1894, the Sierra Club established summit registers and boxes on Mount Dana, Mount Lyell, and four other prominent points. Since then the pages have come to serve as bulletin boards, public forums, and personal ads. Climbing Middle Palisade, which the PCT curls past to the west, Sierra climbing legend Starr penned a simple route description in 1930. Things got weirder as the years passed. "Saw Yeti, abominable snowman on way up," reported a climber on Mount Brewer in 1969. "About to smoke Thailand weed—expect to float down," wrote another.

I was fortunate to commune with my fellow summiteers atop Mount Brewer, because in recent years more and more historic registers have vanished. There are as many theories about what's happening to them as there are about what to do with those that remain. Some think fervent wilderness protectors have tossed them off the mountaintops. Others imagine unscrupulous climbers smuggling them into private collections. Still more believe they may have fallen prey to the elements, human clumsiness, or some combination thereof. The Sierras' summits still harbor a scattering of original or decades-old books, squirreled away like pirate treasure in tobacco tins and film canisters across the Range of Light. But with each tattered slip of yellowed register paper that goes missing, a scrap of history fades like failing alpenglow.

The original Brewer register remained on the eponymous peak for thirty-two years, until climbers took the already historic artifact to the Sierra Club's San Francisco headquarters. Ten years later it was destroyed in the 1906 earthquake and fire. The removal and subsequent demise of Brewer's bottle has been a sticking point for generations of mountaineers. Preservation has long been the Sierra Club's policy for the registers—when an old one fills up, it comes down, replaced by clean sheets. So even if I'd had time that sunny afternoon on the peak, I couldn't have read the full collection of the Mount Brewer registers. Along with books from scores of Sierra summits, those records are kept at the University of California at Berkeley's Bancroft Library.

Each year the Bancroft receives a few more rescued registers, some overflowing with oxygen-deprived ramblings, others in sad shape, like the rusty, battered seventy-seven-year-old tome with the signatures of famous climbers like David Brower (1933) and Steve Roper (1959) plucked off Mount Julius Caesar by a Santa Cruz climber in 2006.

Some, however, believe the books belong on the summits, no matter their condition. "They should stay there forever, so future generations can enjoy them," says guidebook author R. J. Secor, echoing a sentiment voiced in an old Mount Brewer register: "I wonder if those people 50 years ago in this book ever thought their names would be intact today," a climber wrote in 1970. "Fifty years from now I wonder if my name will be intact."

He might well wonder. While some registers have found their way to archives at the Bancroft or in California national park libraries, others—Mount Barnard (east of the PCT at Tyndall Creek Ranger Station), Black Mountain, and Palisade Crest (just north of the PCT), to name a few—have vanished from their mountain homes, practically before peak baggers' eyes. As early as 1934, Brower found many original registers missing and, along with Hervey Voge, removed some himself. Brower and Voge described the various containers they discovered on the more than four dozen summits they bagged during a two-month "knapsacking orgy" that summer: cocoa, sardine, and peanut butter cans; a typewriter ribbon box; and a glass bottle. Over the years registers have also been stored in tubes or cylinders made of brass or iron, in cast-aluminum boxes, and in PVC pipes, then wedged in crevices or tucked under rock cairns.

What comes down also goes up. As I flipped through the Mount Brewer register that day on the peak, books from two nearby summits sat miles away in a park employee's office, waiting for a ride back up to nearby Milestone and North Guard Mountains. They'd been there since the summer of 2006, when rescuers grabbed them to see if a missing climber had made it that far. He had not: A rescue team spotted his body in a steep, narrow chute a couple of hundred feet below where I sat on Mount Brewer, pondering what to write. I scribbled a message to my soon-to-be-born twins, signed my name, and scampered down the mountain.

A few weeks later, my friend Nate Johnson and I ventured to Yosemite National Park to climb the first two peaks to get official Sierra Club registers: Mount Dana and Mount Lyell. As we topped 13,057-foot Dana, the cumulus clouds massed like battleships over the eastern Sierra. We found the register, but fellow climber Hal Borzone, for one, couldn't be bothered.

"I never sign the things," said the sixty-two-year-old schoolteacher, his sunscreen-smeared face a ghostly white. "For me it would be kind of arrogant. When people came up here back in the day, and it took two weeks to get to the base, with mules and fifty-eight-pound packs with skillets they busted their hump to carry, or they were the third person to climb the peak, then they deserved to sign their names." Were any mountaintops worthy of a signature? "Maybe a peak like Black Kaweah," he offered.

We cracked open the stuffed register, the contents of the ammunition box springing out like a jack-in-the-box. It was hard to argue with Borzone. The box held a few years' worth of notebooks, an open invitation to a sexual rendezvous, a student's life plan (budget included), and platitudes passing for wisdom. Signers included professors, a Pilates instructor, and many budding memoirists. Silicon Valley computer geeks, ever networking, dropped in business cards, as if there were a raffle for a free lunch.

The next morning, Johnson and I followed the PCT above tree line. We eventually broke off the packed-dirt path just below Donohue Pass, where the PCT enters Yosemite, to cross granite slabs toward Lyell—at 13,114 feet, Yosemite's highest point. A thousand feet below the summit, we hit snow and then the Sierras' second-largest glacier. We stepped into our crampons and detached our ice axes. The glacier had sprung a million leaks, and the mountaineering gear made our traverse less of a slog.

On top, we found an aluminum box cemented to a granite block just below the summit, where it's sat for more than seven decades.

When Johnson and I opened Lyell's register box, we found a new notebook placed only two weeks before. We added our names, snapped a few pictures, and wended our way back down to the glacier.

~⁂~

Three weeks after I reached the top of Lyell, my friend Jeff Nachtigal and his wife, Sara, join me for the climb up Black Kaweah. We hike in a few miles the night before to cut off some time and distance from the fourteen-mile approach that scales two significant passes just to get to the base of the route. But the next morning we get a late start.

Jeff is stricken with a cold, and as his energy wanes our speed plummets. After crossing the passes and descending into a gorgeous basin known as Little Five Lakes, we split up, my friends encouraging me to push for the summit. I run down the trail, hoping to reach the base by 4:00 PM. Eight hours from camp, I am still a mile from the base of the route and face the reality of at least ten more miles of hiking to go.

At 4:30 I'm still a half hour from the tarn below Black Kaweah's looming southwest face when I meet a climber who warns me off my attempt: "It's suicide if you try to climb Black now," he says.

I wiggle my toes as I consider his advice. He's right. I glance back at the peak and retrace my steps. A gauzy light covers the sky, the sunset reddened by forest fires burning to the south. I face a dilemma: I can either try to return to camp that night or trek to the backcountry ranger's cabin, hoping to sleep there without a sleeping bag.

I push on, passing by three climbers who are already bedded down for the evening. As dark falls, I arrive at the crest of Hands and Knees Pass. By memory, I work my way down the slabs and scree, barely aided by the sliver of blood-orange moonlight. On a ledge, I fasten my helmet and turn on my headlamp, then drop to another ledge.

Where I find myself stuck.

Then something catches my eye. From a few hundred feet below, a light flashes once, then again. I turn my headlamp off and on, signaling back. I take a deep breath and delicately ease myself down the rounded granite wall. I extend far to my left and inch my fingers into a grassy crack. Lowering my left leg, I shift my weight onto my pointed right foot and ease onto another bench. A wave of nausea rises and falls inside me. I'm glad that's over.

It's nearly 9:00 PM by the time I reach level ground. I still have another class 3 pass and two or three hours of stumbling before I reach camp. As I try to visualize the cross-country route we took this morning, the light flashes again, and a voice booms out from fifty feet away: "Campsite over here!" I wobble into camp and am greeted by a gigantic hand, which I shake vigorously. The next thing I know, I am showered with offers of food, water, clothes, and even a tent and sleeping bag.

The next morning I get my first full view of the man attached to the hand. Standing seven feet two inches, Ralph Drollinger is a former pro basketball player (he also played center on John Wooden's last UCLA team to win a national championship). The day before, he led a group of evangelical Christians, including an eleven-year-old boy, to the summit of Black Kaweah. I try to hide my jealousy.

We break camp, and although I am not accustomed to morning hiking prayers, I belt out an "Amen!" at the end of theirs—and add a plea that the register will still be there when I try again.

BAKER'S BLUE-JAY YARN

By Samuel Langhorne Clemens

In 1861, a young Samuel Langhorne Clemens traveled west to Virginia City, Nevada, and for the next several years unsuccessfully tried his hand at prospecting there and in the mines around Angel's Camp on the western slope of the Sierras. It was during these years that he first used his famous pen name, Mark Twain, as he began writing for the Virginia City Territorial Enterprise. *Clemens's experiences in the Sierras provided material for "The Celebrated Jumping Frog of Calaveras County,"* Roughing It, *and many other stories.*

Often published in the Overland Monthly *and other eastern periodicals, Clemens's writing brought the West humorously to life in often exaggerated tales. Set in the oak woodlands not far below the crest, "Baker's Blue-Jay Yarn" describes with as much fanfare as accuracy one of the PCT hiker's most common camp visitors: the raucous blue jay. Depending on your location along the trail, you may find yourself listening to rowdy Steller's jays (*Cyanocitta stelleri*), as in this story, or in lower elevations their sunny cousin the scrub jay (*Aphelocoma californica*). Regardless, many hikers will recognize the lively, loud, and loquacious character of these birds in Clemens's story. In fact, with enough time spent on the trail without many people to talk to, it is possible that you will find yourself beginning to understand the jay's language just as Jim Baker does in this tale.*

A nimals talk to each other, of course. There can be no question about that; but I suppose there are very few people who can understand them. I

SOURCE: Excerpted from *A Tramp Abroad*, by Mark Twain (a.k.a. Samuel Langhorne Clemens) (New York: Penguin, 1997 [1880]).

never knew but one man who could. I knew he could, because he told me so himself. He was a middle-aged, simple-hearted miner who had lived in a lonely corner of California, among the woods and mountains, a good many years, and had studied the ways of his only neighbors, the beasts and the birds, until he believed he could accurately translate any remark which they made. This was Jim Baker. According to Jim Baker, some animals have only a limited education, and use only very simple words, and scarcely ever a comparison or a flowery figure; whereas, certain other animals have a large vocabulary, a fine command of language and a ready and fluent delivery; consequently these latter talk a great deal; they like it; they are conscious of their talent, and they enjoy "showing it off." Baker said, that after long and careful observation, he had come to the conclusion that the bluejays were the best talkers he had found among birds and beasts.

Said he: "There's more to a bluejay than any other creature. He has got more moods, and more different kinds of feelings than other creatures; and, mind you, whatever a bluejay feels, he can put it into language. And no mere commonplace language, either, but rattling, out-and-out book-talk—and bristling with metaphor, too—just bristling! And as for command of language—why you never see a bluejay get stuck for a word. They just boil out of him! And another thing: there's no bird, or cow, or anything that uses as good grammar as a bluejay. You might say a cat uses good grammar. Well, a cat does—but you let a cat get excited once; you let a cat get to pulling fur with another cat on a shed nights, and you'll hear grammar that will give you the lockjaw. Ignorant people think it's the *noise* which fighting cats make that is so aggravating, but it ain't so; it's the sickening grammar they use. Now I've heard a jay use bad grammar but very seldom; and when they do, they are as ashamed as a human; they shut right down and leave.

You may call a jay a bird. Well, so he is, in a measure—because he's got feathers on him, and don't belong to no church, perhaps; but otherwise he is just as much a human as you be. And I'll tell you why. A jay's gifts, and instincts, and feelings, and interests, cover the whole ground. A jay hasn't got any more principle than a Congressman. A jay will lie, a jay will steal, a jay will deceive, a jay will betray; and four times of five, a jay will go back on his solemnest promise. The sacredness of an obligation is a thing which you can't cram into no bluejay's head. Now, on top of all this, there's another thing; a jay can out-swear any gentleman in the mines. And there's yet another thing; in the one little particular of scolding—just good, clean, out-and-out scolding—a bluejay can lay over anything, be it human or divine. Yes, sir, a jay is everything that a man is. A jay can cry, a jay can laugh, a jay can feel shame, a jay can reason and plan and discuss, a jay likes gossip and scandal, a jay has got a sense of humor, a jay knows when he is an ass just as well as you do—maybe better.

Now I'm going to tell you a perfectly true fact bout some bluejays. When I first begun to understand jay language correctly, there was a little incident that happened here. Seven years ago, the last man in this region but me moved away. There stands his house—been empty ever since; a log house, with a plank roof—just one big room, and no more; no ceiling—nothing between the rafters and the floor. Well, one Sunday morning I was sitting out here in front of my cabin taking the sun and thinking of the home away yonder in the states, that I hadn't heard from in thirteen years, when a bluejay lit on that house, with an acorn in his mouth, and says, 'Hello, I reckon I've struck something.' When he spoke, the acorn dropped out of his mouth and rolled down the roof, of course, but he didn't care; his mind was all on the thing he had struck. It was a knothole in the roof. He cocked his head to one side, shut one eye an put the other one to the hole, like a possum looking down a jug; then he glanced up with his bright eyes, gave a wink or two with his wings—which signifies gratification, you understand—and says, 'It looks like a hole, it's located like a hole—blamed if I don't believe it *is* a hole!'

Then he cocked his head down and took another look; he glances up perfectly joyful, this time; winks his wings and his tail both, and says, 'Oh no, this ain't no fat thing, I reckon! If I ain't in luck!—Why it's a perfectly elegant hole!' So he flew down and got that acorn, and fetched it up and dropped it in, and was just tilting his head back, with the heavenliest smile on his face, when all of a sudden he was paralyzed into a listening attitude and that smile faded gradually out of his countenance like a breath off'n a razor, and the queerest look of surprise took its place. Then he sways, 'Why I didn't hear it fall!' He cocked his eye at the hole again, and took a long look; raised up and shook his head; stepped around the other side of the hole and took another look from that side; shook his head again. He studied a while, then he just went into the details—walked round and round the hole and spied into it from every point of the compass. No use. Now he took a thinking attitude on the comb of the roof and scratched the back of his head with his right foot a minute, an finally says, 'Well, it's too many for *me* that's certain; must be a mighty long hole; however, I ain't got no time to fool around here, I got to 'tend to business; I reckon it's all right—I'll chance it, anyway.'

So he flew off and fetched another acorn and dropped it in, and tried to flirt his eye to the hole quick enough to see what become of it, but he was too late. He held his eye there as much as a minute; then he raised up and sighed, and says, 'Confound it, I don't seem to understand this thing, no way; however, I'll tackle her again.' He fetched another acorn, and done his level best to see what become of it, but he couldn't. He says, 'Well, I never struck no such hole as this before; I'm of the opinion it's a totally new kind of hole.' Then he begun to get mad. He held in for a spell, walking up and down the comb of the roof and shaking his head and muttering to himself; but his feelings got the upper hand of him, presently, and he broke loose and cussed himself black in the face. I never see a bird take on so about a little thing. When he got through he walks to the hole and looks in again for half a minute; then he says, 'Well, you're a long hole, and a deep hole, and a mighty singular hole altogether—but I've started in to fill you, and I'm d—d if I *don't* fill you, if it takes a hundred years!'

And with that, away he went. You never see a bird work so since you was born. He laid into his work and the way he shoved acorns into that hole for about two hours and a half was one of the most exciting and astonishing spectacles I ever struck. He never stopped to take a look any more—he just hove 'em in and went for more. Well, at last he could hardly flop his wings, he was so tuckered out. He comes a-drooping down, once more, swearing like an ice-pitcher, drops his acorn and says, 'Now I guess I've got the bulge on you by this time!' So he bent down for a look. If you'll believe me, when his head come up again he was just pale with rage.

He just had strength enough to crawl up on to the comb and lean his back agin' the chimney and then he collected his impressions and begun to free his mind. I see in a second that what I had mistook for profanity in the mines was only just the rudiments, as you may say.

Another jay was going by, and heard him doing his devotions, and stops to inquire what was up. The sufferer told him the whole circumstance, and says, 'Now yonder's the hole, and if you don't believe me, go and look for yourself.'

So this fellow went and looked, and comes back and says, 'How many did you say you put in there?'

'Not any less than two tons,' says the sufferer.

The other jay went and looked again. He couldn't seem to make it out, so he raised a yell, and three more jays come. They all made the sufferer tell it over again, then they all discussed it, and got off as many leather-headed opinions about it as an average crowd of humans could have done.

They called in more jays; then more and more, till pretty soon this whole region 'peared to have a blue flush about it. There must have been five thousand of them; and such another jawing and disputing and ripping and cussing, you never heard. Every jay in the whole lot put his eye to the hole and delivered a more chuckle-headed opinion about the mystery than the jay that went there before him. They examined the house all over, too. The door was standing half open, and at last one old jay happened to go and light on it and look in. Of course, that knocked the mystery galley-west in a second. There lay the acorns, scattered all over the floor. He flopped his wings and raised a whoop. 'Come here!' he says, 'Come here, everybody; hang'd if this fool hasn't been trying to fill up the house with acorns!' They all came a-swooping down like a blue cloud, and as each fellow lit on the door and took a glance, the whole absurdity of the contract that first jay had tackled hit him home and he fell over backward suffocating with laughter, and the next jay took his place and done the same.

Well, sir, they roosted around here on the trees for an hour, and guffawed over that thing like human beings. It ain't any use to tell me a bluejay hasn't got a sense of humor, because I know better. And memory, too. They brought jays here from all over the United States to look at that hole, every summer for three years. Other birds, too. And they could all see the point, except an old owl that come from Nova Scotia to visit the Yosemite, and he took this thing in on his way back. He said he couldn't see anything funny in it. But then he was a good deal disappointed about Yosemite, too."

NORTHERN SIERRA
MOUNTAINS AND RIVERS WITHOUT END

COVERING SECTION I–SECTION M

Tuolumne Meadows—Sonora Pass—Echo Lake
Donner Pass—Yuba River—Feather River Canyon—Belden

THE ADVENTURES OF ZENAS LEONARD, FUR TRADER

By Zenas Leonard

Zenas Leonard's record of the 1833–34 westward journey by Joseph Red-deford Walker's company of mountain men across the Sierra Nevada to the Pacific is regarded by historians as one of the most complete and accurate accounts of such early exploration. Walker's legacy remains, as a number of geographical features linked with the Pacific Crest Trail bear his name, including the well-known Walker Pass in the southern Sierra (marking the end of Section F and the beginning of Section G of the PCT). Walker Pass offered a far easier return route than the pass chosen for the westward crossing documented in Leonard's narrative.

The westward route taken by Walker was most likely along one of the southern tributaries of the East Walker River near the present-day community of Bridgeport. Once over the crest, somewhere near Virginia Pass, they followed the divide between the Merced and Tuolumne Rivers within the area of present-day Yosemite National Park. It is probable that expedition members were the first white men to view the Yosemite Valley. Leonard also documents his early encounters with the giant Sequoia (Sequoiadendron giganteum), as well as the party's attempts to eat juniper berries and their gratitude upon finding acorns from the California black oak in the region.

This excerpt from Leonard's journal begins in mid-October 1833, as the Walker party prepares to cross the Sierras.

SOURCE: Excerpted from *The Adventures of Zenas Leonard, Fur Trader*, ed. John C. Ewers. Copyright © 1959 by the University of Oklahoma Press. By permission of the University of Oklahoma Press.

Today we sent out several scouting parties to search out a pass over the mountain. [. . .] One of them had found an Indian path, which they thought led over the mountain—whereupon it was resolved that in the morning we would take this path as it seemed to be our only prospect of preservation. Accordingly, at an early hour the next morning we started on our journey along the foot of the mountain in search of the path discovered on the previous day, and found it. On examination we found that horses traveled it, and must of course come from the west. This gave us great encouragement, as we were very fearful we would not be able to get our horses over at all. Here we encamped for the night. In the morning we started on our toilsome journey. Ascending the mountain we found to be very difficult from the rocks and its steepness. This day we made but poor speed, and encamped on the side of the mountain.

October 16. Continued our course until the afternoon when we arrived at what we took for the top, where we again encamped, but without anything to eat for our horses, as the ground was covered with a deep snow, which from appearance, lays on the north side of the peaks the whole year around. These peaks are generally covered with rocks and sand, totally incapable of vegetation; except on the south side, where grows a kind of juniper or gin shrub, bearing a berry tasting similar to gin. Here we passed the night without anything to eat except these gin berries, and some of the insects from the lake [described earlier], which our men had got from the Indians. We had not suffered much from cold for several months previous to this; but this night, surrounded as we were with the everlasting snows on the summit of this mountain, the cold was felt with three-fold severity.

In taking a view the next morning of the extensive plains through which we had traveled, its appearance is awfully sublime. As far as the eye can reach, you can see nothing but an unbroken level, tiresome to the eye to behold. To the east the aspect is truly wonderful. [...] The next morning it was with no cheerful prospect that each man prepared himself for traveling, as we had nothing to eat worth mentioning. As we advanced, in the hollows sometimes we would encounter prodigious quantities of snow. When we would come to such places, a certain portion of the men would be appointed alternately to go forward and break the road to enable our horses to get through; and if any of the horses would get swamped, these same men were to get them out. In this tedious and tiresome manner we spent the whole day without going more than eight or ten miles. In some of these ravines where the snow is drifted from the peaks, it never entirely melts, and may be found at this season of the year from ten to one hundred feet deep. From appearance it never melts on the top, but in warm weather the heap sinks by that part melting which lays next [to] the ground. This day's travel was very severe on our horses, as they had not a particle to eat. They began to grow stupid and stiff, and we began to despair of getting them over the mountain. We encamped this night on the south side of one of these peaks or ridges without anything to eat, and almost without fire. To add to the troubles and fatigues which we encountered in the day time, in getting over the rocks and through the snow, we had the mortification this evening to find that some of our men had become almost unmanageable, and were desirous of turning back and retracing our steps to the buffalo country! The voice of the majority, which always directs the movements of such a company, would not pacify them; nor had the earnest appeals of our captain any effect. The distance was too great for them to undertake without being well provided, and the only way they could be prevented was by not letting them have any of the horses or ammunition. Two of our horses were so much reduced that it was thought they would not be able to travel in the morning at all whereupon it was agreed that they should be butchered for the use of the men. This gave our men fresh courage, and we went to bed this night in better spirits than we had done for a long time. Some of the men had fasted so long, and were so much in want of nourishment, that they did not know when they had satisfied the demands of nature, and ate as much and as eagerly of this black, tough, lean, horse flesh, as if it had been the choicest piece of beef steak.

In the morning, after freely partaking of the horse meat, and sharing the remainder to each man, we renewed our journey, now and then coming onto an Indian path, but as they did not lead in the direction we were going, we did not follow them—but for most of the distance we this day traveled, we had to encounter hills, rocks and deep snows. The snow in most of the hollows we this day passed through, looks as if it had remained here all summer, as eight or ten inches from the top it was packed close and firm—the top being loose and light, having fell only a day or two previous. About the middle of the afternoon we arrived at a small lake or pond, where we concluded to encamp, as at this pond we found a small quantity of very indifferent grass, but which our horses cropped off with great eagerness. Here we spent the night, having yet seen nothing to create a hope that we had arrived near the opposite side of the mountain—and what was equally as melancholy, having yet discovered no signs of game.

The next morning we resumed our labor, fortunately finding less snow and more timber, besides a number of small lakes, and some prospect of getting into a country that produced some kind of vegetation. The timber is principally pine, cedar, and red wood, mostly of a scrubby and knotty quality. After traveling a few miles further, however, than any other day since we had reached the top of the mountain, we again encamped on the margin of another small lake, where we also had the good fortune to find some pasture for our horses. This evening it was again decided to kill three more of our horses which had grown entirely worthless from severe traveling and little food. The next morning several parties were dispatched in search of a pass over the mountain, and to make search for game; but they all returned in the evening without finding either. The prospect at this time began to grow somewhat gloomy and threaten us with hard times again. We were at a complete stand. No one was acquainted with the country, nor no person knew how wide the summit of this mountain was. We had traveled for five days since we arrived at what we supposed to be the summit—were now still surrounded with snow and rugged peaks—the vigor of every man almost exhausted—nothing to give our poor horses, which were no longer any assistance to us in traveling, but a burden, for we had to help the most of them along as we would an old and feeble man.

This mountain must be near as high as the main chain of the Rocky Mountains—at least a person would judge so from the vast quantity of snow with which it is covered, and the coldness of the air. The descent from the Rocky Mountains to this is but trifling, and supposed by all the company not to be greater than we had ascended this mountain from the plain—though we had no means of ascertaining the face. It is true, however, that the vast plain through which we had traveled was almost perfectly level, on part of which the water gradually descended to the west, and on the other towards the east.

Our situation was growing more distressing every hour, and all we now thought of was to extricate ourselves from this inhospitable region; and as we were perfectly aware, that to travel on foot was the only way of succeeding, we spent no time in idleness—scarcely stopping in our journey to view an occasional specimen of the wonders of nature's handiwork. We traveled a few miles every day, still on the top of the mountain, and our course continually obstructed with snow, hills and rocks. Here we began to encounter in our path, many small streams which would shoot out from under these high snowbanks, and after running a short distance in deep chasms which they have through ages cut in the rocks, precipitate themselves from one lofty precipice to another, until they are exhausted in rain below. Some of these precipices appeared to us to be more than a mile high. Some of the men thought that if we could succeed in descending one of these precipices to the bottom, we might thus work our way into the valley below—but on making several attempts we found it utterly impossible for a man to descend, to say nothing of our horses. We were then obliged to keep along the top of the dividing ridge between two of these chasms which seemed to lead pretty near in the direction we were going—which was west—in passing over the mountain, supposing it to run north and south. In this manner we continued until the 25th without any particular occurrence, except that of our horses dying daily—the flesh of which we preserved for food. Our course was very rough and tiresome, having to encounter one hill of snow and one ledge of rocks after another. On the 25th every man appeared to be more discouraged and down-spirited than ever, and I thought that our situation would soon be beyond hope if no prospect of getting from the mountain would now be discovered. This day we sent out several parties on discoveries, who returned in the evening without bringing the least good news, except one man, who was last coming, having separated from his companions, brought a basket full of acorns to camp. These were the first acorns we had seen since we left the state of Missouri. These nuts our hunter had got from an Indian who had them on his back traveling as though he was on a journey across the mountain, to the east side. When the Indian seen our hunter he dropped his basket of provision and ran for his life. These nuts caused no little rejoicing in our camp, not only on account of their value as food, but because they gave us the gratifying evidence that a country mild and salubrious enough to produce acorns was not far distant, which must be vastly different from any we had passed through for a long time. We now felt agreeably surprised that we had succeeded so far and so prosperously, in a region of many miles in extent where a native Indian could find nothing to eat in traversing the same route, but acorns. These nuts are quite different from those in Missouri—being much larger and more palatable [...] (though a person subsisting upon very lean horse meat for several days is hardly capable of judging with precision in a case of this kind).

The next morning we resumed our journey somewhat revived with the strong expectation that after a few days more tedious traveling, we would find ourselves in a country producing some kind of game by which we might recruit our languid frames, and pasture to resuscitate the famished condition of our horses. We still found snow in abundance, but our course was not so much obstructed with rocks as formerly. In two or three days we arrived at the brink of the mountain. This at first was a happy sight, but when we approached close, it seemed to be so near perpendicular that it would be folly to attempt a descent. In looking on the plain below with the naked eye, you have one of the most singular prospects in nature; from the great height of the mountain the plain presents a dim yellow appearance; but on taking a view with the spy glass we found it to be a beautiful plain stretched out towards the west until the horizon presents a barrier to the sight. From the spot where we stood to the plain beneath, must at least be a distance of three miles, as it is almost perpendicular a person cannot look down without feeling as if he was wafted to and fro in the air, from the giddy height. [...] Here we encamped for the night, and sent men out to discover some convenient passage down towards the plain—who returned after an absence of a few hours and reported that they had discovered a pass or Indian trail which they thought would answer our purpose, and also some signs of deer and bear, which was equally as joyful news—as we longed to have a taste of some palatable food. The next morning after pursuing our course a few miles along the edge of the mountain top we arrived at the path discovered by our men, and immediately commenced the descent, gladly leaving the cold and famished region of snow behind. The mountain was extremely steep and difficult to descend, and the only way we could come with any speed was by taking a zigzag direction, first climbing along one side and then turning to the other, until we arrived at a ledge or precipice of rocks, of great height, and extending eight or ten miles along the mountain—where we halted and sent men in each direction to ascertain if there was any possibility of getting over this obstruction. In the afternoon of the same day our men returned without finding any safe passage through the rocks—but one man had succeeded in killing a small deer, which he carried all the way to camp on his back—this was dressed, cooked and eat in less time than a hungry wolf would devour a lamb.

This was the first game larger than a rabbit we had killed since the 4th of August when we killed the last buffalo near the Great Salt Lake, and the first we had eat since our dried meat was exhausted (being fourteen days), during which time we lived on stale and forbidden horse flesh. I was conscious that it was not such meat as a dog would feast on, but we were driven to extremes and had either to do this or die. It was the most unwholesome as well as the most unpleasant food I ever eat or ever expect to eat—and I hope that no other person will ever be compelled to go through the same. It seemed to be the greatest cruelty to take your rifle, when your horse sinks to the ground from starvation, but still manifests a desire and willingness to follow you, to shoot him in the head and then cut him up and take such parts of their flesh as extreme hunger alone will render it possible for a human being to eat. This we done several times, and it was the only thing that saved us from death. Twenty-four of our horses died since we arrived on top of the mountain—seventeen of which we eat the best parts.

When our men returned without finding any passage over the rocks, we searched for a place that was as smooth and gradual in the descent as possible, and after finding one we brought our horses, and by fastening ropes round them let them down one at a time without doing them any injury. After we got our horses and baggage all over the rocks we continued our course down the mountain, which still continued very steep and difficulty. The circumstance of one of our men killing a deer greatly cheered the languid spirits of our hunters, and after we got safely over the rocks several of the men started out in search of game, although it was then near night. The main body continued on down until we arrived at some green oak bushes, where we encamped for the night, to wait for our hunters—who returned soon after dark well paid for their labor, having killed two large black-tailed deer and a black bear, all very fat and in good eating order. This night we passed more cheerful and in better heart than any we had spent for a long time. Our meat was dressed and well cooked, and every man felt in good order to partake of it.

In descending the mountain this far we have found but little snow, and began to emerge into a country which had some signs of vegetation—having passed through several groves of green oak bushes, &c. The principal timber which we came across is red wood, white cedar, and the balsam tree. We continued down the side of the mountain at our leisure, finding the timber much larger and better, game more abundant and the soil more fertile. Here we found plenty of oak timber, bearing a large quantity of acorns, though of a different kind from those taken from the Indian on the mountain top. In the evening of the 30th we arrived at the foot or base of this mountain—having spent almost a month in crossing over. Along the base of this mountain it is quite romantic—the soil is very productive—the timber is immensely large and plenty, and game, such as deer, elk, grizzly bear and antelopes are remarkably plenty. [...] In the last two days traveling we have found some trees of the red-wood species, incredibly large—some of which would measure from sixteen to eighteen fathom round the trunk and at the height of a man's head from the ground.

On the 31st we pursued our course towards the plain in a western direction. Now that we had reached a country thickly filled with almost all kinds of game, our men, and particularly those fond of hunting, were in fine spirits.

CLIMBING MATTERHORN PEAK

By Jack Kerouac

Just north of Tuolumne Meadows, Pacific Crest Trail hikers camped at Miller Lake, or passing the Matterhorn Canyon Trail, will see rising to the east, in great saw-toothed ridges of granite, the alpine ridgeline and stark peak of the Sierra Matterhorn. This daunting summit was immortalized in Jack Kerouac's 1958 novel, The Dharma Bums. *In many ways a backcountry version of his earlier work* On the Road, *this Zen- and wilderness-inspired adventure is based on many of the real-life exploits of Kerouac, enacted by Ray Smith in the novel, and California poet Gary Snyder, who is called Japhy Ryder.*

In this excerpt, Japhy and his friend Morley are taking Ray on his first-ever backpacking trip: a weekend summit of the Sierra Matterhorn. In addition to introducing Ray to the rigors of backcountry travel and the awe-inspiring beauty of nights in the high country, Japhy also initiates him into more esoteric practices, like haiku hiking (the impromptu creation of instant haikus as one hikes) and the Zen of mountain climbing. The trip described in The Dharma Bums *has become so popular, in fact, that the camp used by the three men—near an RV-size boulder at the base of the peak itself—has been dubbed Kerouac Camp and is often visited by hikers carrying the text along with them as they retrace their hero's footsteps. This excerpt begins on the second day of the trip, as the three men leave base camp and make their summit attempt.*

SOURCES: Excerpted from *The Dharma Bums*, by Jack Kerouac, copyright © 1958 by Jack Kerouac, © renewed 1986 by Stella Kerouac and Jan Kerouac, used by permission of Penguin, a division of Penguin Group (USA) Inc.; "On Climbing the Sierra Matterhorn Again After Thirty-One Years," from *No Nature*, by Gary Snyder, copyright © 1992 by Gary Snyder, by permission of Pantheon Books, a division of Random House, Inc.

At about noon we started out, leaving our big packs at the camp where nobody was likely to be till next year anyway, and went up the scree valley with just some food and first-aid kits. The valley was longer than it looked. In no time at all it was two o'clock in the afternoon and the sun was getting that later more golden look and a wind was rising and I began to think "By gosh how we ever gonna climb that mountain, tonight?"

I put it up to Japhy who said: "You're right, we'll have to hurry."

"Why don't we just forget it and go home?"

"Aw come on Tiger, we'll make a run up that hill and then we'll go home." The valley was long and long and long. And at the top end of it got very steep and I began to be a little afraid of falling down, the rocks were small and it got slippery and my ankles were in pain from yesterday's muscle strain anyway. But Morley kept walking and talking and I noticed his tremendous endurance. Japhy took his pants off so he could look just like an Indian, I mean stark naked, except for a jockstrap, and hiked almost a quarter-mile ahead of us, sometimes waiting a while, to give us time to catch up, then went on, moving fast, wanting to climb the mountain today. Morley came second, about fifty yards ahead of me all the way. I was in no hurry. Then as it got later afternoon I went faster and decided to pass Morley and join Japhy. Now we were at about eleven thousand feet and it was cold and there was a lot of snow and to the east we could see immense snowcapped ranges of whooee levels of valleyland below them, we were already practically on top of California. At one point I had to scramble, like the others, on a narrow ledge, around a butte of rock, and it really scared me: the fall was a hundred feet, enough to break your neck, with another little ledge letting you bounce a minute preparatory to a nice good bye one-thousand-foot drop. The wind was whipping now. Yet that whole afternoon, even more than the other, was filled with old premonitions or memories, as though I'd been there before, scrambling on these rocks, for other purposes more ancient, more serious, more simple. We finally got to the foot of Matterhorn where there was a most beautiful small lake unknown to the eyes of most men in this world, seen by only a handful of mountain-climbers, a small lake at eleven thousand some odd feet with snow on the edges of it and beautiful flowers and a beautiful meadow, an alpine meadow, flat and dreamy, upon which I immediately threw myself and took my shoes off. Japhy'd been there a half-hour when I made it, and it was cold now and his clothes were on again. Morley came up behind us smiling. We sat there looking up at the imminent steep scree slope of the final crag of the Matterhorn.

"That don't look much, we can do it!" I said glad now.

"No, Ray, that's more than it looks. Do you realize that's a thousand feet more?"

"That much?"

"Unless we make a run up there, double-time, we'll never make it down again to our camp before nightfall and never make it down to the car at the lodge before tomorrow morning at, well midnight."

"Phew."

"I'm tired," said Morley. "I don't think I'll try it."

"Well that's right," I said. "The whole purpose of mountain climbing to me isn't just to show off you can get to the top, it's getting out to this wild country."

"Well I'm gonna go," said Japhy.

"Well if you're gonna go, I'm goin with you."

"Morley?"

"I don't think I can make it. I'll wait here." And that wind was strong, too strong, I felt that as soon as we'd be a few hundred feet up the slope it might hamper our climbing.

Japhy took a small pack of peanuts and raisins and said "This'll be our gasoline, boy. You ready Ray to make a double-time run?"

"Ready. What would I say to the boys in The Place if I came all this way only to give up at the last minute?"

"It's late so let's hurry." Japhy started walking very rapidly and then even running sometimes where the climb had to be to the right or left along ridges of scree. Scree is long landslides of rocks and sand, very difficult to scramble through, always little avalanches going on. At every few steps we took it seemed we were going higher and higher on a terrifying elevator, I gulped when I turned around to look back and see all of the state of California it would seem stretching out in three directions under huge blue skies with frightening planetary space clouds and immense vistas of distant valleys and even plateaus and for all I knew whole Nevadas out there. It was terrifying to look down and see Morley a dreaming spot by the little lake waiting for us. "Oh why didn't I stay with old Henry?" I thought. I now began to be afraid to go any higher from sheer fear of being too high. I began to be afraid of being blown away by the wind. All the nightmares I'd ever had about falling off mountains and precipitous buildings ran through my head in perfect clarity. Also with every twenty steps we took upward we both became completely exhausted.

"That's because of the high altitude Ray," said Japhy sitting beside me panting. "So have raisins and peanuts and you'll see what kick it gives you." And each time it gave us such a tremendous kick we both jumped up without a word and climbed another twenty, thirty steps. Then sat down again, panting, sweating in the cold wind, high on top of the world our noses sniffling like the noses of little boys playing late Saturday afternoon their final little games in winter. Now the wind began to howl like the wind in movies about the Shroud of Tibet. The steepness began to be too much for me; I was afraid now to look back any more; I peeked: I couldn't even make out Morley by the tiny lake.

"Hurry it up," yelled Japhy from a hundred feet ahead. "It's getting awfully late." I looked up to the peak. It was right there. I'd be there in five minutes. "Only a half-hour to go!" yelled Japhy. I didn't believe it. In five minutes of scrambling angrily upward I fell down and looked up and it was still just as far away. What I didn't like about that peak-top was that the clouds of all the world were blowing right through it like fog.

"Wouldn't see anything up there anyway," I muttered. "Oh why did I ever let myself into this?" Japhy was way ahead of me now, he'd left the peanuts and raisins with me, it was with a kind of lonely solemnity now he had decided to rush to the top if it killed him. He didn't sit down any more. Soon he was a whole football field, a hundred yards ahead of me, getting smaller. I looked back and like Lot's wife that did it. *This is too high!* I yelled to Japhy in a panic. He didn't hear me. I raced a few more feet up and fell exhausted on my belly, slipping back just a little. *This is too high!* I yelled. I was really scared. Supposing I'd start to slip back for good, these screes might start sliding any time any way. That damn mountain got Japhy, I could see him jumping through the foggy air up ahead from rock to rock, up, up, just the flash of his boot bottoms. "How can I keep up with a maniac like that?" But with nutty desperation I followed him. Finally I came to the kind of ledge where I could sit at a level angle instead of having to cling not to slip, and I nudged my whole body inside the ledge just to hold me there tight, so the wind would not dislodge me, and I looked down and around I had had it. *I'm staying here!* I yelled to Japhy.

"Come on Smith, only five minutes. I only got a hundred feet to go!"

I'm staying here! It's too high!

He said nothing and went on. I saw him collapse and pant and get up and make his run again.

I nudged myself closer into the ledge and closed my eyes and thought. "Oh what life is this, why do we have to be born in the first place, and only so we can have our poor gentle flesh laid out to such impossible horrors as huge mountains and rock and empty space," and with horror I remembered the famous Zen saying, "When you get to the top of a mountain, keep climbing." The saying made my hair stand on end; it had been such cute poetry sitting on Alvah's straw mats. Now it was enough to make my heart pound and my heart bleed for being born at all. "In fact when Japhy gets to the top of that crag he *will* keep climbing, the way the wind's blowing. Well this old philosopher is staying right here," and I closed my eyes. "Besides," I thought, "rest and be kind, you don't have to prove anything." Suddenly I heard a beautiful broken yodel of strange musical and mystical intensity in the wind, and looked up, and it was Japhy standing on top of Matterhorn peak letting out his triumphant mountain-conquering Buddha Mountain Smashing song of joy. It was beautiful. It was funny, too, up here on the not-so-funny top of California and in all that rushing fog. But I had to hand it to him, the guts, the endurance, the sweat, and now the crazy human singing: whipped cream on top of ice cream. I didn't have enough strength to answer his yodel. He ran around up there and went out of sight to investigate the little flat top of some kind (he said) that ran a few feet west and then dropped sheer back down maybe as far as I care to the sawdust floors of Virginia City. It was insane. I could hear him yelling at me but I just nudged farther into my protective nook, trembling. I looked down at the small lake where Morley was lying on his back with a blade of grass in his mouth and said out loud "Now there's the karma of these three men here: Japhy Ryder gets to his triumphant mountaintop and makes it, I almost make it and have to give up and huddle in a bloody cave, but the smartest of them all is that poet's poet lyin down there with his knees crossed to the sky chewing on a flower dreaming by a gurgling *plage*, goddamit they'll never get me up here again."

I really was amazed by the wisdom of Morley now: "Him with all his goddam pictures of snowcapped Swiss Alps" I thought.

Then suddenly everything was just like jazz: it happened in one insane second or so: I looked up and saw Japhy *running down the mountain* in huge twenty-foot leaps, running, leaping, landing with a great drive of his booted heels, bouncing five feet or so, running, then taking another long crazy yelling yodelaying sail down the sides of the world and in that flash I realized *it's impossible to fall off mountains you fool* and with a yodel of my own I suddenly got up and began running down the mountain after him doing exactly the same huge leaps, the same fantastic runs and jumps, and in the space of about five minutes I'd guess Japhy Ryder and I (in my sneakers, driving the heels of my sneakers right into the sand, rock, boulders, I didn't care any more I was so anxious to get down out of there) came leaping and yelling like mountain goats or I'd say like Chinese lunatics of a thousand years ago, enough to raise the hair on the head of the meditating Morley by the lake, who said he looked up and saw us flying down and couldn't believe it. In fact, with one of my greatest leaps and loudest screams of joy I came flying right down to the edge of the lake and dug my sneakered heels into the mud and just fell sitting there, glad. Japhy was already taking his shoes off and pouring sand and pebbles out. It was great. I took off my sneakers and poured out a couple of buckets of lava dust and said "Ah Japhy you taught me a final lesson of them all, you can't fall off a mountain."

"And that's what they mean by the saying, When you get to the top of the mountain keep climbing, Smith."

Thirty-one years after this climb, the acclaimed California poet Gary Snyder, upon whom Japhy Ryder was based, returned to the Matterhorn. After reaching the summit, Snyder sat down and composed the following haiku-like poem. Today it can still be found, written in black calligraphy on brown, laminated paper, with the peak ledger on the summit. His words echo the feelings of many PCT travelers and backcountry explorers who have spent countless years climbing, hiking, and backpacking through the magnificent mountain ranges of the Pacific Rim.

On Climbing the Sierra Matterhorn Again After Thirty-One Years
Range after range of mountains
Year after year after year.
I am still in love.

4 X 40086, On the summit

ON THE PCT WITHOUT FOOD

By David Horton

When David Horton even talks about competition, running, and records, there is a sense that adrenaline is beginning its mad rush to every part of his body. He speaks and moves with a frenetic energy that seems beyond his power to contain. He gesticulates passionately with his hands and his words contain an infectious enthusiasm. As Horton says, "You can do more than you think you can." This poster child for extreme running completed the Appalachian Trail in record time in 1991, ran across the United States in 1995, and in 2005 established the speed record for completion of the Pacific Crest Trail (which has subsequently been broken by Scott "Bink" Williamson and Adam "Krudmeister" Bradley, who completed the trail in 65 days, 9 hours, and 58 minutes). To do so, Horton averaged the equivalent of running a marathon and a half every day. It was a stunning feat of endurance and determination and his faith.

Horton carried only a small pack and relied on a logistical support team to supply most of his needs. For the most part, this plan worked flawlessly until they reached the section of trail between Tuolumne Meadows and Sonora Pass. As Horton's story describes, a failed resupply left him and his hiking partner with the daunting decision to either admit defeat or to continue on their trek, without food. Either way, the failed resupply left them with empty packs and stomachs, deep in the backcountry. While an ordinary hike on the PCT can be challenging, a high-speed thru hike—especially without food—takes this challenge to new heights.

In the summer of 2005 I was on the Pacific Crest Trail with the goal of breaking the 83-day speed record for completing the trail. I had previously set the speed record on the Appalachian Trail at 52 days and 9 hours, averaging just over 40 miles per day. I thought I could achieve that on the PCT as well.

From the Mexican border to Kennedy Meadows, I had averaged over 43.7 miles per day. I knew this would not continue as I took on the High Sierra. The previous winter had seen the highest snowfall in the last eighty years. Most thru hikers that season skipped ahead of that section to bypass the snow and returned later in the season to complete the trail. In addition to the challenge created by the snowpack, for the 238 miles from Kennedy Meadows north to Highway 120 at Tuolumne Meadows, there were no road crossings, and that created extra logistical challenges. All of this elevated the level of difficulty.

Brian Robinson was going to accompany me from Kennedy Meadows until Sonora Pass to aid in routefinding and to assist me. Brian had previously completed the Triple Crown in one year (the Appalachian Trail, the Continental Divide Trail, and the Pacific Crest Trail), the first to ever do that.

I had planned on doing that long section in 6 days. With the level of snow, it took longer, 2 days longer. One day we went 19 miles in 13 hours and were totally wiped out.

Finally making it to Tuolumne Meadows was a relief, but we were both physically whipped and behind schedule. I had wanted to complete the 75 miles from there to Sonora Pass in 2 days. Based upon the amount of snow that we had come through and what we anticipated lay ahead, we both knew it would take 3 days.

The start of the next section was nice and easy enough. That soon changed, however, as we reached the snow. I remember going down through Kerrick Canyon on solid snow, on a very steep, off-camber trail with the cold rushing stream below us. It was difficult to stay upright and not plunge down the mountainside into the bone-chilling waters.

We camped the first night after covering about 30 miles. After a frigid night and a couple of intensely cold and unnerving stream crossings, we made it to Wilma Lake and the junction of Jack Main Canyon Trail. Josh Yeoman, one of my crew members, was going to meet us there to resupply us with food for the next day and a half. We arrived there around 3:00 PM. We had eaten the last of our food at 2:00 PM, thinking that we would get more soon.

The area around Wilma Lake was covered in huge mounds of snow, many feet high. Most of the trail signs were almost completely covered in snow. Josh was hiking in from Hetch Hetchy, more than 15 miles from the lake.

We waited, and we looked for Josh and any markings he might have left. We could not find any sign of anyone being there at all. I had a satellite phone and called my crew. They said that Josh was unable to make it in—he had gone back out to the road, with the food we needed.

I asked Brian what he thought we should do. Our options were to hike out to Hetch Hetchy, more than 15 miles downhill, and then later hike back over those same miles. Or, we could go on without food. This was a very difficult decision. We were consuming about six thousand calories daily, so how would we make it over 24 hours and 30 miles without food? Brian thought we could do it. The trail was well marked and far less rugged than the terrain down to Hetch Hetchy, and continuing on meant we wouldn't have to backtrack, which neither of us wanted to do. I hesitated. Then I agreed. "Let's go on without food," I told him. I called our crew and told them to drive to Sonora Pass and hike back along the trail with food, to meet us the next day.

We continued on, heading north for 6 miles and stopping around 6:00 PM in the stunning glaciated valley that is home to Grace Meadow. I carefully went through my pack, searching every pocket, but found no food. Brian rifled his pack and unearthed two ounces of olive oil and a small handful of beef jerky. We split this between us, maybe 150 calories each, and went to bed an hour later.

It was one of the longest and coldest nights I have ever spent. I could not get warm. I was wearing every stitch of clothing I had and was in a 15-degree sleeping bag. Brian recommended curling up in a ball, but that made little difference. I thought about suggesting that we share one sleeping bag, but my pride kept me from posing that option. When you are cold and low on energy you get extremely cold. I was so glad when morning came—it was such a relief to get moving and get warm.

It was a very long day as we walked north with no food. I never got light-headed or dizzy, but I spent considerable time fantasizing about large milkshakes and hamburgers. Walking was tiring, and I could not enjoy the beauty of my surroundings. At one point, Brian pointed out the 1000-mile mark. I said that I could not care less about what mile we had crossed.

During that tiring day, I made up my mind that I was quitting when we finished that day. I did not say anything to Brian about this, but I mentally made plans to fly home and be with my family and enjoy myself and not suffer anymore on this stupid trail.

As we were climbing the last high ridge of the volcanic terrain south of Sonora Pass—a spectacular area—I got to thinking about taking a day off. Instead of quitting, maybe if I took a day off I might be able to finish the PCT. I was mentally and physically annihilated. I gave it over to the Lord and said, if I take this day off and you can change my attitude, I will continue.

Finally, we got to a notch in the mountain and Josh met us a little over 4 miles from Sonora Pass—he had a lot of food, amazing food. It was 4:30 PM and we hadn't eaten in 26.5 hours. We were ravenous, and we inhaled everything Josh handed us. When we got to the pass, I told them that I was going to take the next day off and then maybe continue on.

We spent much of the next 2 days in Bridgeport. I don't think I have ever eaten so much in my life. Hamburgers. Milkshakes. More hamburgers. More milkshakes. We ate and slept and ate and slept. That full day off was glorious. It was so special. Over the course of the day my spirits lifted—I would go on. I never revealed that I had planned on quitting.

Brian left me the next morning and I continued north from Sonora Pass. He had been with me for more than 300 of the toughest miles on the PCT. I would not have made it without him. In fact, I got lost during the next 2 days without him. In the end, I had taken 2 days more than planned from Kennedy Meadows to Tuolumne Meadows, 1 more day from Tuolumne Meadows to Sonora Pass, and 1 rest day—4 extra days total. I never took another day off after that or failed to achieve my desired daily mileage. My total time was 66 days, 7 hours, and 15 minutes.

Now, four years later, I think back to that special trip. The hunger and the pain are long gone, but the memories of the spectacular vistas and the unique challenges of the PCT will last. I have been back on the trail each year since then and, for whatever reason, I continually challenge myself to pursue multiday adventures. I feel certain that I will always push myself to achieve ever greater goals. The drive seems to be part passion, part compulsion, with a pinch of insanity—something I learned that many Pacific Crest Trail hikers understand.

A SIERRA STORM

By "No Way" Ray Echols

On May 15, 2006, "No Way" Ray Echols fell to his death from the crumbling segment of the Pacific Crest Trail that clings to the cliffs above Deep Creek, about trail mile 301. Alice Tulloch, Ray's spouse and hiking partner, and Ray had begun a thru hike just three weeks earlier. As Alice comments, "We were finally free of careers, kids and car payments. He bubbled with excitement each day."

Ray had been a lifelong hiker. He chose his profession as a schoolteacher partly because he would have summers off for hiking. "Every summer," Alice remembers, "was the answer to the question of 'Where are we hiking next?'" Following his death, Alice compiled his writings into A Thru-Hiker's Heart, *which she concluded with a short afterword. "Late in summer," she wrote, "the weather becomes increasingly unstable over the High Sierra. Moist warm ocean air collides with granite. Afternoon thunderstorms release the energy. The clouds roil over the ridges. Sunshine and shadow play on the ragged white blocks. . . . The vivid light and the tumultuous weather marked the time No Way Ray best loved being in the Sierras. Hunkered down in the lee of a rock or cozy in a tent, he would watch the light show with pure delight."*

This excerpt from A Thru-Hiker's Heart *captures this sense of respect for, and awe of, the humbling power and majesty of the Sierra storm that we all should have . . . and the peace and light that follows.*

"The lightning splinters on the peaks, and rocks shiver, and great crashes
split the air and go rolling and tumbling into every cave and hollow; and
the darkness is filled with overwhelming noise and sudden light."
(*The Hobbit*, J. R. R. Tolkien)

It always amazes me…how quietly it begins, with the smallest and simplest of things…like the gentle brush of a butterfly's wings or the first rays of sunrise. It's early morning, and I notice a small puff of a cloud, a nascent cumulus, riding low and all alone on the southern horizon. [...]

By mid-morning the larger brothers of this insignificant, nearly unnoticeable cotton ball have gathered to fill half of the sky. I walk towards Ebbetts Pass, sometimes in windy, chilling shade, sometimes in glaring sun. Suddenly, clouds sweep over the sun and a biting wind drives a light rain across me. For the fifth time in six days I have experienced this early ephemeral shower. The first couple of days out of Tuolumne I donned my rain gear only to remove it minutes later as the clouds and sun again played hide-and-seek, at least for a few hours, until playing ceased. And so I know this momentary rain is but a taste of what is to come.

I travel on down the seven miles to Ebbetts Pass. By now the clouds have coalesced and cover most of the sky. To the northeast, virga (trailing rain that evaporates before it hits the ground) reaches its gray, gossamer fingers down towards the summits of Highland and Silver Peaks, both nearly 11,000 feet tall.

I arrive at the highway near Ebbetts Pass a little after 1:30. Sitting on a large, friendly rock just above the trail, I watch cars roar by. Civilization is too noisy…too fast. [...] A faint rumble of distant thunder reminds me that I also should be hurrying, so I gather up my gear and head up and around Ebbetts Peak. Within minutes, the trail breaks into the open, and the view sweeps out and around me in full circle.

By now, it's hide-and-seek in earnest. The clouds are definitely it, and the sun is busy hiding. Dark and foreboding, they cover the heavens. A second rumble undulates across the sky, tumbling and reverberating among the peaks. A minute later the thunder is louder and louder and seems closer, so I stop to look for lightning. To the south, from where I have just come, I see a flash and count…thirty seconds, about six miles. More to the west, lightning flashes over some closer peaks…fifteen seconds, three miles.

It's coming on fast, so I stop to check my pack. My gear is protected from the elements by an *innie*, a tough, plastic trash-compactor bag inside my pack.

With all my gear stowed inside it, the pack itself will get wet, but the contents stay nice and dry.

Now the trail begins to descend and wind its way through a maze of granite slopes, ledges, and boulders. The rain begins, still tentative but with obvious intent, so I stop next to Sherrold Lake and don my rain gear. The lightning and thunder are five seconds apart...a mile and counting. And I lose the trail. I walk back and forth and range outward and back—no trail. Checking the Guidebook, I see it say the "often faint" trail "snakes northwest...ducking in and around obstacles," and I can't find it—no ducks and too many obstacles.

The rain has now decided to get serious, and actual lightning bolts are visible, though still a mile or so away. I begin to feel some concern, more for my inability to find the trail than from the storm. The Guidebook says the trail follows the "path of least resistance," and somehow I convince myself that must mean down. Kinney Reservoir is visible, four hundred vertical feet below me, and that's down, so I drop into a steep ravine that falls towards its dark waters. After descending a hundred or so ticklish vertical feet, I come to my senses and head back up to where I know the trail must surely be.

The rain is coming hard, and lightning and thunder are only two and three seconds apart. The area is dotted with savagely gnarled lodgepole pine trees, none very tall, but many of respectable girth. I pick one and sit down on my pack. The wind, blowing strongly out of the west, drives the rain aslant, and here, sheltered in the lee of this venerable tree, I am fairly well protected. Hunched down, I look around and see that, of the dozens of trees about, including the one giving me shelter, all have tops that are split and shattered and dead...signs of lightning strikes. Truly, it's not the most comforting of sights.

I have always loved the storms, the fierce winds and raging elements, and although not much afraid, I confess to feeling some small disquiet as light and sound edge closer to becoming one. Over the years, I have waited out these mountain storms many times and have come to accept that there isn't really much one can do about them other than stay home. Obviously there are certain precautions that may be taken: don't hang onto metal, try to get off of ridges and peaks early, don't be the highest thing around, don't hide under tall trees, don't go into caves, try to contact the ground as little as possible, try to camouflage yourself in a grove of moderate-sized trees, don't fly a kite...and so on. Wisdom changes though, for the rock hut on the summit of Mount Whitney was constructed in 1909 as a shelter from lightning as a direct result of a death on its top, three years earlier. Now, caves are out, and a rock hut and a cave differ in little more than name. An old mountaineering book of mine from the 1950s suggests lying down on the ground; now the recommendation is to squat down, contacting the ground with as little of one's self as possible.

All precautions aside, by and large you are, as Homer says, in the hands of Zeus Who Loves the Thunder. You will either be struck or not, die or not, so you may as well sit back and enjoy the marvelous show. It's out of your hands. I have found that there is great serenity to be gained in knowing that there is nothing that can be done. And, after all, the probability of being struck is remotely small. That being said, I recall the wry statement of writer Douglas Adams, "The more unlikely an event is, the more likely it is to happen immediately," and make a passing nod to St. Barbara, a patron saint to those besieged by lightning. Life is full of incongruities. Isn't it marvelous?

Head down and supported by elbows on knees, my seated position feels comfortable, so I close my eyes and begin to . . . not doze really, but . . . withdraw from it all. My mind travels back to other places and times, to other storms. One from long ago comes to mind, a beautiful series of rolling cells that raged up the Sierra crest. My wife and I were camped in a little dome tent. The cells were coming from the south, and bumped along the crest about every half hour for three or four hours. You could hear them coming . . . thunder at first distant and lightning faint. Then, they would become brighter and louder until the crescendo, and it was upon us in all its fury. Passing on and to the north, it would gradually fade and give way to a new set from the south. The lightning was so fierce that I could see the fiberglass poles of the tent . . . through closed eyes.

Before that even, in 1972, my wife and I hiked the John Muir Trail. Coming up and out of LeConte Canyon, we traversed Dusy Basin and went over Bishop Pass to a food re-supply. Just over and down from the pass, a storm began in earnest. At the base of the pass, we saw a small tent over by Saddlerock Lake. Nestled among the rocks on a tiny peninsula that jutted out toward one of two islands, it looked small and insignificant below storm-wracked Mount Goode, towering nearly two thousand feet above.

After our re-supply and a zero day, we returned to the trailhead. At road's end there were ten or fifteen cars with people swarming everywhere, checking gear and shouldering packs. Asking what was the matter, we learned that two hikers were overdue. [. . .] Five days later, we heard from other hikers that the two had been found . . . struck by lightning and killed and lying in a small, insignificant tent on the shores of Saddlerock Lake.

A bright flash, followed in only two seconds by the thunderclap, startles me momentarily. Still adequately distant . . . almost. I hunker down and let my mind float free again. Another time, on another hike of the John Muir Trail, my son and I endured six days of the most ferocious thunderstorms I have yet to see. Going over Pinchot Pass, a storm caught my son and me down a couple of miles on its north side. We sought cover in a sparse, stunted forest near the Taboose Pass trail junction. North and down across the south fork of the Kings River, the trail broke out of the trees and traced a clear track up a long moraine to Mather Pass. Fully a mile away, we could see the tiny, dark forms of three hikers coming down. Suddenly, there was a burst of lightning. It came down seemingly directly toward the hikers, and to this day I swear that I saw it abruptly change direction so that it appeared to travel level with the ground and right over their heads. The hikers ran jerkily in all directions, scurrying about like Keystone Cops. I counted forty-three lightning strikes that were three seconds (less than half a mile) or closer within a half hour.

Another year, we climbed Mount Whitney arriving in mid-afternoon, but didn't stay long for the clouds were gathering. Whitney, being Whitney, had a dozen or two people lounging around on its top. We headed down and got onto the long south ridge. Within a few minutes, we felt every hair on our bodies begin to stand up. There was a raw humming in the air. Throwing off my all-metal Kelty pack frame, I bounded west down the bouldery slopes. Within seconds there was a thunderclap so loud that my ears rang. The sharp smell of ozone cut the air. I looked to the summit and saw a dozen people, apparently auditioning for a part in St. Vitus' Dance, the musical.

Moments after thinking of that time, I feel a familiar sensation as I begin to tingle over my entire body. Like the scarcely perceived sounds of a distant ringing telephone that somehow instantly and seamlessly become incorporated in your dream, Zeus has sculpted my reverie to warn me. Barely having time to act, I cram my fingers in my ears and hope for the best. Immediately, it goes off. If you've ever spent time in a foxhole, or gone fishing with dynamite, or had lightning strike right on top of you, you know the feeling—the light and sound and pressure. Stunned, I look around, expecting to see a nearby tree smoldering, standing in a shower of bark with a long scar winding around its trunk to the ground. But no, I can't see much, nor am I much inclined to explore.

This last seems to be the storm's hurrah, for no more strikes come closer than two or three seconds, and they begin to travel further afield. Mighty Zeus, having proofed me, no doubt searches for other hikers to assay.

In minutes, the rain begins to lessen, and within a quarter hour I am up and looking for the trail. And here it is, plain for those less harried to see. Another hour passes, and I am walking along the base of a stark serried, volcanic ridge, headed towards Reynolds Peak. The sun, newly coaxed from its hiding place, illuminates the land. Everything is wet and luminescent. A beautiful pink Indian paintbrush glows in the gray sage. A little further and I come to a field of dusky, green mule-ears, their golden-yellow flowers shining fiercely in the sun's lambent rays. Among them, white and blue lupine sway in the late afternoon breeze. Another Sierra storm has come and gone. The world has been created anew. Nearby, a bird makes a few tentative inquiries and, apparently satisfied with the answer, bursts into song. I head on up the trail.

SNOW-SHOE THOMPSON

By Dan DeQuille

The challenges, casualties, and conquests in these mountains have firmly established names like Muir, LeConte, Donner, and Carson in the lexicon of the High Sierra. But there are other lesser-known individuals who should be part of this mountain lore. And there may be no person more deserving of being elevated from mere mortal to legend than Snow-Shoe Thompson. No ordinary mailman, Thompson's primary route took him over the Old Emigrant Trail, which left Markleyville and summited the Sierras in the area of Border Ruffian Pass before dropping west to Hermit Valley. The Pacific Crest Trail crosses this area south of the Blue Lakes and the Nipple, both prominent features on this stretch of trail. For twenty winters, Thompson delivered the mail over this rugged route.

Dan DeQuille, a pseudonym for William Wright, was an associate and friend of Mark Twain. The "snowshoes" Thompson crafted, as DeQuille describes them, were much like rudimentary cross-country skis, while Thompson's method of backcountry travel can be likened to today's telemark skiers, who switch from cross-country to downhill skiing. Thompson also appears to have been an early adopter of the go-light philosophy.

DeQuille also mentions George W. Chorpenning Jr., who pioneered the transportation of mail, freight, and passengers to California (and other areas of the West). In 1851, Chorpenning contracted with the US Postal Service to deliver mail between Salt Lake City and Sacramento. Silver Mountain, which is mentioned in this tale, once the site of a booming prospecting town, is just east of Ebbetts Pass.

Source: Excerpted from "Snow-Shoe Thompson," by Dan DeQuille, *Sierra Club Bulletin* 20 (1935), reprinted from the *Overland Monthly* (October 1886): 419–35.

John A. Thompson, the man to whom the people of the Pacific Coast gave the name of "Snow-shoe Thompson," was born [...] [in] Norway, April 30, 1827; and died, May 15, 1876, after an illness of but a few days.

Mr. Thompson was a man of splendid physique, standing six feet in his stockings, and weighing 180 pounds. He had the blonde hair and beard, and fair skin and blue eyes of his Scandinavian ancestors; and looked a true descendant of the sea-roving Northmen of old.

At the age of forty-nine years, he seemed in the very prime of his life. His eye was bright as that of a hawk, his cheeks were ruddy, his frame muscular, and his *tout ensemble* that of a hardy mountaineer, ready to take the field, and face the dangers of the wilderness and the elements, at a moment's notice. His face wore that look of repose, and he had that calmness of manner, which are the result of perfect self-reliance, and a feeling of confidence in the possession of the powers to conquer.

In the year 1837, when ten years of age, Thompson left his native land, and with his father and family came to the United States. In 1851, Mr. Thompson was smitten with the "gold fever," and came across the plains to California. He landed at Hangtown, now known as Placerville. He presently became dissatisfied with the life and luck of a miner, and concluded to try the valleys. He went to Putah Creek, Sacramento Valley, and set up as a ranchman, but his eyes were constantly turned eastward toward the mountains—toward where the snowy peaks glittered against the deep blue sky.

Early in the winter of 1856, Mr. Thompson read in the papers of the trouble experienced in getting the mail across the snowy summit of the Sierra Nevada. What he heard and read of the difficulties encountered in the mountains, on account of the great depth of the snow, set him to thinking. When he was a boy, in Norway, snow-shoes were objects as familiar to him as ordinary shoes are to the children of other lands. He determined to make a pair of snow-shoes out of oak timber. Although he was but ten years of age at the time he left his native land, his recollections of the shoes he had seen there were in the main correct. Nevertheless, the shoes he made were such as would at the present day be considered much too heavy, and somewhat clumsy. They were ten feet in length, were four inches in width behind the part on which the feet rest, and in front were four inches and a quarter wide.

Having completed his snow-shoes to the best of his knowledge, Thompson at once set out for Placerville, in order to make experiments with them. Being made out of green oak, Thompson's first shoes were very heavy [...] he put them upon a pair of scales, and found that they weighed twenty-five pounds. They were ponderous affairs, but their owner was a man of giant strength, and he was too eager to be up and doing to lose time in making another pair out of lighter wood.

When he made his first public appearance, he was already able to perform such feats as astonished all who beheld them. His were the first Norwegian snow-shoes ever seen in California. At that time, the only snow-shoes known were those of the Canadian pattern. Mounted upon his shoes—which were not unlike thick sled runners in appearance—and with his long balance-pole in his hands, he dashed down the sides of the mountains at such a fearful rate of speed as to cause many to characterize the performance as fool-hardy. Snow-shoe Thompson did not ride astride his guide-pole, nor trail it by his side in the snow, as is the practice of other snow-shoers when descending a steep mountain, but held it horizontally before him, after the manner of a tight-rope walker. His appearance was most graceful when seen darting down the face of a steep mountain, swaying his long balance-pole now to this side and now to that, as a soaring eagle moves its wings.

His first trip was made in January, 1856. He went from Placerville to Carson Valley, a distance of ninety miles. With the mail bags strapped upon his back, he glided over fields of snow that were in places from thirty to fifty feet in depth, his long Norwegian shoes bearing him safely and swiftly along upon the surface of the great drifts. Having successfully made the trip to Carson Valley and back to Placerville, Snow-shoe Thompson became a necessity, and was soon a fixed institution of the mountains. He carried the mail between the two points all winter. Through him was kept up the only land communication there was between the Atlantic States and California.

The loads that Snow-shoe Thompson carried strapped upon his back would have broken down an ordinary man, though wearing common shoes and traveling on solid ground. The weight of the bags he carried was ordinarily from sixty to eighty pounds; but one winter, when he carried mail for Chorpenning, his load often weighed over one hundred pounds.

In going from Placerville to Carson Valley, owing to the great amount of uphill traveling, three days were consumed; whereas, he was able to go from Carson Valley to Placerville in two days, making forty-five miles a day. Not a house was then found in all that distance. Between the two points all was a wilderness.

While traveling in the mountains, Snow-shoe Thompson never carried blankets, nor did he even wear an overcoat. The weight and bulk of such articles would have encumbered and discommoded him. Exercise kept him warm while traveling, and when encamped he always built a fire. He carried as little as possible beside the bags containing the mail.

At the time Thompson began snow-shoeing in the Sierras, nothing was known of the mysteries of "dope"—a preparation of pitch, tallow, and other ingredients, which, being applied to the bottom of the shoes, enables the wearer to lightly glide over snow softened by the rays of the sun. It is made of different qualities, and different degrees of hardness and softness. Each California snow-shoe runner has his "dope secret," or his "pet" dope, and some are so nice in this respect as to carry with them dope for different hours of the day; using one quality in the morning, when the snow is frozen, and others later on, as the snow becomes soft. As Thompson used no dope, soft snow stuck to and so clogged his shoes that it was sometimes impossible for him to travel over it. Thus, it frequently happened that he was obliged to halt for several hours during the day, and resume his journey at night, when a crust was frozen on the snow.

Snow-shoe Thompson's night camps—whenever the night was such as prevented him from pursuing his journey, or when it was necessary for him to obtain sleep—were generally made wherever he happened to be at the moment. He did not push forward to reach particular points. He was always able to substitute snow for water, without feeling any bad effect. He always tried, however, to find the stump of a dead pine, at which to make his camp. After setting fire to the dry stump he collected a quantity of fir or spruce boughs, with which he constructed a sort of rude couch or platform on the snow. Stretched upon his bed of boughs, with his feet to his fire, and his head resting upon one of Uncle Sam's mail bags, he slept as soundly as if occupying the best bed ever made; though, perhaps, beneath his couch there was a depth of from ten to thirty feet of snow.

When Snow-shoe Thompson was carrying the mail to Murphy's Camp, California, he traveled by way of Hermit Valley. At Hermit Valley were some deserted houses, and occasionally he found it convenient to lodge for a night in one of these. The snow was frequently so deep in that elevated region that it was a difficult matter to find the houses, so completely were they buried beneath the great drifts. He was obliged to prospect for the buildings, by probing the snow with his balance-pole.

At times, when traveling at night, Thompson was overtaken by blizzards, when the air would be so filled with snow, and the darkness so great, that he could not see to proceed. On such occasions, he would get on top of some big rock, which the winds kept clear of snow, and there dance until daylight appeared; the lateness of the hour and the blinding storm preventing his making one of his usual camps.

If not the swiftest, it was universally conceded that, even up to the time of his death, Thompson was the most expert snow-shoe runner in the Sierra Nevada. At Silver Mountain, Alpine County, California, in 1870, when he was forty-three years of age, he ran a distance of sixteen hundred feet in twenty-one seconds. There were many snow-shoers at that place, but in daring Thompson surpassed them all. Near the town was a big mountain, where the people of the place were wont to assemble on bright days in winter, to the number of two or three hundred. The ordinary snow-shoers would go part way up the mountain to where there was a bench, and then glide down a beaten path. This was too tame for Thompson. He would make a circuit of over a mile, and come out on the top of the mountain. When he appeared on the peak he would give one of his wild High-Sierra whoops, poise his balance-pole, and dart down the face of the mountain at lightning speed, leaping all the terraces from top to bottom, and gliding far out on the level before halting.

Snow-shoe Thompson seldom performed any feat for the mere name and fame of doing a difficult and daring thing; yet W. P. Merrill, postmaster at Woodford's, Alpine County, writes me as follows, in speaking of some of Thompson's achievements: "He at one time [...] made a jump of one hundred and eighty feet without a break." This seems almost incredible, but Mr. Merrill is a reliable man. I spoke of this feat to Mr. C. P. Gregory, formerly Thompson's neighbor in the mountains, and he answered that although he had never heard of that particular leap, he did not doubt what Mr. Merrill said. "I know," said Mr. Gregory, "that at Silver Mountain he often made clear jumps of fifty and sixty feet."

Postmaster Merrill says: "A few years before his death, Thompson one winter made a trip from here [Woodford's] up into Sierra County on his snow-shoes, to run a race with the snow-shoers up there. But he would not run their way. They had a track beaten down the hill where they ran. They would then squat down on their shoes, and run down along the prepared course. Thompson offered to put up money and go out upon the highest mountains, where there was no track made, and run and jump with them, but no one would take him up. "That style of snow-shoe racing" Thompson said "is nothing more than coasting on snow-shoes," and in Alpine County is not dignified with the name of snow-shoeing.

John A. Thompson was the father of all the race of snow-shoers in the Sierra Nevada; and in those mountains he was the pioneer of the pack train, the stage coach, and the locomotive. On the Pacific Coast his equal in his peculiar line will probably never again be seen. The times and conditions are past and gone that called for men possessing the special qualifications that made him famous. It would be hard to find another man combining his courage, physique, and powers of endurance—a man with such sinews, controlled by such a will.

JUNE 28, BARKER PASS:
CONFESSIONS OF A DAY HIKER

By Chris Robertson

In athletics we often speak of "muscle memory"—the body's ability to remember specific and precise movements, especially those practiced repetitively, such as swinging a tennis racket, riding a bicycle, swimming or walking. Pacific Crest Trail hikers are similarly familiar with the sensation of lying stretched out on a sleeping bag after a long day on the trail while the muscles of the legs continue to twitch and spasm in a remembered rhythm of walking. Here, Chris Robertson reminds us that our regular memory is itself just like a muscle, one that strengthens through practice and exercise and that weakens with age and disuse. Many PCT hikers who return to the trail year after year have experienced this weakening of the memory's muscle, as wildflowers and wildlife that were known at the end of the last season must be looked up again at the beginning of this one. Since even the sharpest memories and the most memorable experiences can fade over time, we often record them in our trail journals and collect these stories in anthologies like this one—wordy forget-me-nots left behind like trail markers for the mind to follow so that we lose less to the passage of time.

> *"The memory is a muscle. The memory is a muscle."*
> —The Bootstrappers

We see him walking toward us on the trail. He's maybe thirty, still fresh faced, smiling. His gaze settles on a point above the trees, where forest meets sky. He's carrying a full pack. His step is light, even without hiking poles. He's swatting at bugs. "Thru hiker," I say.

"Yep," says John, who announced last night over beers that someday—soon, next summer or the summer after that—he wants to hike the length of the PCT.

"How's the trail?" I ask. When we meet hikers, we smile, offer a friendly but reserved hello. Most people want the trail to themselves. Mostly, so do we. Today I'm curious. The hiker stops, smiles, I do see collapsible poles, strapped to the back of his pack.

"Well," he says, "mosquitoes are bad from here to Richardson Lake, real bad down by Bear Lake Creek." John nods, gives me a look. "But, they were hellacious in Yosemite," Adam continues, "so it's relative."

"Are you from around here?" I ask. Adam tells us he's from Oklahoma. He's been planning this trip for five years.

"I sold my construction business, everything in my house. Then I sold my house," he says.

"Way to go," John says.

"I kept looking at topo maps," Adam says. "I knew it was now or never." We nod. I can tell John is checking out Adam's pack, gauging weight, thinking a season ahead.

"How is it, carrying that much weight?" John asks.

"My pack's at twenty-eight pounds, which isn't too bad," Adam says. "I've shipped some gear home." He shifts under the load, takes a step back. "I'm heavier after a resupply, but I get light again pretty quick. Guess I should get moving." We wish him a good walk. He gives us a wave, heads up the trail.

This afternoon—our twelfth wedding anniversary—we've hooked onto the PCT at Barker Pass. I'm carrying a topo map of Lake Tahoe basin, my Sierra flower guide, fleece pants, vest, slicker, journal, two liters of water, an orange, a peanut butter sandwich, my baseball hat, matches, emergency blanket, a hank of rope, sunscreen, bite gel, lip balm, extra wool socks, toilet paper, trowel, two baggies. Travel light? Not me. Three miles, seven, sixteen, my pack shows who I am: a girl raised on bad weather, bugs, wind, summer snow, and a better than average chance of getting stranded.

"If we thru hike you won't be able to carry all that weight," John tells me, not for the first time, his own pack slim, light as a wing.

"You know I'm a lost cause for thru hiking," I say. "How's about I'm your trail angel. I'll meet you at Sonora Pass. I'll meet you here. Which way do you want to go?"

"You choose," he says.

Barker Pass is a hub of dirt roads, used by the Forest Service and all kinds of recreators. There's a paved road right to the top, making access to the trailhead, at 7650 feet, easy. You can head south toward Desolation Wilderness or north toward Twin Peaks.

To the south I spy a mariposa lily, its pale yellow petals cupping all procreation, pistil and stamen and pollen, smoky red and gold, blooming in dry rocky soil. Where there's one, there's more. "This way," I point, and start walking.

"Adam says the bugs are bad," John says.

"You'll be hiking through peak mosquito season when you do the PCT," I say. "We'll turn around if they get bad." It's only been the past few seasons that we've hiked on the PCT while much of anything was in bloom. John, a salt lick for mosquitoes, favors fall hiking—you see fewer hikers, even fewer bugs, hillsides of aspen quaking gold, orange, red, then purply brown. And the plants have shriveled by then, gone to seed and dun. So when I finally picked up a Sierra Nevada guide and saw color plates of wildflowers I'd only heard rumors about—hillsides of balsamroot, Sierra violet, grass-of-Parnassus, early summer creeks crowded with monkey flower, stands of larkspur, seams of corn lily, a bog ringed by a meadow thick with shooting star—I was forced into heady, cold-hearted math. I divided John's potential future bites into the numbers of flowers I'd already missed. Tidy and incontrovertible sum in hand, I bought him a hat with a net and vowed to carry repellents and salves. Now, we lace up our boots in mid-June.

The trail descends, curves into woods. I fall in behind John and the rhythm of my boots and hiking poles soon sets my breath free. Like my pack, though, my mind is overfull. A few weeks' back, my father's doctor told him, no mincing words, he's got early Alzheimer's. "I'm going to give you three words to remember," he told him early in his physical. "Fair enough," said my father. Twenty minutes later, the doctor asked him for the words. Simple, working words, like ladder, apple, walk. My father lost two of them.

Each time we talk I ask, "Dad, are you taking your walks?"

"Not much," he says. "I get to thinking too much." Like father, like daughter. Yet what I also know about putting one foot in front of the other is that, sure as lupine pods will turn brown and snap open, casting black, pebbled seeds into late summer's parched air, a few miles down the trail my feet will set my head free. We reach a section of trail that cuts through forested bog lush with corn lilies set to bloom in mid-July. It's been a wet spring up in the Sierras. Not enough snow and rain to make up for another dry winter, but enough, at least, to bring on flowers. More wildflowers than I have names for. Cinquefoil and forget-me-not grow thick along the west side of the trail. Forget-me-not, "mouse ear," from the Greek *myosotis*, winds up grassy ravines, fills hollows, turns meadows a shaggy blue. A water-loving borage, here in the Sierras the tiny, periwinkle, five-petaled flower thrives while streams run but almost always dies back by mid-July.

Forget-me-not grows like a weed in my father's backyard. A few weeks ago, after talking with my brother about Dad's faltering memory, I flew to British Columbia for a visit. My father couldn't remember where he left his shovel, or his gloves, but he recited the Latin names for half a dozen plants growing in his garden. We were helping him clean up the backyard, take it back from half a year of weeds and neglect. "Pull out all that forget-me-not, will you?" he'd directed me, waving his hand at a glorious patch standing tall in the middle of his garden.

"You want me to pull out all this forget-me-not?" I said. "Why, Dad?"

"It's a damned weed," he shrugged. "It'll take over if you let it."

And so I did as he asked. I razed the whole patch, crushing stalks and tiny blue flowers in my fingers. My father tossed the plants onto a heap at the edge of the yard. Then he showed my brother and me how to dig up iris bulbs and how to split them, trim them, tuck them into dirt. "Not too deep," he said, "or they won't overwinter." He gave us each a sack of bulbs to plant in our own gardens. Later still, over grilled trout and beer, he said, "Did I show you, I dug up all the irises along the wall this afternoon."

Now John and I, we're hiking in mountains older than human memory, so old their granite ridges gleam in sunlight, a bleached and knotty and twisted spine. Before settler cultures arrived, indigenous peoples, the Martis and Paiute among them, traveled and lived among these peaks and valleys. Speaking of the nineteenth-century summer days he spent exploring the Sierras, John Muir says, "No pain here, no dull empty hours, no fear of the past, no fear of the future." More than 150 years on, legions of us take to trails in the Range of Light like bumblebees to heather, hummingbirds to paintbrush, nutcrackers to whitebark pine.

On another day, south of here, as John and I stood on the rocky saddle of Virginia Pass looking down at Virginia Canyon, bathed in dawn, we shifted our gaze north to Virginia Peak, volcanic red in every kind of light, and the Sierra Nevada claimed me, aching knees and pumping heart, as one of its own. Here, like nowhere else, I'm home. And so today, like always, a mile or two into our hike I'm taken over by the tug of the trail. Ahead, John reaches a creek, finds the crossing rocks, waits on the other side. The trail opens up to meadow, soft and muddy. Mosquitoes cloud around him, descend. John trots, shakes his head, stops, raises a pole, swipes at the air. "I'm getting pummeled," he says.

"Let's turn around and check out the trail that goes to Twin Peaks," I say. We retrace our steps, reach the parking lot, head north.

Here's a conversation we sometimes have on the trail. I say, "If I become an invalid or lose my marbles, you know what to do, right?"

"Right," John says. "Take you up to Ebbetts Pass, walk you into the woods, and leave you there with blankets, food, and water."

"You got it," I say.

"I'm with you," he says.

"Right," I say. "It's settled, then." Neither of us is joking. Not really.

When he was in his sixties, John's father had a series of strokes and then a quadruple bypass; his short-term memory vanished. My grandmother lost her memory in her fifties. Her mother died recognizing no one.

My father is seventy-four. His doctor tells him, "Jack, you've got the heart of a sixty-four year old." But my father knows he's losing names, bits of the conversation he's having with you. He tells me, laughing sadly, "My body's going to outlast my mind. I'll give you trouble yet, kid."

In the trees, the trail follows a rise. Forget-me-not, lush and blue, skirts the trail. Rounding a corner, we see it—a red flash on the wing. "Who's that?" John asks.

"Woodpecker?"

"Nope," he says. "Blunt bill. Red breast, some gray. Wing bars. I've got him." He hands me the binoculars. I look, but I'm stumped.

"We'll check the book," I say. Have I forgotten this bird? For all he's lost, my father remembers every plant or bird he ever knew. My parents stayed together forty years, until my mother's death. They didn't hike, but they learned the flowers and the birds.

On a scree slope we meet Adam. He's not alone. "Hello again," he says. He introduces us to Highlander, whose off-trail name is also Adam. It's sunny, almost hot. We're standing on an exposed slope. The two Adams seem happy to talk. Highlander is hiking with his girlfriend, Gingersnap, a ways behind.

"She's having a hard day," Highlander says. Two years ago they hiked the Appalachian Trail. He's made for thru hiking: he's lean, tall, young, smiling. He can't be more than twenty-seven.

"Did you guys see a red bird a bit ago?" I ask.

"No," says Highlander, "but if you run into Gingersnap, ask her. She knows her birds."

"So, does news travel fast on the trail?" John asks.

"Yeah, even if it's not true." Adam says. He tells us, then, how a few weeks' back word got out about a young preacher, engaged to be married, hiking the trail. Adam met him, hiked with him for a week. "I finally asked him, 'Are you a preacher? Are you engaged?' He said, 'No, I just graduated from college.' "

Everyone laughs. I have another question. Their faces are sunburned. "Where are your hats?"

In unison they say, "We sent them home."

"Extra weight?" John says.

"Exactly."

We wish them well. Adam and Highlander head north, we head south. Soon we run into Gingersnap. Red-faced, slogging along, she still smiles. She hasn't seen the red bird. John asks about her shoe covers. She says, "They keep rocks and dust from getting into your shoes."

John nods, taking mental note. "Well," she says, "I need to keep going. Lots of miles left today."

"Have a good walk," I tell her. I'm glad she's wearing a hat.

The last mile we walk through trees. I'm thinking about the name of the bird. I'm thinking about how the body, not just the mind, caches memories. Our days turn into sinew and bone. I know John is thinking ahead to his own PCT hike. That summer, I'll be his trail angel. I'll hike close to home. Walking on the PCT, for a day, a week, a summer, you join a tribe, a pilgrimage. This walk is a cultural story.

The name of the stunning red bird? Pine grosbeak. Forget me not.

WINTER ON DONNER PASS

By Moses Schallenberger

The story of Donner Pass has been dominated by the ill-fated trans-Sierra journey of the Donner Party during the winter of 1847. The tragic conclusion of their trip has been well documented in the diaries of Patrick Breen, Virginia Reed Murphy, Sarah Graves Fosdick, and others.

The troubles of the Donner Party had their roots in their slow progress across the West. Winter came early in 1846, and by November 4 eighty-one people were living in two camps and were prevented from moving across the pass by snow. One of the cabins occupied by the Breen family had been constructed the prior winter by Joseph Foster, Allen Montgomery, and Moses Schallenberger. Schallenberger was barely eighteen years old when he arrived at present-day Donner Lake as a member of the Stephens-Townsend-Murphy Party. He volunteered (along with Foster and Montgomery) to remain behind and guard six wagons as the rest of the party rushed to cross the Sierras before winter made the mountains impassable. Schallenberger's account of his ordeal, while lesser known, is no less compelling than the dramatic tale of the Donner Party.

On June 22, 1847, after remnants of human bodies had been collected and buried, the cabin was burned, apparently as a kind of purification ceremony. The site of the cabin is near the present Donner Monument east of the pass. Present-day PCT hikers will see Donner Lake off to the east and can imagine, as they trudge the upper elevations of Donner Pass, how difficult it must have been to travel this mountain wilderness in winter, with little food, and even less gear.

Here is some of Schallenberger's story.

Source: Excerpted from *The Opening of the California Trail*, by Moses Schallenberger, ed. George R. Stewart. Copyright © 1953 by the Regents of the University of California, © renewed 1981 by Theodosia Stewart. Published by the University of California Press. Reprinted by permission of the University of California Press.

They left us two cows, so worn out and poor that they could go no further. We did not care for them to leave us any cattle for food, for [...] there seemed to be plenty of game, and we were all good hunters, well furnished with ammunition, so we had no apprehension that we would not have plenty to eat, that is, plenty of meat. Bread we had not tasted for many weeks, and had no desire for it. We had used up all our supply of buffalo meat, and had been living on fresh beef and bacon, which seemed to satisfy us completely.

[...] Foster, Montgomery and myself set about making a cabin, for we determined to make ourselves as comfortable as possible, even if it was for a short time. We cut saplings and yoked up our poor cows and hauled them together. These we formed into a rude house, and covered it with rawhides and pine bush. The size was about twelve by fourteen feet. We made a chimney of logs eight or ten feet high, on the outside, and used some large stones for the jambs and back. We had no windows; neither was the house chinked or daubed, as is usual in log-houses, but we notched the logs down so close that they nearly or quite touched. A hole was cut for a door, which was never closed. We left it open in the day-time to give us light, and as we had plenty of good beds and bedding that had been left with the wagons, and were not afraid of burglars, we left it open at night also. [...]

On the evening of the day we finished our little house it began to snow, and that night it fell to a depth of three feet. This prevented a hunt which we had in contemplation for the next day. It did not worry us much, however, for the weather was not at all cold, and we thought the snow would soon melt. But we were doomed to disappointment. A week passed, and instead of any snow going off more came. At last we were compelled to kill our cows, for the snow was so deep that they could not get around to eat. They were nothing but skin and bones, but we killed the poor things to keep them from starving to death. We hung them up on the north side of the house and covered them with pine brush. That night the meat froze, and as the weather was just cold enough to keep it frozen, it remained fresh without salt. It kept on snowing continually, and our little cabin was almost covered. It was now about the last of November or first of December, and we began to fear that we should all perish in the snow.

The snow was so light and frosty that it would not bear us up, therefore we were not able to go out at all except to cut wood for the fire; and if that had not been near at hand I do not know what we should have done. None of us had ever seen snow-shoes, and of course had no idea how to make them, but finally Foster and Montgomery managed to make something they called a snow-shoe.

[...] Their method of construction was this: taking some of our wagon bows, which were of hickory and about half an inch thick, they bent them into an oblong shape forming a sort of hoop. This they filled with a network of rawhide. We were now able to walk on the snow to bring in our wood, and that was about all there was to do. There was no game. We went out several times but never saw anything. What could we expect to find in ten feet of snow? It would sometimes thaw a little during the day and freeze at night, which made a crust on the snow sufficiently thick to bear the weight of a coyote, or a fox, and we used sometimes to see the tracks of these animals, but we were never fortunate enough to get a sight of the animals themselves.

We now began to feel very blue, for there seemed no possible hope for us. We had already eaten about half our meat, and with the snow on the ground getting deeper and deeper each day, there was no chance for game. Death, the fearful, agonizing death by starvation, literally stared us in the face. At last, after due consideration, we determined to start for California on foot. Accordingly we dried some of our beef, and each of us carrying ten pounds of meat, a pair of blankets, a rifle and ammunition, we set out on our perilous journey. Not knowing how to fasten snow-shoes to our feet made it very fatiguing to walk with them. We fastened them heel and toe, and thus had to lift the whole weight of the shoe at every step, and the shoe would necessarily sink down somewhat, the snow would crumble in on top of it, and in a short time each shoe weighed about ten pounds.

Foster and Montgomery were matured men, and could consequently stand a greater amount of hardship than I, who was still a growing boy with weak muscles and a huge appetite, both of which were being used in exactly the reverse order designed by nature. Consequently, when we reached the summit of the mountain about sunset that night, having traveled a distance of about fifteen miles, I was scarcely able to drag one foot after the other. The day had been a hard one for us all, but particularly painful to me. The awkward manner in which our snow-shoes were fastened to our feet made the mere act of walking the hardest kind of work. In addition to this, about the middle of the afternoon I was seized with cramps. I fell down with them several times, and my companions had to wait for me, for it was impossible for me to move until the paroxysm had passed off. After each attack I would summon all my will power and press on, trying to keep up with the others. Towards evening, however, the attacks became more frequent and painful, and I could not walk more than fifty yards without stopping to rest.

When night came on we cut down a tree and with it built a fire on top of the snow. We then spread some pine brush for our beds, and after eating a little of our jerky and standing round our fire in a vain attempt to get warm, we laid down and tried to sleep. Although we were thoroughly exhausted, sleep would not come. Anxiety as to what might have been the fate of those who had preceded us, as well as uncertainty as to our fate, kept us awake all night. Every now and then one of us would rise to replenish the fire, which, though it kept us from freezing, could not make us comfortable. When daylight came we found that our fire had melted the snow in a circle of about fifteen feet in diameter, and had sunk to the ground a distance also of about fifteen feet. The fire was so far down that we could not get to it, but as we had nothing to cook, it made but little difference. We ate our jerky while we deliberated as to what we should do next. I was so stiff that I could hardly move, and my companions had grave doubts as to whether I could stand the journey. If I should give out they could afford me no assistance, and I would necessarily be left to perish in the snow. I fully realized the situation, and told them that I would return to the cabin and live as long as possible on the quarter of beef that was still there, and when it was all gone I would start out again alone for California. They reluctantly assented to my plan, and promised that if they ever got to California and it was possible to get back, they would return to my assistance.

We did not say much at [this] parting. Our hearts were too full for that. There was simply a warm clasp of the hand accompanied by the familiar word, "Good-by," which we all felt might be the last words we should ever speak to each other. The feeling of loneliness that came over me as the two men turned away I cannot express, though it will never be forgotten, while the, "Good-by, Mose," so sadly and reluctantly spoken rings in my ears to-day.

My companions had not been long out of sight before my spirits began to revive. [...] I strapped on my blankets and dried beef, shouldered my gun, and began to retrace my steps to the cabin. It had frozen during the night and this enabled me to walk on our trail without the snowshoes. This was a great relief, but the exertion and sickness of the day before had so weakened me that I think I was never so tired in my life as when, just before dark, I came in sight of the cabin. The door-sill was only nine inches high, but I could not step over it without taking my hands to raise my leg. As soon as I was able to crawl around the next morning I put on snow-shoes, and taking my rifle, scoured the country thoroughly for foxes. The result was as I had expected—just as it had always been—plenty of tracks, but no fox.

Discouraged and sick at heart, I came in from my fruitless search and prepared to pass another night of agony. As I put my gun in the corner, my eyes fell upon some steel traps that Captain Stevens had brought with him and left behind in his wagon. In an instant the thought flashed across my mind, 'If I can't shoot a coyote or fox, why not trap one.' There was inspiration in the thought, and my spirits began to rise immediately. The heads of the two cows I cut to pieces for bait, and, having raked the snow from some fallen trees, and found other sheltered places, I set my traps. That night I went to bed with a lighter heart, and was able to get some sleep.

As soon as daylight came I was out to inspect the traps. I was anxious to see them and still I dreaded to look. After some hesitation I commenced the examination, and to my great delight I found in one of them a starved coyote. I soon had his hide off and his flesh roasted in a Dutch oven. I ate this meat, but it was horrible. I next tried boiling him, but it did not improve the flavor. I cooked him in every possible manner my imagination, spurred by hunger, could suggest, but could not get him into a condition where he could be eaten without revolting my stomach. But for three days this was all I had to eat. On the third night I caught two foxes. I roasted one of them, and the meat, though entirely devoid of fat, was delicious. I was so hungry that I could easily have eaten a fox at two meals, but I made one last me two days.

I often took my gun and tried to find something to shoot, but in vain. Once I shot a crow that seemed to have got out of his latitude and stopped on a tree near the cabin. I stewed the crow, but it was difficult for me to decide which I liked best, crow or coyote. I now gave my whole attention to trapping, having found how useless it was to hunt for game. I caught, on an average, a fox in two days, and every now and then a coyote. These last-named animals I carefully hung up under the brush shed on the north side of the cabin, but I never got hungry enough to eat one of them again. There were eleven hanging there when I came away. I never really suffered for something to eat, but was in almost continual anxiety for fear the supply would give out. For instance, as soon as one meal was finished I began to be distressed for fear I could not get another one. My only hope was that the supply of foxes would not become exhausted. [...] It is strange that I never craved anything to eat but good fat meat. For bread or vegetables I had no desire. Salt I had plenty, but never used. I had just coffee enough for one cup, and that I saved for Christmas.

My life was more miserable than I can describe. The daily struggle for life and the uncertainty under which I labored were very wearing. I was always worried and anxious, not about myself alone, but in regard to the fate of those who had gone forward. I would lie awake nights and think of these things, and revolve in my mind what I would do when the supply of foxes became exhausted. The quarter of beef I had not touched, and I resolved to dry it, and, when the foxes were all gone, to take my gun, blankets, and dried beef and follow in the footsteps of my former companions.

Fortunately, I had plenty of books, Dr. Townsend having brought out quite a library. I used often to read aloud, for I longed for some sound to break the oppressive stillness. For the same reason, I would talk aloud to myself. At night I built large fires and read by the light of the pine knots as late as possible, in order that I might sleep late the next morning, and thus cause the days to seem shorter. What I wanted most was enough to eat, and the next thing I tried hardest to do was to kill time. I thought the snow would never leave the ground, and the few months I had been living here seemed years.

One evening, a little before sunset, about the last of February, as I was standing a short distance from my cabin, I thought I could distinguish the form of a man moving towards me. I first thought it was an Indian, but very soon I recognized the familiar face of Dennis Martin. My feelings can be better imagined than described. He relieved my anxiety about those of our party who had gone forward with the wagons. They had all arrived safely in California and were then in camp on the Yuba. They were all safe, although some of them had suffered much from hunger. [...] My sister, Mrs. Townsend, hearing that Mr. Martin was about to return to pilot the emigrants out of the wilderness, begged him to extend his journey a little farther and lend a helping hand to her brother Moses. He consented to do so, and here he was. Being a Canadian, he was accustomed to snow-shoes, and soon showed me how to fix mine so I could travel with less than half the labor. He made the shoe a little narrower, and fastened it to the foot only at the toe, thus making the heel a little heavier, so that the shoe would drag on the snow instead of having to be lifted at every step.

The next morning, Martin and Schallenberger began their journey. Although Schallenberger's weakened condition made this an ordeal for him, they emerged safely from the mountains. Schallenberger lived much of his life near San Jose, where he died in 1909.

FOOTPRINTS

By Corey Lee Lewis

One of the most commonly cited and treasured experiences to be had along the Pacific Crest Trail is that of solitude. Many PCT aficionados, whether ardent thru hikers or frequent day-trippers, enjoy the long stretches of lonely trail and uninhabited wilderness, the silence and peace that come from escaping the flatlander crowds and climbing high into the clouds. And yet, many others write and talk about the trail culture, the people they met along the way, those they hiked and talked with, and those that gave them rides to resupply or to a well-known trail angel's house. In this piece, Corey Lewis takes to the trail to find solitude but instead finds himself reflecting on the long history of trail culture surrounding the PCT, the countless number of explorers, activists, and trail crew members that it took to create—and that it takes to maintain—this two-thousand-mile trail.

I came out here to be alone—to lose even the company of my shadow in the solitude and darkness of wilderness night hiking—but, instead, I find I am walking in well-worn footsteps, surrounded by the ghosts of those who have gone before me.

As I hike north from the bustle and business of the Interstate 80 corridor, I leave the constant hiss and hum of traffic behind. Soon, the sounds of the wind whispering through the long needles of the pine and the short strings of the fir, are the only music I hear, and I am reminded of John Muir's travels through these same forests. These soft symphonies, although newer to my ears, have

SOURCE: The poetry excerpt in this essay is from "Kusiwoqqobi," from *No Nature*, by Gary Snyder. Copyright © 1992 Gary Snyder. Used by permission of Pantheon Books, a division of Random House, Inc.

been enjoyed by generations of concertgoers before me; ancient "Æolian harps" Muir called these musical giants as they sang to him softly in the Sierra wind so many years ago. As I leave the light pollution of the highway behind me, Orion the Hunter looks on from the heavens above, while Ursa Major spoons out inky blackness into the sky and Ursa Minor guides me on my way north.

Night hiking usually offers an extra degree of solitude, especially because you cease to rely so heavily on sight, your dominant sense. Sounds erupt with significance, and even the rhythmic thumping of your feet begins to affect the direction of your thoughts. While wilderness experiences like my time on the PCT are becoming increasingly rare in our urbanized world, experiences of wild, untrammeled night are perhaps even less common and thus more valuable. Even busy stretches of the PCT are deserted at night. You can hike for long miles with only your thoughts and shadow for company and conversation along the trail. But, as I'm beginning to find out, they alone can be quite a crowd.

As I pass the Sierra Club's Peter Grubb Hut, warm rectangles of light, voices, and laughter escape from its open windows, and my thoughts move from Muir to David Brower, the Sierra Club, and the countless activists it took to preserve and protect this wild corridor through which I now hike. Although I'm alone now and farther north, I think about William Colby leading that first Sierra Club High Trip in 1901 with ninety-six people up to the Pacific Crest overlooking Yosemite. I recall with gratitude that if it weren't for the tireless efforts of people like him, or Senator William J. Carr, and Forest Service Supervisor Fred W. Cleator, this trail simply would not exist.

As I put one beat-up boot down in front of the other on the well-worn tread, my mind wanders backward, into the past, tracing the trail's origins and construction: From Theodore Solomons's first dreams of a Sierra crest trail in 1884 to Catherine Montgomery's full-fledged 1926 vision of a "high winding trail down the heights of our western mountains with mile markers and shelter huts...from the Canadian border to the Mexican boundary line!" My solitary footsteps along this lonely stretch of trail, ring with the echoes and memories of thousands of trail crews, those I've worked on and those countless others that built this trail before me.

As I ascend the west side of Basin Peak and climb to over 8000 feet elevation, I take note of the carefully constructed retaining walls holding the switchbacks in place and begin to get dizzy, not so much from the altitude but from trying to imagine the sheer amount of labor it took to build this entire trail. As a former trail crew member, I know well the slow, rhythmic days of hauling and chipping rock that it takes just to build a few feet of trail. And I know from reading, and hiking other sections of the trail, that some parts were blasted out of solid rock and others riprapped cobble by cobble on faces of slick granite, while other heavily wooded sections to my north are blocked each season by falling trees and eroding trail beds. Hiking alone, I find myself immersed in the trail's early history, giving thanks with each step for the countless number of Civilian Conservation Corps members and volunteers who constructed this trail, stone by stone, switchback by switchback, and mile by mile.

Initially I decided to take this solo hike as a reprieve from the fast pace and heavy demands of graduate school and wilderness advocacy work, a chance to spend some time alone in the Sierras and on the trail that I love. But I seem to have brought my studies and my work with me. Everywhere I look, each step I take and each landmark I see, seems laden with memories, crowded by the ever-present past.

As I pass an old-growth Jeffrey pine, one almost three feet in diameter at breast height and at least several hundred years old, I press my nose into its cracked and plated bark, and soon I am swimming in memories made of vanilla and pineapple: "Wow, it does smell just like ice cream!" I exclaimed to my older brother. We were just children, being introduced to the Jeffrey pine for the first time in our lives. A forest ranger stood beside me smiling, perhaps recalling her first encounter with the child-famous "ice cream trees" of the West. And then, in a flash, with my nose still in the bark, I'm an adult and I'm hearing Gary Snyder read his poem "Kusiwoqqobi" to a packed audience in the ballroom of a Sacramento hotel:

> *Sweet smell of the pine.*
> *Delicious! Like pineapple!*
> *What did the Piute children think of,*
> *Smelling Kusiwoqqobi,*
> *What did they say?*

As I step back from the towering tree, I'm surrounded by generations of Piute, the first travelers of these trails, and I become aware that the thread of history I am following is very long indeed, and the trail more crowded with traffic than I had ever imagined.

As I hike through the dappled moonlight and shadows, I imagine the Pacific Crest Trail as a long thread, stretching from south to north, weaving itself deep within the tapestry of American history and culture. Even the names of the surrounding areas are rich with history: Haypress Valley, Wild Plum Creek, Dead Horse Canyon, Henness Pass, Yuba River. As Henry Nash Smith observed in *Wilderness and the American Mind*, the frontier wilderness and our experiences of it, form a major part of the American character and culture. We would not be the same people we are without our wilderness areas and the wildlands of the West. Even easterners like Emerson and Thoreau recognized this and wrote of the need for an increasingly urban population to get outside and experience nature in her grandest, wildest, and freest forms.

On the trail, I'm completely alone, even losing my faint moon shadow from time to time, but still I find myself carrying these historic figures with me. Or, perhaps, it is more accurate to say they were carrying me. As in the famous poem "Footsteps in the Sand," although we carry the memories of these forbearers, it is they who carry us. It was they who imagined the trail, protected and preserved its corridor, built and maintained its eroding routes, and passed all this knowledge and their stories on to us. I suddenly realize that none of us, even the purest solo thru hiker, ever hikes the PCT alone. Each of us is carried along the trail by these hiking partners of both past and present.

The next day, I climb down from the PCT and thread my way to the banks of the North Fork of the Yuba River, and I can see us all flowing through time. The Yuba's rolling waters and clear currents boil and bubble before me, dropping down an endless cascade of boulders, pools, braided channels, and free-flowing streams in a constant and clear symphony of sound. As I slip into the icy stream, I imagine myself as a single drop of water, joining the throng of drops that have come before me, until we are one, a single river of hikers, of heart and soul, flowing through space and across time.

After a long and luxurious swim, and plenty of playful splashing and otter-like sliding down smoothed stream channels, I sit in the sun to dry off. Quartz, feldspar, and mica glitter from the granite below, twinkling like the stars above that have watched over me on this hike. I hoist my pack and return to the trail, knowing that this time I'm not hiking alone. There are still miles to cover and work to do, trails to maintain, rivers to free, wilderness to protect, and there are generations of hikers to come who are counting on us to leave footsteps for them to follow.

They are all hiking with me, and I'm grateful for the company: the deer and bear that first scouted these routes, the Piute who connected them from village to village, and the early immigrants and explorers who named the passes and crossings of the crest. And along with them walk the trail's early advocates and proponents, the trail workers and volunteers, who laid the tread and built the bridges on which I walk, and the trail angels who guide and support me along the way. They too are coming with me. The generations of hikers who have shared their stories, offered advice and hard-won wisdom, have also joined my hiking party. In a long and dusty line, we head off over the horizon, hiking with the hope that by following in each others footsteps we will find our own way, together, into the future.

A WIND-STORM IN THE FORESTS

By John Muir

Pacific Crest Trail hikers resupplying at Wild Plum Campground or Sierra City will soon find themselves in the Yuba watershed, hiking along some of the same ridges that John Muir explored and captured in his acclaimed 1894 publication, The Mountains of California. *PCT hikers and backcountry enthusiasts owe most of their protected public lands to the efforts of John Muir—founder of the Sierra Club and often called the father of both our national park and national forest systems. A dedicated environmentalist and hardy mountain climber, Muir studied and explored the Sierras tirelessly, often hiking for days with nothing but a cup and a loaf of bread tied to his belt. In this excerpt from* The Mountains of California, *Muir describes climbing to the top of a massive Douglas spruce in order to enjoy a violent Sierra windstorm and he reflects on both the natural history of, and our kinship with, the diverse conifers of the California mountains. No anthology about walking the mountains of the West would be complete without the words of John Muir.*

One of the most beautiful and exhilarating storms I ever enjoyed in the Sierra occurred in December, 1874, when I happened to be exploring one of the tributary valleys of the Yuba River. The sky and the ground and the trees had been thoroughly rain-washed and were dry again. The day was intensely pure, one of those incomparable bits of California winter, warm and balmy and full of white sparkling sunshine, redolent of all the purest influences of the spring, and at the same time enlivened with one of the most bracing wind-

SOURCE: Excerpted from *The Mountains of California*, by John Muir (New York: The Century Company, 1907), 248–57.

storms conceivable. Instead of camping out, as I usually do, I then chanced to be stopping at the house of a friend. But when the storm began to sound, I lost no time in pushing out into the woods to enjoy it. For on such occasions Nature has always something rare to show us, and the danger to life and limb is hardly greater than one would experience crouching deprecatingly beneath a roof.

It was still early morning when I found myself fairly adrift. Delicious sunshine came pouring over the hills, lighting the tops of the pines, and setting free a steam of summery fragrance that contrasted strangely with the wild tones of the storm. The air was mottled with pine-tassels and bright green plumes, that went flashing past in the sunlight like birds pursued. But there was not the slightest dustiness, nothing less pure than leaves, and ripe pollen, and flecks of withered bracken and moss. I heard trees falling for hours at the rate of one every two or three minutes; some uprooted, partly on account of the loose, water-soaked condition of the ground; others broken straight across, where some weakness caused by fire had determined the spot. The gestures of the various trees made a delightful study. Young Sugar Pines, light and feathery as squirrel-tails, were bowing almost to the ground; while the grand old patriarchs, whose massive boles had been tried in a hundred storms, waved solemnly above them, their long, arching branches streaming fluently on the gale, and every needle thrilling and ringing and shedding off keen lances of light like a diamond. The Douglas Spruces, with long sprays drawn out in level tresses, and needles massed in a gray, shimmering glow, presented a most striking appearance as they stood in bold relief along the hilltops. The madroños in the dells, with their red bark and large glossy leaves tilted every way, reflected the sunshine in throbbing spangles like those one so often sees on the rippled surface of a glacier lake. But the Silver Pines were now the most impressively beautiful of all. Colossal spires 200 feet in height waved like supple goldenrods chanting and bowing low as if in worship, while the whole mass of their long, tremulous foliage was kindled into one continuous blaze of white sun-fire. The force of the gale was such that the most steadfast monarch of them all rocked down to its roots with a motion plainly perceptible when one leaned against it. Nature was holding high festival, and every fiber of the most rigid giants thrilled with glad excitement.

I drifted on through the midst of this passionate music and motion, across many a glen, from ridge to ridge; often halting in the lee of a rock for shelter, or to gaze and listen. Even when the grand anthem had swelled to its highest pitch, I could distinctly hear the varying tones of individual trees—Spruce and Fir and Pine, and leafless Oak—and even the infinitely gentle rustle of the withered grasses at my feet. Each was expressing itself in its own way,—singing its own song, and making its own peculiar gestures,—manifesting a richness of variety to be found in no other forest I have yet seen. The coniferous woods of Canada, and the Carolinas, and Florida, are made up of trees that resemble one another about as nearly as blades of grass, and grow close together in much the same way. Coniferous trees, in general, seldom possess individual character, such as is manifest among Oaks and Elms. But the California forests are made up of a greater number of distinct species than any other in the world. And in them we find, not only a marked differentiation into special groups, but also a marked individuality in almost every tree, giving rise to storm effects indescribably glorious.

Toward midday, after a long, tingling scramble through copses of hazel and ceanothus, I gained the summit of the highest ridge in the neighborhood; and then it occurred to me that it would be a fine thing to climb one of the trees to obtain a wider outlook and get my ear close to the Æolian music of its topmost needles. But under the circumstances the choice of a tree was a serious matter. One whose instep was not very strong seemed in danger of being blown down, or of being struck by others in case they should fall; another was branchless to a considerable height above the ground, and at the same time too large to be grasped with arms and legs in climbing; while others were not favorably situated for clear views. After cautiously casting about, I made choice of the tallest of a group of Douglas Spruces that were growing close together like a tuft of grass, no one of which seemed likely to fall unless all the rest fell with it. Though comparatively young, they were about 100 feet high, and their lithe, brushy tops were rocking and swirling in wild ecstasy. Being accustomed to climb trees in making botanical studies, I experienced no difficulty in reaching the top of this one, and never before did I enjoy so noble an exhilaration of motion. The slender tops fairly flapped and swished in the passionate torrent, bending and swirling backward and forward, round and round, tracing indescribable combinations of vertical and horizontal curves, while I clung with muscles firm braced, like a bobo-link on a reed.

In its widest sweeps my tree-top described an arc of from twenty to thirty degrees, but I felt sure of its elastic temper, having seen others of the same species still more severely tried—bent almost to the ground indeed, in heavy snows—without breaking a fiber. I was therefore safe, and free to take the wind into my pulses and enjoy the excited forest from my superb outlook.

The view from here must be extremely beautiful in any weather. Now my eye roved over the piny hills and dales as over fields of waving grain, and felt the light running in ripples and broad swelling undulations across the valleys from ridge to ridge, as the shining foliage was stirred by corresponding waves of air. Oftentimes these waves of reflected light would break up suddenly into a kind of beaten foam, and again, after chasing one another in regular order, they would seem to bend forward in concentric curves, and disappear on some hillside, like sea-waves on a shelving shore. The quantity of light reflected from the bent needles was so great as to make whole groves appear as if covered with snow, while the black shadows beneath the trees greatly enhanced the effect of the silvery splendor.

Excepting only the shadows there was nothing somber in all this wild sea of pines. On the contrary, notwithstanding this was the winter season, the colors were remarkably beautiful. The shafts of the pine and libocedrus were brown and purple, and most of the foliage was well tinged with yellow; the laurel groves, with the pale undersides of their leaves turned upward, made masses of gray; and then there was many a dash of chocolate color from clumps of manzanita, and jet of vivid crimson from the bark of the madroños, while the ground on the hillsides, appearing here and there through openings between the groves, displayed masses of pale purple and brown.

The sounds of the storm corresponded gloriously with this wild exuberance of light and motion. The profound bass of the naked branches and boles booming like waterfalls; the quick, tense vibrations of the pine-needles, now rising to a shrill, whistling hiss, now falling to a silky murmur; the rustling of laurel groves in the dells, and the keen metallic click of leaf on leaf—all this was heard in easy analysis when the attention was calmly bent.

The varied gestures of the multitude were seen to fine advantage, so that one could recognize the different species at a distance of several miles by this means alone, as well as by their forms and colors, and the way they reflected the light. All seemed strong and comfortable, as if really enjoying the storm, while responding to its most enthusiastic greetings. We hear much nowadays concerning the universal struggle for existence, but no struggle in the common meaning of the word was manifest here; no recognition of danger by any tree; no deprecation; but rather an invincible gladness as remote from exultation as from fear.

I kept my lofty perch for hours, frequently closing my eyes to enjoy the music by itself, or to feast quietly on the delicious fragrance that was streaming past. The fragrance of the woods was less marked than that produced during warm rain, when so many balsamic buds and leaves are steeped like tea; but, from the chafing of resiny branches against each other, and the incessant attrition of myriads of needles, the gale was spiced to a very tonic degree. And besides the fragrance from these local sources there were traces of scents brought from afar. For this wind came first from the sea, rubbing against its fresh, briny waves, then distilled through the redwoods, threading rich ferny gulches, and spreading itself in broad undulating currents over many a flower-enameled ridge of the coast mountains, then across the golden plains, up the purple foot-hills, and into these piny woods with the varied incense gathered by the way.

Winds are advertisements of all they touch, however much or little we may be able to read them; telling their wanderings even by their scents alone. Mariners detect the flowery perfume of land-winds far at sea, and sea-winds carry the fragrance of copse and tangle far inland, where it is quickly recognized, though mingled with the scents of a thousand land-flowers. As an illustration of this, I may tell here that I breathed sea-air on the Firth of Forth, in Scotland, while a boy; then was taken to Wisconsin, where I remained nineteen years; then, without in all this time having breathed one breath of the sea, I walked quietly, alone, from the middle of the Mississippi Valley to the Gulf of Mexico, on a botanical excursion, and while in Florida, far from the coast, my attention wholly bent on the splendid tropical vegetation about me, I suddenly recognized a sea-breeze, as it came sifting through the palmettos and blooming vine-tangles, which at once awakened and set free a thousand dormant associations, and made me a boy again in Scotland, as if all the intervening years had been annihilated.

Most people like to look at mountain rivers, and bear them in mind; but few care to look at the winds, though far more beautiful and sublime, and though they become at times about as visible as flowing water. When the north winds in winter are making upward sweeps over the curving summits of the High Sierra, the fact is sometimes published with flying snow-banners a mile long. Those portions of the winds thus embodied can scarce be wholly invisible, even to the darkest imagination. And when we look around over an agitated forest, we may see something of the wind that stirs it, by its effects upon the trees. Yonder it descends in a rush of water-like ripples, and sweeps over the bending pines from hill to hill. Nearer, we see detached plumes and leaves, now speeding by on level currents, now whirling in eddies, or, escaping over the edges of the whirls, soaring aloft on grand, upswelling domes of air, or tossing on flame-like crests. Smooth, deep currents, cascades, falls, and swirling eddies, sing around every tree and leaf, and over all the varied topography of the region with telling changes of form, like mountain rivers conforming to the features of their channels.

After tracing the Sierra streams from their fountains to the plains, marking where they bloom white in falls, glide in crystal plumes, surge gray and foam-filled in boulder-choked gorges, and slip through the woods in long, tranquil reaches—after thus learning their language and forms in detail, we may at length hear them chanting all together in one grand anthem, and comprehend them all in clear inner vision, covering the range like lace. But even this spectacle is far less sublime and not a whit more substantial than what we may behold of these storm-streams of air in the mountain woods.

We all travel the milky way together, trees and men; but it never occurred to me until this storm-day, while swinging in the wind, that trees are travelers, in the ordinary sense. They make many journeys, not extensive ones, it is true; but our own little journeys, away and back again, are only little more than tree-wavings—many of them not so much.

When the storm began to abate, I dismounted and sauntered down through the calming woods. The storm-tones died away, and, turning toward the east, I beheld the countless hosts of the forests hushed and tranquil, towering above one another on the slopes of the hills like a devout audience. The setting sun filled them with amber light, and seemed to say, while they listened, "My peace I give unto you."

As I gazed on the impressive scene, all the so called ruin of the storm was forgotten, and never before did these noble woods appear so fresh, so joyous, so immortal.

RIPRAP

By Gary Snyder

The poem "Riprap" was written during Gary Snyder's days working as a trail crew member in Yosemite National Park. As a long-time resident of San Juan Ridge, high above the Yuba River drainage, Snyder has long been an explorer and defender of the Pacific Crest region, most well known for his work as an environmental poet and philosopher. For Pacific Crest Trail hikers, Snyder's description of riprap—a cobble of stone used to build trail base and to provide footing for horses on slick granite—will prove familiar. For the Buddhist poet, however, riprapping trail becomes a meditative experience, a chance to reflect upon the careful construction of poetry as well as the intricate interconnections between everything in the universe. Lost in the meditative silence of ascending or descending steep switchbacks built out of riprap, many PCT hikers may find themselves taking similarly philosophical journeys as the rhythm of walking and reading moves the mind as well as the body.

RIPRAP

Lay down these words
Before your mind like rocks.
    placed solid, by hands
In choice of place, set
Before the body of the mind
    in space and time:
Solidity of bark, leaf, or wall
    riprap of things:
Cobble of milky way,
    straying planets,
These poems, people,
    lost ponies with
Dragging saddles
    and rocky sure-foot trails.
The worlds like an endless
    four-dimensional
Game of *Go*.
    ants and pebbles
In the thin loam, each rock a word
    a creek-washed stone
Granite: ingrained
    with torment of fire and weight
Crystal and sediment linked hot
    all change, in thoughts,
As well as things.

WALKING

By Hank Meals

Pacific Crest Trail hikers—along with devotees of our nation's other long scenic trails—more than any other group, perhaps, appreciate the many different aspects of walking. From its meditative qualities and robust physical benefits to its significant place in our evolutionary and cultural history, walking has occupied the thoughts of many a PCT hiker. In this excerpt from Yuba Trails, *Hank Meals explores walking's many different roles and meanings in our long history as bipedal hominids wandering the earth. A rooted resident of the Yuba watershed in the northern Sierras, Hank lives on San Juan Ridge near Nevada City, California, and provides in* Yuba Trails *in-depth history and descriptions of the many trails connecting to the PCT in this area.*

After it crosses the swath of Interstate 80 and heads northwest, leaving Donner Pass and the Sierra Club's Peter Grubb Hut behind, the PCT enters the headwaters of the Yuba River—a country filled with streams that cascade through boulder-strewn riverbeds from white pine, fir, and hemlock in the higher elevations to flow among California black oak and Pacific madrone along the lower slopes. Depending on how many miles PCT hikers have put on their trail shoes, and how many blisters are on their feet, they may find themselves agreeing with the author that walking is a great panacea or crying and swearing that it is a curse from Pandora.

*A*ustralopithecus was the first real walker. During the reign of this early ancestor the pelvis and foot were restructured from those of a forest ape to

Source: Excerpted from *Yuba Trails 2*, by Hank Meals (self-published, 2001). Reprinted by permission of the author.

a walker on the plains. Paleontologist Mary Leakey wrote: "One cannot overemphasize the role of bipedalism in hominid development. It stands as perhaps the salient point that differentiates the forebears of man from other primates."

This new creature had freed its hands for other pursuits. After about four million years we could talk about our walks. The greatest events in the history of our species have been sustained walks, or migrations. We walked out of Africa and Asia, and when the Rhine, Danube, Moldau and Seine Rivers froze, we walked across Europe. Eventually, by crossing what is now the Bering Strait, hunters and gatherers took thousands of years meandering south to reach Tierra del Fuego.

Those first walks were to find food. While following either a herd or the ripening of plants, the earliest walkers embodied Carl Franz's well-worn phrase, "wherever you go, there you are." As seasons changed and animals migrated, opportunistic humans changed locale by following the food. With the development of agriculture people were bound to a particular place like never before, but they continued to explore.

Walking is fundamentally exploration and as such is part of the human psyche. Before written history nameless populations walked the earth for thousands of years. In the historic period we find Marco Polo walking from Venice to Peking, Romans walking to the British Isles, and Crusaders walking from Europe to the Middle East, to name only a few.

According to Henry David Thoreau, the word *sauntering* came from "idlers" who roamed Europe in the Middle Ages asking for charity under the guise of going "a la Sainte Terre," or to the Holy Land. The pilgrim or wanderer came to be known as a "Sainte Terrer" or a Holy Lander. In his essay, *Walking*, Thoreau was as passionate as an Earth Firster when he proclaimed, "For every walk is a sort of crusade preached by some Peter the Hermit in us, to go forth and re-conquer this Holy Land from the hands of the Infidels." Another possible origin of the word *sauntering* is "sans terre," without land or home.

Walking was the fundamental mode of transportation [until] [...] about 3000 years ago when the horse and donkey, domesticated for hauling 2000 years before, were mounted for a ride. Horses with their speed, responsiveness and bulk were especially valued for the advantage they offered in warfare. Because of this, horsemen were instantly identified with power and privilege while the far more numerous foot soldiers were looked down upon both literally and figuratively. In time, for a fee people could be transported by wagons, carriages and coaches. Those who could not afford a ride walked and were assumed to be inferior. We still see the quality of our transportation, be it a Mercedes or a first-class airplane ticket, as an indication of worth.

At the same time that Asians and Europeans were trying to master horseback riding, small groups of hunters and gatherers were walking both sides of the Sierra Nevada summit near the Feather, Yuba, Bear and American rivers. It has been a distinct pleasure to find their stone tools in remote and rugged landscapes.

In the foothills, where acorns were a reliable food source, the indigenous people (the Nisenan) were hesitant to travel very far from home. Stephen Powers, pioneering ethnographer and author of *Tribes of California*, recorded the Nisenan word *u yem*, or "to walk," in the Bear River watershed in 1877. There is ample archeological evidence of the presence of native people in the spectacular settings and on peaks and ridges with terrific views. For non-scientific and poetic insight into journeying with California Indians, read Jaime d'Angulo's *Indian Tales*. Ishi, the last of the Yahi, walked to Oroville and into the twentieth century in August of 1911. He was turned over to anthropologists at the University of California, where he lived for the remaining five years of his life. Dr. Saxon Pope, a medical doctor, described how Ishi, a tireless walker, walked:

> *He springs from the great toe which is wonderfully strong in its plantar flexion and abduction. His method of locomotion is that of rather short steps, each foot sliding along the ground as it touches. Neither the heel nor the ball of the foot seems to receive the jar of the step. The foot is placed in position cautiously, not slammed or jammed down. He progresses rather pigeon-toed and approximates crossing the line of his progress each step.*

If you have not read *Ishi in Two Worlds* by Theodore Kroeber, you cannot call yourself educated, at least by California standards.

The literature of walking is full of prodigious walkers like Dr. Barbara Moore, "the walking vegetarian" who in 1960 walked from San Francisco to Times Square in 85 days. In 1909, 71-year-old Edward P. Weston made the same trip in 105 days. Charles Lummis walked the 3507 miles between Cincinnati and Los Angeles in 1884, taking 143 days. At age 81 Plennie Wingo walked the 452 miles between Santa Monica and San Francisco. There are obviously thousands more, named and unnamed, who have walked long distances just for the pleasure of it.

This notion of taking pleasure in walking for its own sake came of age in the late eighteenth century when William Wordsworth and his sister Dorothy elevated walking to an aesthetic, or cultural experience. Thomas De Quincey estimated that Wordsworth "must have traversed a distance of 175[000] to 180,000 English miles." In Rebecca Solnit's thoughtful book *Wanderlust: A History of Walking*, she says: "For Wordsworth, walking was a mode not of traveling, but of being" and "He is the figure to which posterity looks in tracing the history of walking in the landscape: he has become a trailside god."

Solnit's phrase "walking in the landscape" makes an important distinction in this age of efficient exercise machines. As you know, people pay to walk in place on a treadmill for health benefits alone. In a recent treadmill review *Time* magazine explained that there are 10,000 steps in 5 miles, and those steps burn 500 calories—that's one way to look at walking. Both the treadmill and the stationary cycle can now be found in casinos, where customers can "sweat and bet" at the same time. These "multi-task machines" are made by Fitness Gaming Corporation, whose motto is "Put your heart into gambling." Am I missing something? Most of the people I know are trying to get off the treadmill.

Exercise alone has its place, and if you can only devote a short time to it— well, so be it. But you are leaving out fresh air, ominous clouds, scrambling in scree, woodpeckers, wolf moss, hot stillness, rattlesnakes, wildflowers, black oaks, rushing water, windy ridges, ice, bedrock mortars, and heart-opening vistas, among many other things. Technology moves forward with efficiency and achievement as its goals but leaves the soul starving for beauty and grace. For walking to be nutritious you have to leave the landscape in.

Former Associate Justice of the Supreme Court, William O. Douglas, at age sixty-six had this to say about strolling: "A stroll is not a hike. Strolling is indeed tiring. Why, I'm not sure, but a bracing hike is invigorating and while one comes in weary, a thirty-mile hike will give his body a good tone for several days."

Hiking, no matter how rigorous, is seen as play, while a *pilgrimage* is a journey to a specific power spot with the vague goal of transformation. There is definitely some notion that the long walk is spiritual, and it has been around for a long time. Muslims traveling to Mecca, Christians and Jews on their way to Jerusalem, Hispanic Catholics walking to Chimayo, New Mexico, and Huichols headed for the San Luis Potosi desert to collect peyote are all on pilgrimages. Until recently travel to these places was arduous and involved long walks.

Among the Sufis there is the concept of *Siyahat* or "errance," in which the rhythm of walking is used as a technique for dissolving the attachments of the world. Back-country Buddhists, the Yamabushi, make walking and climbing a major part of their practice. Nobel Prize nominee and Buddhist monk Thich Nhat Hanh offers instruction in *Walking Meditation* while "Vision Quests" are increasingly popular.

Because "spirituality" has become a commodity, the word seems inadequate to describe the experience of walking in the landscape. What a walk in nature offers is perspective. No matter what terrors the mind can manufacture, the natural world has a way of mitigating pain. The simple act of moving through beauty soothes pain, restores balance and reminds you that life goes on. When I lost my sweet wife Susan, only walking brought me peace and eventual healing. Walking the landscape, experiencing it through the soles to the soul, feels like an appropriate way to pay respect for all of this splendor.

JIM BECKWOURTH: LARGER THAN LIFE

By Andy Hammond

Hikers on the Pacific Crest Trail east of Bucks Lake will encounter a section of an 1851 emigrant wagon road known as the Beckwourth Trail. The remnants of the Beckwourth Trail lie just south of where the PCT crosses the highway connecting Quincy with Bucks Lake and Oroville. As the original Beckwourth Trail climbs the slope of the Big Creek drainage to the east, it is easy to conceive of the difficulties emigrants faced in getting their wagons to Bucks Summit.

A few hundred yards south of the highway, hikers will find a trail marker made of railroad rail marking the approximate spot where the two trails separate, with the Beckwourth going west while the PCT continues north. The inscription on the trail marker reads as follows:

BECKWOURTH TRAIL—BUCKS SUMMIT

TRAIL ROUTE, 1851–1855. HERE EMIGRANTS COMPLETED THE

STEEP TWO-MILE CLIMB UP FROM BIG CREEK AND TURNED

DOWN TO RICH VALLEY AND BUCKS RANCH, NOW SUBMERGED

UNDER BUCKS LAKE.

The Beckwourth Trail was more or less abandoned after 1855 when a toll road was constructed so as to bypass the difficult Big Creek route. This toll road basically followed the course of the modern highway and by about 1858 ceased to be an emigrant road. Behind the establishment of the Beckwourth Trail was a legendary mountain man, Jim Beckwourth, who in an era of colorful, almost mythical characters, was truly larger than life.

Jim Beckwourth was a trapper, explorer, trader, guide, scout, teamster, inter-preter, raconteur, and, in the eyes of some, a "gaudy liar." While much about his life is sketchy and often contradictory, there is no question that Beckwourth led a life of extraordinary adventure. He was a mountain man in the true sense: a phantom of the frontier and a wanderer who was at home with everyone and with no one. Historian Elinor Wilson, in her biography of Beckwourth, char-acterized him as loving song and merriment, as kindly and open, with a passion for storytelling. She noted that his language was much superior to that usually heard in his era. His knowledge of Indian ways was superb and he often dressed in Indian costume, with elaborately beaded and embroidered buckskin and long hair either braided into long rolls or tied at his neck with a gaudy ribbon. He loved personal ornaments such as gold chains, buttons, and earrings (with his ears pierced in several places).

The words of those who met him help form an image of Jim Beckwourth. Ina Coolbrith, who later became the first poet laureate of California, encoun-tered him in 1851 and remembered him as "one of the most beautiful creatures that ever lived. He was rather dark and wore his hair in two long braids, twisted with colored cord that gave him a picturesque appearance. He wore a leather coat, moccasins and rode a horse without a saddle." A storekeeper at Mormon Bar recounted seeing Beckwourth "approaching the store, a strange looking being, mounted on a gray horse, a poncho thrown over his shoulder, over which slung a huge rifle, skins wrapped around his legs, a pair of Mexican spurs on, and a slouched hat which partially obscured his copper complexion." Another person remembered him chilling "the blood of the green young miner, who, unacquainted with the arts of war and subjugation congregate around him, by the cold blooded manner in which he relates the Indian fights that he has been engaged in." A sense of awe pervaded every observation.

James Pearson Beckwith was born in Virginia in 1798 to a white planta-tion owner, Sir Jennings Beckwith, who traced his ancestry back to the first king of Scotland. However, because his mother was a slave, Jim began his life as a slave. When Jim was seven or eight years old, Sir Jennings moved his household to Missouri, settling near St. Louis. There, Jim attended school for a brief time before being apprenticed to a blacksmith. Following an altercation with his employer, Jim ran off. But he returned a few years later, expressing a desire to go west, and Sir Jennings gave Jim his freedom via a declaration of emancipation. How Beckwith became Beckwourth has never been clear, but in his memoirs—*The Life and Adventures of James P.*

Beckwourth, as Told to Thomas Bonner (1856)—his name appeared as Beckwourth rather than Beckwith.

Jim's adventures began when he joined William Ashley's fur-trapping party in 1824 and ended when he died in Montana in 1866. The interim was rich with experience, as the peripatetic Beckwourth crisscrossed the West. In 1828 Jim was captured by the Crow Indians, who believed he was one of their own who had been taken as a child and raised by whites. For several years he lived with the Crow, where his bravery led to his attaining the exalted title of War Chief. In 1843 he set out with a pack train, bringing trade goods from Santa Fe and arriving in California for the first time in early 1844.

Throughout this period he developed the fine art of storytelling, often exaggerating his own role such that it is difficult to distill truth from tall tale. For example, he left California in 1845 because of the increasing American-Mexican hostilities, claiming to have stolen eighteen hundred head of Spanish horses as a departing gesture. And three years later, he returned to California with a party delivering dispatches from Fort Leavenworth to Monterey, presenting himself as having been in charge (while he was probably serving as guide).

Beckwourth joined the surge of gold seekers in 1850, during which time he discovered what is now Beckwourth Pass as a new road to the diggings. "From some of the elevations over which we passed," Beckwourth wrote in his memoirs,

> *I remarked a place far away that seemed lower than any other [and] thought that at some future time I would examine into it farther. I continued on to Shasta and returned after a fruitless journey [of] eighteen days. After a short stay in the American Valley I again started out with a prospecting party of twelve men. We proceeded in an easterly direction, and all busied themselves in searching for gold; but my errand was of a different character: I had come to discover what I suspected to be a pass. It was the latter end of April when we entered upon an extensive valley [and] struck across this beautiful valley to the waters of the Yuba, from thence to the waters of the Truchy [Truckee], which latter flowed in an easterly direction, telling us that we were on the eastern slope of the mountain range. This, I at once saw, would afford the best wagon-road into the American Valley approaching from the eastward.*

Returning to the American Valley, then to Bidwells Bar—one of the many short-lived communities that blossomed with gold fever—and finally to

Marysville, Beckwourth found great enthusiasm for the road. In Marysville, the mayor assured him that "the benefits accruing to the city would be incalculable" and that Beckwourth would be well paid if he would open his proposed road.

At the time, Marysville was the shipping point for all goods going to the northern mines and, although a wagon road was in place between Marysville and Bidwells Bar, from there on the only "roads" were Indian trails. In addition, those heading for the American Valley or the mines on the Feather River had to follow the circuitous route over Donner or Carson Pass to Sacramento and then to Bidwells Bar and pack from there, loading their goods on their own backs or on those of temperamental mules.

To open his road, Beckwourth hired men to hack out enough of a path to allow the passage of wagons; the first wagon trail reached Marysville over the route in late August or early September of 1851. Unfortunately, Marysville burned about that time and Beckwourth was never paid. He then returned to Sierra Valley, where he established his ranch and trading post. "[The] sixteen hundred dollars I expended upon the road," he wrote in his memoirs,

> is forever gone, but those who derive advantage from this outlay and loss of time devote no thought to the discoverer; nor do I see clearly how I am to help myself, for every one knows I can not roll a mountain into the passes and shut it up. But there is one thing certain: although I recognize no superior in love of country, and feel in all its force the obligation imposed upon me to advance her interests, still, when I go out hunting in the mountains a road for every body to pass through, and expending my time and capital upon an object from which I shall derive no benefit, it will be because I have nothing better to do.

Beckwourth's trading post was not a great moneymaker, although it was visited by most of the emigrants and gold seekers who passed by. Few had money, and even many of those who did simply took advantage of Beckwourth's kindness and generosity. Beckwourth's character is well illustrated in the 1852 diary of Henry Taylor, whose wagon train, having nothing to eat, reached Beckwourth's post about midnight:

> I went with Turner up to the house [where] through the window [we] could see the dim light of a tallow candle. We knocked at the door, and a rough old voice bade us come in. Beckweth was laying on his counter,

behind which were some shelves, on which were a few bottles contain-
ing whiskey. After shaking hands all around, Beckweth curled up in one
corner of the room, telling Turner to help himself and wait on the boys,
saying also, 'Boys, I have nothing to eat, but drink all you want, only leave
me enough for tomorrow, for the train will be here then, and I will have
plenty.' Then he dropped on his buffalo cot, but raised again saying to
Turner, 'Jim, you're welcome to go down to the corral and kill a beef.'

Because Beckwourth Pass is at a low elevation (5212 feet), in fact the lowest
crossing of the Sierras, many have assumed that the entire route was easy. It was
not. And for that reason it saw a decline in use once an easier route was opened.
As John Clark observed regarding the challenges of the Beckwourth Trail in
his 1852 diary,

Seeing the many teams winding up the heights as if they were making
for the clouds, we just stop a while, throw away all the spare donage &
prepare the lash; for it took awful cracking to get up the 2 miles in Six
and a half hours. Many teams with eight & ten yoke were seven hours. I
saw one long team that stuck on the brink. They had to run a line from
the forward yoke, make fast to a tree so as to hold, while the cattle could
rest. Other teams, many oxen, would be on their knees holding while the
drivers would whip & pound until the poor beasts would bawl under the
lash, before they could raise & go forward.

This reality is reinforced from the vantage point of Bucks Summit and the
view east from the Pacific Crest Trail.

In 1852 Beckwourth was reported to have said that he had traveled across
the mountains fourteen times and expected to cross them twenty-four times
more. So, not surprisingly, his last years were spent wandering: to St. Louis
in 1858, back to Colorado, and again working as a guide for the US military,
which included involvement in the horrific Sand Creek Massacre of 1864 in
Colorado, to his final days with the Crow Indians in Montana.

Jim Beckwourth's footprints are long gone from these mountains. But
like his contemporaries—Kit Carson, Jim Bridger, and Jedediah Smith—
his legacy of courage and bravery and exploration deserves to be a part of
western history.

A RITE OF MASCULINITY

By John Henry Smihula

At the northern end of the Sierra Nevada, one does not encounter the staggering beauty typical of southern sections like Kings Canyon and the Hoover Wilderness. What one finds is a relatively modest, gentle landscape: lower elevations, smaller mountains, dense expansive forest, moderate ascents and descents—a region more reminiscent, perhaps, of the Appalachian Trail. In fact, the difference in scale and scenery of the northern Sierra makes many hikers believe they are in a liminal region between the Sierras and Cascades. When not awestruck or overwhelmed by what John Muir called "the most divinely beautiful of all the mountain-chains I have ever seen," when topographical distractions are minimal, the hiker may more easily turn inward to introspection, meditation, or reflection. One such rumination can spring from a basic demographic question: who is on the trail? And this can lead to considering such matters as age, race, class, and gender. Why, for example, are there so few children, so few people of color, so few working-class people on the trail? Gender is a subject John Smihula ponders as he heads southward and sees few women but comes upon a phalanx of thru-hiking men trudging resolutely northward.

"If I don't reach Canada before the snow starts to fall, I'm screwed," declared the middle-aged man while adjusting his glasses and glancing nervously at a hot, cloudless midsummer sky in northern California. He stood sweating by Lookout Rock, hunched under a heavy pack, and saw only the Canadian border. He was walking in August and thinking of October. He anticipated the autumnal lowering of sky and felt the cold north wind, but he didn't seem to notice the two red-tailed hawks wheeling about a hundred feet above him.

Though peculiar, he was no anomaly. I hiked south from Bucks Summit to the Middle Fork of the Feather River, Lakes Basin, and Sierra Buttes. Destination: girlfriend and beer in little Sierra City. I passed a few dozen stouthearted thru hikers who had, like this man, started from the Mexican border in early May with a vision of Canada before their eyes. What I encountered was a kind of seasonal migration or ritual: the five-month, 2650-mile slog northward along the entire PCT.

They were all men, remarkably similar in appearance—all but one white, most in their twenties and early thirties, most evidently middle class; and in manner—gaunt and tense, preternaturally earnest, more or less obsessive-compulsive, preoccupied with time and mileage and finding water. To me, because of their demeanor, each seemed to bear a cross on his back, as penance for some unspeakable crime. Surely, I thought, the sun was meant to shine on enterprises more cheerful than this—hiking the trail is not supposed to be punishment. The youngest man I met was also probably the poorest. Recently unemployed from a menial job, he rested in the shade, scruffily smoking a cigarette. His clothes were army surplus—the opposite of the latest ultralight-weight, ultraexpensive gear donned by the bourgeois hiker. His boots were worn out, and so were his feet, which were covered with blisters, dried blood, and duct tape. He was wholly unconcerned about them; his thoughts were instead fixed on reaching Canada, its border shimmering before his weary eyes. California, Oregon, and Washington were only obstacles to overcome.

Men on the trail: what a strange and intriguing phenomenon, and so different from women on the trail! After graduating college, my partner Wendy and her girlfriend Bailey hiked 350 miles of the PCT through the northern and central Sierra, during which they too saw only male thru hikers (all looking "haunted"). Wendy and Bailey had a simple, easygoing agenda: to see beautiful lands, experience the wilderness, and have fun. For them, time exerted little pressure. "We had no mission, nothing to prove," Wendy says. She and Bailey fished, identified birds and wildflowers, took side trips, and occasionally met friends and family members along the trail. They, as well as Cindy Ross, were amazed by how "serious" and "driven" men were on the trail. Over two seasons, Ross hiked the entire PCT to escape the tedium of her working-class "subservient" life and to enjoy the freedom and adventure of the wilderness—she describes her trips in her 1987 book, *Journey on the Crest* (excerpted in the Oregon/Washington volume of the *Trailside Reader*). Women, it seems, are not on the trail to realize or test their womanhood—whatever this means. Who has ever heard of a woman striving to attain womanhood? Who has ever heard of a "crisis of femininity"? Feminism as a movement may seem to be in crisis, but femininity is not. The only crisis women collectively face is that generated by patriarchy or masculinism. Yet the notion of a "crisis of masculinity"—what is a man? what makes a man? how shall a man live?—has been for a generation bruited about, particularly in America, where this crisis was actually first proclaimed over a century ago by the hypermasculinist and militarist Teddy Roosevelt, vilifying what he deemed an effete urban-industrial civilization.

The men I observed on the PCT were on a mission or crusade as metaphysical as it was physical. Whatever the crisis of masculinity, these men strove to solve it. Being enacted before me was a rite of masculinity, a male imperative to resurrect an atavistic impulse to journey on foot great distances, to meet the challenge of open space, to test one's will and fortitude. Retrieving the "inner warrior," or "Wild Man energy," is what the poet Robert Bly would call it. In his primer for the remasculinization of men, *Iron John*, he urges his readers to overcome the gentle, overrefined "soft male" and to realize the fierce, Paleolithic "deep male." Such a transformation is essentially a rite of passage, from boyhood to manhood, from a partial life to a complete life.

Although Bly's book includes much New Age nonsense, and his essentialism (men are by nature like *this* and women like *that*) is largely untenable, and more than a little phallocratic, his fundamental point is valid: "we have no ideas at all on how to produce men." It is a problem that begins with socialization—boys raised to compete, not cooperate; to dominate, not deliberate—and this too often results in an arbitrary imposing of will on the external world. During my week on the trail, I saw the consequences of this problem, of male energy misdirected: a labyrinth of unpaved roads to give people (i.e., men) access to remote areas without having to use their legs; hillsides disfigured by truck, dirt bike, and ATV tracks; trail signs blasted apart by gunfire or torn from the ground; millions of trees marked with blue paint for cutting, sacrificed on the altar of profit; a speeding logging truck nearly running me down; piles of trash and spent rifle cartridges defiling the landscape. I spent much of my hike in a state of either shock or sadness. I struggled more with despair than fatigue—a feeling I often have in the wild when I discover that I haven't escaped entirely the taint of civilization. Encountering a dumpsite, or a campsite littered with shattered glass, or a truck gashing the earth, or a hunter with death in his eyes, I recall what Sergeant Colby says to the young Marine Philip Caputo in Caputo's Vietnam War memoir, *A Rumor of War*: "Before you leave here, sir, you're going to learn that one of the most brutal things in the world is your average nineteen-year-old American boy." This boy may kill and torture in a foreign land, or he may desecrate and destroy some part of the natural world at home.

If such brutality represents male energy misdirected, thru hiking one of America's great trails represents a more proper and salutary application of it. Walking across the land is not the same as tearing it up with a machine; carrying a pack is not the same as carrying a gun. On the PCT, I was witnessing men exercising mobility—our *kinesthetic* sense. Long ago Ralph Waldo Emerson lamented that "the civilized man has built a coach, but has lost the use of his feet," and here were men using their feet, practicing the noble art of walking. How novel this is at a time when most Americans use their feet only to reach their automobiles or refrigerators. I admired the resolve and hardiness of these thru hikers but questioned their method and mind-set. Rather than being in the moment, they were preoccupied with that future moment when they would reach their destination. Most evinced little awareness of, or connection to, the land they traversed; a few even had iPods and headphones, which isolated them in a private sound world as they tramped mechanically from Point A (Mexican border) to Point B (Canadian border). I prefer the method of Matsuo Basho, the seventeenth-century Japanese haiku poet and pilgrim, whose book of travel sketches I carried with me. Basho followed no itinerary; he went where desire led him, such as high into the mountains to watch the full moon rise over the peaks or down into valleys to witness the blooming of cherry blossoms.

Nonetheless, as I considered all the thru hikers on the trail, I grew wistful, for I did not have the time or physical health to spend one month on the trail, let alone five; and I regretted again that I hadn't been able, thirteen years before, to hike the John Muir Trail because my friend had been stricken with severe altitude sickness. I haven't had a second chance.

Fortunately I have been able, over the years, to periodically satisfy my wanderlust—or what the late travel writer Bruce Chatwin called our "innate migratory impulse"—on major trails like the Appalachian, Pacific Crest, Tahoe Rim, and Toiyabe Crest. I am grateful for such trails—capillaries on the body of the earth—that I can follow into the wilderness, where civilization and its white noise vanish and I can listen to the trilling of birds, the creaking of trees, the rushing of mountain water, the falling of rain and snow; or, like Basho, can watch the full moon rise above the peaks. All it takes to get there is a pair of legs and a pack of necessaries.

Walking is self-reliance, a test of stamina and resourcefulness, and it is a delightful *slowing down*, to a mere two or three miles per hour, in—or apart from, or *against*—a society moving frenetically at the speed of airliners and automobiles. It is restorative, returning us to a more natural and healthful rhythm of life. Walking is in essence a countercultural activity: exquisitely simple and implicitly or incipiently revolutionary—a quiet, ambulatory revolution.

When I set out on a trail, I am never quite sure which is the principal motive: is it an *escape from* or a *journey to*? Is it a furlough or a pilgrimage? Ultimately it does not matter; what matters is being on the trail, and going beyond the pale, one way or the other.

I left the PCT at lovely Lakes Basin, descending a ravine and intersecting another trail, to go to a favorite spot of mine: Rock Lake. It is not the prettiest lake in the area but it has splendid views and cliffs from which you can jump thirty or forty feet into the water. On a warm, dry, calm day, the jumping and swimming are especially exhilarating and rejuvenating. I passed a popular camping spot, marred by burnt wood and broken glass, but no one was there. I was alone. I sat down on a granite slope, leaning against my pack, feeling the hot midday sun on my face, and remained silent and still for several minutes as I breathed out the tension and anxiety of life in civilization and breathed in the peace and quietude of the wilderness.

CASCADES AND THE KLAMATH KNOT
THE REALM OF FIRE

COVERING SECTION N–SECTION R

Belden—Feather River Canyon—Lassen Peak—Burney Falls
Castle Crags—Etna Summit—Seiad Valley—Siskiyou Summit

LASSEN PEAK: THE BIG BLOWOUT

*Based on accounts collected by Alan W. Willendrup and B. F. Loomis,
compiled by Rees Hughes*

*In the past century there have been only two active volcanoes in the Lower
48—Mount St. Helens erupted in 1980 and Lassen Peak blew between
1914 and 1917. The route of the Pacific Crest Trail provides a superb
perspective of both. (See also Ursula Le Guin's commentary on the violent eruption of Mount St. Helens in "A Very Warm Mountain" which is
included in the Oregon/Washington volume.) During the three years of
Lassen Peak's volatility, the most powerful explosions took place between
May 19 and May 22, 1915. Nearby areas were devastated and volcanic
ash rained down as far away as two hundred miles to the east. The impact
was focused on the northeastern flank of the volcano and the Hat and Lost
Creek drainages. As the PCT crosses the Lassen Volcanic National Park
and ultimately climbs the Hat Creek Rim, this now century-old drama
unfolds in the panorama before you. This essay tells the accounts of three
households whose lives were inextricably linked on the night of May 19,
1915, and concludes by introducing B. F. Loomis, who did much to document Lassen Peak's reawakening.*

Sources: Compiled from G. R. Milford to J. S. Diller of the Geological Survey, Nov. 16, 1917, letter
reproduced in *The Volcanic Activity and Hot Springs of Lassen Peak*, by Arthur L. Day and E. T. Allen
(Carnegie Institution of Washington, 1925), 16–17; Alan Wayne Willendrup, "The Lassen Peak Eruptions
and Their Lingering Legacy," Occasional Publication No. 8 (Association for Northern California Records
and Research, 1983), 118–20, 121–24, reprinted by permission of the Association of Northern California
Historical Research; and B. F. Loomis, *Pictorial History of the Lassen Volcano* (Anderson Valley News Press,
1926), copyright transferred to the Loomis Museum Association, Lassen Volcanic National Park, reprinted
by permission of the Loomis Museum Association.

Among the closest inhabitants to Lassen Peak on May 19, 1915, were two homesteaders, Harvey Wilcox and Elmer Sorahan, who worked adjoining plots of land in the Upper Hat Creek Valley, some ten miles from the base of the mountain. Wilcox had constructed a cabin that took advantage of the picturesque setting while Sorahan had yet to build a home. Downstream, the next farm was owned by the Wid Hall family. The valley between was dotted with lava fields and outcroppings; it was not until farther north that the valley permanently broadened.

Although those nearby were unable to see the Peak, observers much farther away reported seeing a bright glow appearing around the rim of the mountain's crater. G. R. Milford, from his vantage point some twenty miles away, recounted the sight this way: "The whole rim of the crater facing us was marked by a bright red fiery line which wavered for an instant and then, in a deep red sheet, broke over the lower part of the lip and was lost to sight for a moment, only to reappear in the form of countless red globules of fire about 500 feet below the crater's lip."

The discharge melted the thickly packed snow, which combined with the volcanic debris and ash to create a supercharged mudflow that accelerated as it raced down Lassen's northeastern slope heading for an unsuspecting Harvey Wilcox, Elmer Sorahan, and the Wid Hall family. What follows are their accounts of the wild night of May 19, 1915.

HARVEY WILCOX CHEATS DEATH:
AS TOLD TO ALAN WAYNE WILLENDRUP

"It had been a particularly busy day for forty-eight year old Harvey Wilcox. At long last he was ready to move into the cabin he had just finished building on his homestead. Some of its furnishings were still stacked in the corral area close by. Shortly before 10:00 PM the tired homesteader retired to his lean-to for the night. It did not take him long to doze off. It would not be a long sleep, however. Less than one hour later Wilcox's peaceful slumber was rudely interrupted by the thundering hoofs of the four horses in his corral. Two of them, a big black saddle horse and a pack mare, belonged to his neighbor, Sorahan, who did not have a fenced in area to keep them. The other two horses, owned by Wilcox, were two old pensioners, nearly thirty years old. But at the moment Wilcox was jolted out of his sleep, his old chargers were too terror-stricken to feel the rigors of age. The four horses went streaking by his lean-to towards the northern edge of the homestead. The startled Wilcox popped his head out into the cold mountain night to see what was 'spooking' his horses. One look and he was suddenly very wide awake. A twenty foot wall of mud was roaring down the picturesque canyon Wilcox had so often admired, directly towards him and his flimsy lean-to. He did not have to hesitate. In one motion Wilcox swooped up his overalls as he rushed by his bed towards the outer flap of his lean-to. Making a dash towards the higher ground on the west side of his homestead, Wilcox took a quick look back. The onrushing flood was demolishing his newly built home. Wilcox later recalled that the logs from his cabin were 'flying through the air like match sticks.' But at that moment the fate of his cabin was of secondary importance to Wilcox. His only chance to avoid being swept away by the rushing torrent was to get to higher ground. He would have to crawl over a jagged lava bed, which was a difficult trek for a middle-aged man, especially at night. Compounding Wilcox's woes was the condition of his feet. In the hasty departure from his lean-to, he had forgotten to take his boots. Consequently, his bare-footed ascent over the jagged lava rock was all the more arduous. [As] he looked down towards his spread, he could see little in the inky blackness of midnight. It was just as well, Wilcox's cabin, the product of months of hard toil, had been reduced to splintered firewood."

A CLOSE CALL FOR SORAHAN TOO:
AS TOLD TO ALAN WAYNE WILLENDRUP

"Harvey Wilcox's brush with death was over, but Elmer Sorahan's ordeal was just beginning. He had closed the flap of his tent at about 10:00 PM but an [hour] later he still had not fallen asleep. Outside all appeared normal. The quiet mountain air was only mildly disturbed by the gentle flow of Hat Creek, a mere twenty feet away from the twenty-five year old homesteader's tent. But something was wrong and Sorahan knew it. Or to be more precise, his dog knew it. Normally, his bloodhound would be sleeping contently by his master's cot. But tonight the dog was restless. Several times in the past hour the bloodhound had nervously trotted out of the tent. When Sorahan would call him back, the dog would obey, only to repeat the nervous habit several minutes later. Finally, in disgust, Sorahan got up from the warm confines of his cot, put on his high-topped boots, and went outside to investigate.

"When Sorahan opened the flap of his tent he heard the unfamiliar and disturbing sound of wire screeching through the staples of his fence at the edge of Wilcox's homestead, a quarter of a mile away. He did not know it at the time, but this screeching sound was caused by the impact of his 1200-pound, terror-stricken pack mare hitting the fence in full stride. Sorahan's anxiety increased seconds later when he heard another sound, which he later described as 'cracking' and 'popping,' coming from nearby Hat Creek. This 'cracking-popping' sound was actually rocks in the creek striking each other as they rolled ahead of the on-coming flood. Sorahan was still not fully aware of the cause of these unusual sounds until he actually saw a sudden physical change in the creek. He caught sight of ripples of water, getting higher and higher, as they swirled down the creek. That was enough for Sorahan. He knew instantaneously what was happening. Rushing into his tent he paused, possibly out of habit to blow out a flickering candle flame. Swooping up his sweater and hat in one motion, Sorahan rushed out of his tent on a mad dash north. His destination was the Wid Hall ranch, nestled down the uneven valley.

"As he started his sprint, Sorahan coolly sized up his predicament. At this point he knew he was in no immediate danger. Unlike Wilcox's homestead, his land did not rest at the edge of a narrow canyon. It was located on flatter terrain where the valley widened out for about one half mile. So when the mud flow reached Sorahan's homestead it was only several feet deep. But the young mountain resident knew that a mile further down the valley the flat terrain would again narrow. The mud flow would build up again before it reached the Hall ranch. He knew he must reach his neighbors to warn them. Calling on reserves of energy he did not believe he possessed, Sorahan quickened his pace.

"He opted not to follow the [meandering] mountain road. Instead he elected to take a more direct route over a jagged bed of lava. Despite this difficult trek, Sorahan gained valuable time on the flood.

"When the exhausted young man reached the edge of the Hall ranch, he noticed a stile between the wire fence. Without hesitating Sorahan bounded over the stile in two leaping strides, tumbling into the soft alfalfa field at the edge of the ranch. By now he was breathing in short fast spurts. Realizing that his mission was nearly accomplished, Sorahan forced himself to his feet and staggered on towards the Hall cabin.

"Inside the cabin, Wid Hall, his wife, Emily, and two young daughters, Marian and Evelyn, were sleeping, oblivious to the on-rushing havoc. Reasoning that his bad manners would be forgiven in view of the circumstances, Sorahan burst into the Hall homestead. Mrs. Hall was the first to react to the sudden intrusion. Her exhausted neighbor quickly told her of the impending disaster. Without hesitating Mrs. Hall took the telephone receiver off the dial and placed a call to the nearby Hat Creek ranger station to flash the warning."

WID HALL'S ESCAPE: AS TOLD TO B. F. LOOMIS

"Mr. Elmer Sorahan was a homesteader living in a tent about a mile and a half above here on Hat Creek. In the night his dog barked, raved, and stuck his paws against him in the bed to wake him up. Elmer thought it might be some kind of animal, a bear or panther, so he got up and dressed, put on his high top boots and laced them up. He put his gun by the bed, then peeped out to see what the dog was barking at.

"He saw the mud flow coming like a wave about twelve feet high which looked like a white streak on top. The flood made a roar something like a gale of wind in the trees, with a crash and boom of the logs and rocks as they came tumbling along in the flood. He realized that it must be a flood coming and ran down the creek to awaken those who lived below him on the creek.

"It was about eleven or twelve o'clock when the flood reached our place. Elmer came with a rush, and he was perhaps five minutes ahead of the wave that struck our house. He gave a yell that startled us, and we all jumped up in a hurry. Frank Bartlett happened to be sleeping in the barn across the creek, 150 yards distant. Elmer then ran across the creek to awaken him and just got back across the creek when the bridge went out. Frank remained on the other side. In the meantime, Mrs. Hall telephoned to the people below on the creek that the flood was coming.

"As soon as Elmer returned he took the two girls, one by each hand, and beat it for higher ground. The crash and roar of the flood was so intense that you could hardly hear one yell even at a short distance.

"After we went to the woods it began to rain, so we went to the high ground, and made our camp under a tree. I had just two stubs of matches in my pockets, and we managed to get a fire.

"About three o'clock we tried to get back to the house, which had moved 53 feet and lodged against a tree and the yard fence, but could not reach it at that time. The mud flow looked more like mortar than water where it ran over the ground it left it slick and smooth like a pavement.

"During the day we put in a temporary bridge across the creek so we could get to the barn where the horses were, so if anything serious should happen we could get away. On their way over, the younger girl, Evelyn, saw a small pool of muddy water and asked if she could wade through it. And when she did so, found that the water was warm, something more than 'milk' warm, and that was in the afternoon of May 20th.

'I saw the form of a fish in the mud, and scraped the mud off with my foot, when the skin slipped off the fish, and it looked like it had been baked in the mud,' said Hall."

B. F. LOOMIS' STORY

The pyrotechnics were far from done. On May 22, there followed a massive eruption that propelled volcanic ash, rock fragments, and gas more than 30,000 feet into the air—a cloud visible from 150 miles away. This created one of the two craters near the summit today and a devastated area still sparsely populated with trees. B. F. Loomis, local lumberman and amateur photographer, had been instrumental in documenting the volcano's return to life.

As a small boy Benjamin Franklin Loomis had traveled west by covered wagon with his family. In 1874 he built a small cabin near Manzanita Lake and eventually homesteaded in the present-day Viola, just west of Lassen Peak. For much of his life he made a living making and selling wood shakes. In 1910 Loomis purchased the Vilas Mill and began a large-scale lumber business. By the time of the Lassen Peak eruptions, Loomis had spent many years documenting with photographs the region's natural and man-made features, his lumbering business, and his family. On May 22, 1915, as he was returning home, he witnessed,

> the largest eruption of Lassen Peak which ever occurred. . . . The eruption came on gradually at first, getting larger and larger until finally it broke out in a roar like thunder; the smoke cloud was hurled with tremendous velocity many miles high, and the rocks thrown from the crater were seen to fly way below the timber line before they struck the ground. As the rocks emerged from the smoke cloud they were followed by a comet-like tail of smoke which enabled us to tell definitely the path of their flight. For a short time the smoke cloud ran down the mountain side, melting snow very fast, and the water could be seen running down the mountain side in a rush.

Loomis captured this tumult with his camera. (See previous page.)

Loomis was also a strong advocate for the formation of Lassen Volcanic National Park. When his daughter, Louisa Mae, died at age twenty, he built the Louisa Mae Loomis Memorial Museum at Manzanita Lake to house and showcase his collection of photographs and artifacts for the public. Loomis deeded the museum, seismograph station, and surrounding forty acres to the national park in 1929.

A SPRING SAGA

Georgi "FireFly" Heitman

Hubris can be a backpacker's greatest liability. It is difficult to know when to turn back, to modify long-established plans, to defer a dream for yet another day…especially when you have already hiked hundreds of Pacific Crest Trail miles. Countless obstacles can stop even the most carefully planned hikes and impassioned hikers. Whether a late-season snowfall, a reroute because of forest fire, or an untimely illness or injury, often there is nothing to do but accept the new reality. This, however, is never easy to do. "A Spring Saga" recounts the tale of a determined hiker named Sagebrush from the perspective of the Heitmans, his guardian trail angels who do everything in their power to support his stubborn commitment to walk from Belden to Castle Crags despite a daunting snowpack.

Easter Sunday came late that year, April 16 to be exact. In fact, ten days later I left for my first-ever PCT Kickoff. My alarm went off just before 5:00 AM, as I was to meet friends at the sunrise service at church in my little town of Old Station. I reached for the cord to raise my window shades, expecting to see the same starlit skies I had seen when I retired the night before. What I saw was snow, *tons* of it cascading from the sky, landing on top of the abundance that had already fallen. My flowerbed, which had been showing the green shoots of emerging daffodils only yesterday, was covered with snow deeper than I'd seen in the thirteen winters we'd lived out here at what my husband and I call the Hideaway, in the back of beyond at more than 4500 feet elevation. A yardstick dropped off our front porch confirmed my suspicions— it disappeared completely.

Fast-forward to June 10 when a car pulled up and parked at our place. Out climbed a balding man, middle fifties give or take, with a few, though not too many, pounds to lose. He introduced himself as Sagebrush, a PCT hiker from Texas. He explained that he had been struggling through the late-spring snow-pack farther south for what seemed like weeks. He was sick to death of it and, on the advice of a seasoned PCT veteran, had driven north to "get above the snow." He asked if he could get a ride south to Belden, from where he intended to hike the ninety miles north to Old Station and back to the Hideaway, where he would retrieve his rental car. He was already pulling his pack and trekking poles from the car. He knew he would be encountering some snow but, after what he had been through, Sagebrush opined that it wouldn't be that onerous.

"Well, fine," I said, " except the highway south through Lassen Volcanic National Park isn't open yet." In fact, due to the Easter surprise that dumped more than fourteen feet of snow on Lassen Peak, the national park was forecasting that the road might not open until mid-July. While we could get him to Belden by other roads, we counseled Sagebrush quite frankly that we did not think he could get here from there. After all, the PCT rises quickly from the Feather River and summits above 7000 feet as it passes along the eastern flank of Lassen Peak. He assured us that we were wrong. Even a call to the Park Service rangers, confirming our doubts, didn't slow him down.

Perhaps we were unable to be sufficiently convincing because, even though we had hosted many hikers, we had not hiked the PCT. As a result, the next morning Sagebrush and I took off for Belden and Little Haven, the home of the Braatens, another trail angel refuge. The Braatens fed us a lovely lunch and, although they were very skeptical about our hiker's chances, Sagebrush still assured us, "No worries." The Braatens had only recently relocated, after all, and were not really current on the snowpack situation. Sagebrush shouldered his pack. I left.

Three or four days later I came home to find FireWalker (my husband) gone. He showed up later with none other than Sagebrush in the pickup. Sagebrush's story went something like this: He ran into deep snow at about the 6000-foot level as he climbed up the trail from Belden. He knew he still had significantly more climbing to do before he would be able to drop down to Highway 36 in the Chester area. He struggled on. He was GPS loaded and well mapped to boot, so even though he was pretty sure that he was off the trail, he had a reasonably good idea where he was. He could see that he might travel cross-country to a Forest Service road that would lead him down. So that's what he did. He eventually found a place where he thought he could safely glissade down quite a way, saving some time and a lot of energy. Cool. Unfortunately, when he came to the bottom of the chute, either a snow bridge collapsed under him or he had misjudged the drop at the bottom. The result was a hard landing on a large boulder, which severely bruised his thigh, cut his chin, and left him with other bruises and contusions. It took him until the next day to locate what he hoped was the Forest Service road. The snow was deep enough to make walking very difficult. And, successfully navigating this stretch of terrain would only get him part of the way back to Old Station.

He realized just how totally exhausted he had become and how cold and how wet he was, how painful his injuries were, and how deep the snow seemed. Then he got lucky. He heard the sound of an engine, and along came a pickup with two occupants. They were driving a company vehicle—no unauthorized passengers, with significant consequences for violations. With Chester still a good fifteen miles away, Sagebrush pleaded with them to take him. "You'll be responsible for my dying out here!" They relented and carried him and his pack to the outskirts of town, where they had him walk into town to avoid trouble with their company. Once in Chester, Sagebrush spent the night and then called us. For the next several, maybe three, days he cured in our hot tub. The size and colors of the bruise on his thigh made me wince each time I saw it. The cut on his chin was healing. Then he got out his maps and began plotting his next venture. FireWalker and I cringed.

I was beginning to smarten up a bit, so I stopped by our local weekly newspaper and copied a recent article about a Redding woman who had attempted to walk the PCT between Burney Falls and Castle Crags State Park in late May. She was an experienced solo hiker but ran into "up to 10 feet of snow." She dropped down to a road that she knew paralleled the trail at a lower elevation but remained unsure that she was on the right road. She continued on in what seemed the right direction but was running out of food and strength. As her trip extended, she tried to signal a low-flying aircraft that she assumed was searching for her. She built a signal fire, but low cloud cover prevented it from being seen. Her new enemy became the snowmelt-fed raging streams. Ultimately she came across a set of tire tracks and followed them, meeting a fellow who was out unlocking gates so searchers could get into the area to look for her. She had planned for a seven-day trip and was out for a total of eleven.

When Sagebrush outlined his next plan—he intended to hike from our Hideaway to Castle Crags—I hauled out the article. "That was weeks ago," he protested. "The snow must be gone by now." Besides, he continued, "it's been really hot out lately." He'd leave the next morning armed with upgraded GPS, maps, and his cell phone despite our warning that we didn't think he could get there from here.

Hours later we received a call from a ranger at Burney Falls, who reported that four hikers had arrived after completing their PCT journey from Castle Crags by helicopter. Abundant snow had made trail finding very challenging if not impossible. We started trying to reach Sagebrush on his trusty cell phone, which had clear access to a repeater on the Hat Creek Rim, over which he was currently hiking. No answers, no return phone calls. We kept trying...

We received a call from our Burney Falls contact, who reported that she had found Sagebrush and had warned him of trail conditions ahead and the recent rescue. She also mentioned that we had tried for three days to reach him by cell phone. He said it had "been acting up" and, again, brushed off the words of caution. "He looked at his watch," she commented, "and said he was right on time and headed up the trail." We mused at just how pig-headed some people could be, unwittingly or unwillingly incapable of recognizing that they were mortal.

It was another two days after he left Burney Falls before we heard again from Sagebrush. Again, FireWalker took the call. It seemed that Sagebrush's phone had miraculously recovered just as he needed to call for help a second time. FireWalker drove fifty miles up Highway 89 to rescue Sagebrush from alongside the highway. That Texan was whupped!

From the comfort of our hot tub, he told us he'd run into a "solid wall of snow at 6000 feet" and had kept going until he was too tired. He knew if he hiked east he would find Highway 89 and safety, so that's what he did. He practically lived in our hot tub for the next couple of days.

Sagebrush was not the only confident PCT hiker humbled that June. We had several more rescues and served as the infirmary for their recharge and recovery too. Perhaps it is the human curse to have to learn everything for ourselves. But, though we didn't experience the PCT firsthand, FireWalker and I will never forget the lessons of that spring's saga.

PISS-FIR WILLIE

By Jim Dodge

While the destructive legacy of uncontrolled logging mars long stretches of the wildlands the Pacific Crest Trail passes through in northern Califor-nia (Section O in particular) and in the Pacific Northwest (most notori-ously, the Stampede Pass area), these areas are also marked by the effects of massive tree-planting projects. The "planters," in fact, make up as much of the culture here as the loggers, wildfire fighters, and fishermen—a rough and rude crew who endure all kinds of weather and grueling work to get the job done. In these two poems, northern California poet Jim Dodge captures both the experience of working as a planter and the experience of knowing one in his renditions of Piss-Fir Willie. Part mythical creature, part real-live person, a Piss-Fir Willie can be found in almost every tree-planting or trail-building crew in the backcountry: a seasoned veteran, as tough as the work is itself.

In the first poem, "Green Side Up," Dodge captures the visceral sensa-tions of planting for hours on steep, muddy slopes in the incessant rain. For the PCT hiker slogging through constant rain, up and down endless passes and through long stretches of forest, these sensations will be all too famil-iar. Since planters are paid by how many trees they put in the ground, such fortitude is absolutely necessary and pays off in dollars—just like the long-distance PCT hiker gets rewarded in miles. The second poem, "Getting After It," illustrates the all-or-nothing, no-holds-barred attitude common in tree planting. For the PCT hiker, especially the thru hiker, this attitude will certainly resonate.

SOURCE: "Green Side Up" and "Getting After It," from *Rain on the River*, by Jim Dodge (Grove Press, 2002). Copyright © 2002 by Jim Dodge. Reprinted by permission of the author.

GREEN SIDE UP

Kid, there's only two things a tree planter needs to know:
The green side goes up, and ain't no raingear in the world that'll keep you dry.
—Piss-Fir Willie

Once you're soaked
It doesn't matter
If it's raining.

The trees go in
One by one by one
And you go on

Borne and lost in
The mindless rhythm,
Bent to the task.

No time at all
You forget the rain,
Blur into its

Monotony.
Between root and breath,
No difference—

It's all hard work.
Your wet body burns
From the bones out.

GETTING AFTER IT
    All the planters on our crew
    Packed double tree-bags.
    Piss-Fir Willie harnessed three,
    And stuffed another 20 bare root stock
    In a day-pack with his lunch.
    When Timothy ragged him one morning—
    "Geez, Willie, you could probably get
    Another six down each pants leg
    And a dozen between your teeth"—

    Willie turned to him and said,
    Loud enough for us all to hear,
    "I'll tell you what my daddy told me:
    Son, if you're gonna be a bear,
    Be a grizzly."

LEMURIA: MYSTERIES OF MOUNT SHASTA

By Maurice Doreal

Mount Shasta is a picturesque presence for some three hundred trail miles as the Pacific Crest Trail makes its long traverse west around the massive peak. Such prominence has made Mount Shasta a mystical, spiritual icon for many who have lived in its shadow, experienced its moods, or witnessed its majesty. No legend is more fascinating than the relationship between Mount Shasta and the lost lands of Atlantis and Lemuria.

Originally hypothesized by zoologist Philip Sclater in 1864 as an explanation for the wide distribution of fossilized remains of lemurs, Lemuria was one of many land bridges and continents whose existence was suggested during the nineteenth century to account for the present distribution of species. Later that century, though Lemuria disappeared from conventional scientific consideration, it was embraced by occult writers, who suggested that the people of Lemuria were highly advanced beings.

In 1894, Frederick Spencer Oliver, the famed author and channeler, described a secret city beneath Mount Shasta and in passing mentioned Lemuria. These beliefs have been repeated and enhanced by occultists such as Maurice Doreal. Doreal founded the Brotherhood of the White Temple in 1930, an organization that continues today in order to bring "the Ancient Wisdom to mankind." The Brotherhood's headquarters and spiritual center is in the Rocky Mountains not far from Denver.

When I was in Los Angeles in 1931 it was my good fortune to make a personal, physical visit to the colonies in Mt. Shasta. [...] It is the common

Source: Excerpted from *Mysteries of Mt. Shasta*, by Dr. Maurice Doreal (Brotherhood of the White Temple, n.d.). Reprinted by permission of the Brotherhood of the White Temple.

assumption that the inhabitants of that mountain are Lemurians. That is, that they are the last descendents of the great Race which occupied the ancient continent of Lemuria, which existed in the South Pacific ocean. That continent occupied a very vast space in what now is the approximate location of the Caroline Islands. [...] The Caroline Islands are the last traces of the mountain peaks of Lemuria that rise above the surface of the water.

[...] Before the sinking of Lemuria and Atlantis, there was an Atlantean colony in northern California. When the great flood came which submerged Atlantis and Lemuria, those who were able fled to the highest mountains and established a colony in the mountainous country. [...]

Today, the remains of [the temples of Lemuria] may be seen in the Caroline Islands, a city large enough to have several million inhabitants. [...] The great space beneath Lemuria was used by the Lemurians as a pleasure place. They had a vast knowledge of science, unparalleled in modern times. [...] When Lemuria sank and it was destroyed in the great war with Atlantis, [...] the priest-kings of Lemuria and the nobles retreated in their underground palaces and shut themselves off from the outer circle of the world. They live there today, approximately four and a half million of them living beneath the surface of the earth today. Someday, they might break forth. [...]

The Atlantean colony in northern California was given the duty of guarding the entrance to the prison in which the Lemurians were bound because after they had retreated the Atlanteans sealed the entrance and set a guard to see that they never broke out again. [...]

When I was lecturing in Los Angeles, in 1931, two of the inhabitants of Mt. Shasta came to Los Angeles and attended my lectures and they were there for a week before they let me know who they were and then, one Friday evening, they introduced themselves to me and they told me I could visit them at Mt. Shasta. I told them it was impossible for me to go there and get back in time for my lecture. They said, "We have another way of going," so we took a car out into the hills, just off Cahuenga Boulevard. [...] They gave me a little thin mask almost like cellophane. We did not have cellophane at that time, at least not much, and it had no chemicals and they told me to put that over my face and I did. Then they gave me a belt with two little pockets on the side and a row of buttons. I did not know what was going to happen. Each one took me by the arm and told me to press certain buttons and I went up through the air like a rocket plane and we rose until the earth looked like it was almost fading out, we breathed perfectly because something in that mask over my face condensed the small amount of oxygen so we could breathe and it seemed that around us there was a shell of some kind of force, because I could hear a humming noise all the time.

When we came down it seemed like almost no time had passed; probably, fifteen or twenty minutes. We landed about two thirds up the side of Mt. Shasta—we landed in front of a small building. The building itself was not large, made out of a kind of rose colored stone. We went inside. It was perfectly bare, nothing in it and as we stood there a stone slid out from the side of the door and covered it and then it seemed as if the whole room was shaking back and forth. [. . .]

Then we went down through the rock [. . .] until we were approximately seven miles below the surface of the earth. The space we came into was about two miles in height and about twenty miles long and fifteen miles wide and it was as light as a bright summer day, because suspended, almost in the center of that great cavern of space was a giant glowing mass of light. It was not radio active but it seemed to have qualities in it that caused your entire body to tingle. [. . .]

They told me later that it was condensed from a blending of the rays of the sun and the moon and that it had all of the harmful rays in it extracted and only the life-giving and beneficial energies left. They told me, at certain places on the mountains that they had power houses that they concealed during the time when they were not in use, that would sink through the ground and the ground close over them, that they were so fixed that they would descend in elevators and would be hidden from anyone who would casually stumble onto them. [. . .]

About a mile and a half from the elevator was a small city of beautiful white houses formed of marble and other stone and they were so beautiful that they almost blinded the eye. They had such beautiful lines and architecture that the most beautiful temples of ancient Greece were rough caricatures of those cities. There was one large building and a number of others, about four hundred. The rest of the entire underground space which we could see clearly when we first came out of the cavern, was laid out in gardens—it seemed just like tropical forests, beautiful trees, and parks and places where vegetables were growing and fruit trees bearing fruit that are unlike any upon the face of the earth today, because they have preserved there the plants and even some of the animals that were before the time of the sinking of Atlantis and Lemuria.

[. . .] They told me how the different energies that they had controlled caused the plants to grow perfectly. From time to time they would condense moisture and cause it to rain when they wished and cause it to stop when they wanted it to.

They told me that ordinarily, they were never sick, unless from accident and they lived approximately 150 years and then passed of their own free will. They laid down their body and went elsewhere and everyone there had chosen to do that work for a period of time, that everyone of them were illumined souls that had chosen to carry out the necessary work.

Then they led me to various caves in the walls. They showed me caves in which they performed what we would call today, Alchemistry. They transmuted the materials they needed from the earth and stone itself. I saw one as an experiment pour a shovel full of sand into a curious little box and put it into a furnace and let it stay for five minutes and pull it out as gold [...] and they showed me how they could make from common earth or stone any metal they needed.

Then they took me into another place [...] where they made clothes and I saw clothes made in a way that I would like to be able to make them here. They would make a picture of the design of the costume that they wanted for themselves, then they placed it in a projecto-scope, an invisible ray of energy would shoot out and then on a screen would form a kind of misty figure of the figure they were projecting and that would become more and more solid until there would fall on the floor, the garment they desired. Everything which exists is merely energy with particles of primal substance gathered around it. [...]

Then, after they had shown me these they took me into the largest building which was the temple [...] those who live there do not worship anything. They have no religion. They have passed beyond the need of religion. They know God and when one knows God they do not need religion or dogma or creed of any kind, they had no form, no ceremony. Everything was just as simple as it could possible be.

It was a temple but it was a school at the same time, and occasionally, from the outer world, they bring certain chosen ones whom they instruct in certain work they would have to do [...] during the remaining time that I spent, they gave me instruction, and this instruction was of things which of course I cannot tell you. [...]

After they had finished they showed me certain things in the Great Plan and outlined work for me to do in the outer world, which I am doing now, so that gradually the consciousness of man could be made more and more aware of the great mysteries behind matter and substance and behind life.

After they had finished, they took me back the same way we had come.

The mountain has spawned many other legends and beliefs. You may find the St. Germain Foundation and the "I AM" Activity to be of special interest. Both were founded by Guy Warren Ballard, a mining engineer by training, who while hiking on Mount Shasta in 1930 had an encounter with another hiker, who identified himself as St. Germain, an "ascended master and cosmic messenger." The white-and-purple-clad followers converge on Mount Shasta each August to this day for the annual "I AM" Pageant.

A BLISTERED KIND OF TOGETHERNESS

By Duffy and Angela Ballard

For six years, Angela Ballad served as editor of The Communicator, *the primary voice of the Pacific Crest Trail Association (PCTA). The PCTA strives to protect, preserve, and promote the PCT for the enjoyment of hikers and equestrians and for the value of wild and scenic lands.* The Communicator *has published many wonderful trail stories and serves as a written repository for trail lore, history, and culture.*

During the summer of 2000, Duffy and Angela Ballard hiked 2300 miles of the Pacific Crest Trail. Approximately one year later, they were married. And in 2003 their PCT adventure was recounted in the award-winning book A Blistered Kind of Love: One Couple's Trial by Trail. *In* Blistered, *the Ballards show two different perspectives on trail life in their "he said/she said" style, each tackling alternating chapters. For this anthology, they have written in a similar manner, starting with Duffy...*

DUFFY

While the Pacific Crest Trail does not actually climb Mount Shasta, the 14,162-foot peak is a beacon for thru hikers. It looms on the horizon, visible from the trail for three hundred miles. During their hikes, some PCT trekkers accept the mountain's challenge and veer off-trail to climb it, but most stay true to their northward goal. When we hiked the PCT in 2000, Angela and I often gazed at Shasta's snowcapped spire and wondered. ... In 2002, under the loose guidance of an REI climbing guide, we returned, in search of a Shasta summit. It was our most ambitious expedition since the PCT and it nearly became *my final* expedition.

In retrospect, the shortcomings of our plan were obvious. I had worked a night shift in the hospital's Emergency Department the night prior to our departure and slept only briefly and fitfully on the long car ride from Sacramento to the mountain. After driving for nearly four hours, we then climbed to 10,000 feet and camped. At 3:00 AM we awoke, put on crampons for the first time ever, and headed upward, planning to scale the Hotlum-Bolam route to the mountain's peak. Our guide had described this route as "advanced beginner," but on this particular day it was far trickier than that.

For the first couple hours we made steady progress. Then, at 12,500 feet, with Angela climbing about fifty feet behind, I faced a steep and slippery slab of glacier. Our guide had long since forged ahead, depositing only a series of orange flags in his wake. The route he'd marked didn't seem promising; to my left gaped a large crevasse waiting to gobble up imprudent climbers and to my right was a thin strip of scree and rock, a brown stripe in an otherwise white landscape. The orange flags led along the upper margin of the crevasse, where a misstep would have dire consequences. At first, I stepped methodically toward the flags, but soon impatience took over and I started to climb quickly, ice ax over foot. Bad mountaineering, and a bad idea.

My right crampon didn't purchase, then my left crampon came off my boot, and in a flash I was sliding on my stomach down a two-thousand-foot expanse of glacier. I must have slid twenty feet before I even realized I'd slipped. I sped right past Angela, who seemed to be screaming something, I couldn't hear what. I slid another ten feet before I positioned my ax for self-arrest. I'd visualized myself performing self-arrest many times and I'd practiced it on powdery bunny slopes back home in Philadelphia, but this was completely different. I drove the pick of my ax into the hard ice with my right arm. It made a grating sound and chunks of ice sprayed up and around me. This seemed to go on for minutes, but must have been only milliseconds, and then I abruptly stopped. I looked down in time to see my water bottle rocketing down the hill, flipping over and over again—moving like a tumbleweed in a fierce gale.

At this point, I got up and did what any reasonable mountaineer-in-training would do: started climbing back up. When I caught up with Angela, she was ashen and did not want to continue. Nonsense, I said, as stoically as I could, considering that I'd just been sliding full-speed down a glacier. Without waiting, I continued up the ice, this time adjusting my route so that I was only a few feet from the scree, hoping it would be less slippery there. When I reached the elevation where I'd initially lost my balance, I started systematically testing each foothold. Systematically, my crampons were denied. Now, instead of cutting steps with my ax (the appropriate ice-climbing technique), I got frustrated and started jamming my crampons into the ice, harder and harder; a foolish tactic leading to a predictable result.

Again I fell, hard, but this time I brought my ax down immediately. Unfortunately, while my progress was slowed, it wasn't stopped, and, even worse, I was thrown onto the scree. Now my ax and my butt were dragging through rock and frozen rubble. During several terrifying seconds I thought that I wasn't going to stop, that I'd hit more ice and just keep going until I flew off the mountain or collided with something very unforgiving. For the first time in my life I really believed I was going to die.

Fifty yards down the strip of scree, and not far from where it met snow and ice again, I somehow rolled to a stop. I was dazed and shaking—shaking like an alcoholic twelve hours from his last drink. My back and right thigh throbbed and my elbow stung. My right glove had been completely ripped open and my hand was oozing blood. I tried to stand up and was shocked, not to mention grateful, that I could. I looked up and saw Angela picking her way down the glacier, looking even more concerned than before. And I loved her immensely for that.

I should have felt disappointed, or ashamed—our summit bid had been denied because of my carelessness. And I should have been scared—I was 12,000 feet up a mountain, surrounded by slippery terrain and unsure how hurt I was. Already, I could feel a grapefruit-sized bruise underneath the skin of my right buttock. Instead, I just felt thankful. Thankful to be alive and thankful to have a companion looking out for me, one who knew when it was time to call it quits. This time, when Angela suggested, actually stated, that we were heading down the mountain, I did not argue.

ANGELA

When Duffy and I hiked the PCT, there were a number of times when I knew one or both of us was in danger: when we ran out of water in 110-degree heat in southern California; when we were lost, off-trail for nearly twenty-four hours north of Kennedy Meadows; when raging snowmelt-fed creeks threatened to drag us under in the Sierras; and when we fought to stay dry and warm in hypothermic conditions in Washington. In each of these instances, I feared that we could get really sick, or hurt, or be forced to quit—but it wasn't until a couple years later, when we attempted to climb Mount Shasta, that I experienced true terror on the trail—a moment when I thought that the person I loved most in the world was going to die right in front of me.

As Duffy struggled to ram his ice ax into Shasta's ice-crusted flank, I watched, helpless, as he hurtled down the mountain. First he was above me and next he was within arm's reach. Poised on the slope, crampons just barely dug in, I reached out to grab him, but as I did so, voices behind me, two friends in unison, screamed "NOOOOOO!" And it hit me: I could grab Duffy but I couldn't save him. We'd both end up a tangled mess of crampons, axes, and limbs hurtling downward. So I stopped reaching. I watched. I screamed. And then I collapsed in relief when Duffy finally managed to get his ax into the ice and jolt to a stop.

My heart nearly beat its way out of my chest as I scrambled down to tell Duffy, "Forget it, it's too icy out here for us, we're not mountaineers, I want to go home." Duffy, however, was frustrated, determined, and deaf to my reasoning. Nonsense, he said, and started climbing again. So I had no choice but to clamber up Shasta's crusty flank behind him. I think I've blocked out his second fall. I couldn't believe I was watching him plummet toward certain death again! Of course I screamed, but this time I had no hope of catching him even if I wanted to. And when he landed in a bloody heap in the scree, I landed in a heap too. I'd nearly lost him a second time, and that was too much to bear. We had not hiked more than two thousand miles together to be separated now.

Ideal hiking partnerships are mutually beneficial, such that each member of the party contributes to the experience of the other. Partners split decision making and burdens; lend each other encouragement; and share their thoughts, feelings, fears, and hopes. "A good partnership," writes old-time PCT guru Ray Jardine in *Beyond Backpacking*, "leads to a deeper knowledge of oneself and one's companion, as well as a better understanding of the journey as a whole, its hardships, triumphs, and daily delights." For couples this can be a make-or-break proposition because on-trail they face extremes they'd probably never encounter at home. This makes teamwork crucial not only for physical survival but for the survival of the relationship and the journey as a whole.

As the ten-year anniversary of our PCT thru hike approaches, it's becoming more and more clear that our journey along a winding path from Mexico to Canada is the foundation of our marriage. Together, Duffy and I climbed the tallest mountain in the contiguous United States (but never Shasta; maybe some day we'll try a less technical route); we struggled through thirty-mile days; we held hands across ice, snow, and streams, knowing that our lives might depend on our grip; and we carried extra weight when the other person was hurting. We fought, we bickered, I cried, and blisters were formed and incised and formed again. But it was more than worth it—it was the adventure of a lifetime with the love of a lifetime. We forged a partnership on the PCT that I don't know if we could have created any other way.

Thru hiking isn't *romantic* as the typical person would define the word, and the challenges that long-distance hiking places on a relationship are innumerable. Take your significant other out hiking for a few hundred miles and you'll soon discover things about him or her (and you) that you never imagined. From the metaphysical (How flexible are your visions of the ideal thru hike? What is more important to you: the other person or the hike?), to the practical (How do you each react to extreme hunger, thirst, exhaustion, pain, stress, and isolation? How much food do you like to carry and eat? Can you scoot over in the tent?), to the distasteful (What will you think when your honey starts to smell like vinegar? How will your relationship fare without friends, family, employment, and other distractions to dilute the annoying idiosyncrasies of your personalities?). Relationships in the backcountry are stretched, tested, and tumbled. Some break, but others emerge like river rocks—more polished and beautiful than when they began.

Duffy and I learned life-changing lessons on the PCT. We each found inner strength we didn't know we had, and we gathered perspective that has shaped our lives. I'm sure that we would have gained a lot had we each hiked the PCT alone, but by doing it together we gained even more—we gained each other.

On a slippery mountainside, in a fire-hot desert, or in a rain-soaked tent, we weren't always in perfect sync; but as we faced physical challenges, inner demons, and personality clashes, it was clear—life in the backcountry and then back in the "real" world was best with each other in it.

Nearly a decade later, our memories of the trail hold us together when the day-to-day grind threatens to drag us apart—the children may throw tantrums, the house may be messy, the dog may vomit on the white carpet—but we have known better, and we have known worse. And whenever our foundation needs shoring up, we know where to go.

THE BATTLE OF CASTLE CRAGS

By Joaquin Miller

Part fiction and part fact, this is Joaquin Miller's account of an 1855 skirmish between local American Indians and immigrants. As Miller explains, the fight occurred in the saddle region of the ridgeline separating Castle Lake and a feature he calls Battle Rock, a thumblike spire in the northwest section of Castle Crags. The Pacific Crest Trail, which winds up the south and west side of Castle Crags, traverses this same ridgeline.

Both Miller and Captain Gibson (in the story) acknowledged the devastating impact the influx of gold miners had on the rivers and traditional fisheries of the indigenous communities. The outrage of the Modoc people was certainly understandable. In Captain Gibson's short summary of the battle, which Miller includes in his account, the captain acknowledges this detrimental impact on the Modoc culture and food supply: "In the year 1855, there being a great rush of miners here, the Sacramento River and other streams became muddy, and thereby obstructing the run of fish. The Indians became very indignant on account of it stopping the run of fish, which was their principal living. They commenced making preparations for hostilities by getting into strongholds, the principal one being the Castle Crags."

Joaquin Miller, the "Poet of the Sierras," was sympathetic to the plight of the Indians. As documented in Life Amongst the Modocs: Unwritten History, *Miller lived from 1854 to 1857 in the shadows of Mount Shasta. For a year he lived with an Indian wife completely isolated from white society, which gave him an unparalleled insight into relations between indigenous people and white settlers. "I must write of myself," noted Miller, "because I was among these people of whom*

SOURCE: Excerpted from "The Battle of Castle Crags," from *Selected Writings of Joaquin Miller*, ed. Alan Rosenus (Urion Press, 1977). Reprinted by permission of Alan Rosenus and Urion Press.

I write, though often in the background, giving place to the inner and actual lives of a silent and mysterious people, a race of prophets; poets without the gift of expression—a race that has often, almost always, been mistreated, and never understood—a race that is moving noiselessly from the face of the earth."

Miller, who achieved much of his celebrity in England in the 1870s, was a colorful but often underappreciated presence in California until his death in 1913. In this piece, he describes the similarly eccentric "Mountain Joe," one of the many untamed mountain guides who blazed trails through this section of rugged high country.

At what date Mountain Joe located Lower Soda Springs Ranch, now known as Castle Crag Tavern, I am not certain. [...] It is equitable to set Mountain Joe down as the first earnest and permanent proprietor of all this region round about here, for he tilled the soil, built some houses and kept a sort of hotel, and guided people to the top of Mount Shasta, to say nothing of his ugly battles with the Indians for his home.

I first saw this strange man at his own campfire when a school-lad at home in Oregon, where he had camped near our place with his pack-train. He told us he was in the habit of going to Mexico for half-wild horses, driving them up to Oregon, and then packing them back to California, by which time they were tamed and ready for sale. He told my brother and me most wondrous tales about his Soda Springs, Mount Shasta, the Lost Cabin, and a secret mine of gold. [...] But what won my heart entirely was the ease with which he reached his left hand, and taking "Di Bella Galica" from my father, divided "Gaul in three parts" in the ashes of the campfire as he read and translated the mighty Roman by the roaring Oregon. He was a learned foreigner, of noble birth, it was said, certainly of noble nature. I could not forget Mountain Joe and his red men, and his Mexicans and mules and horses; and so, in the fall of 1854, I ran away from school and joined him at Soda Springs, now Castle Crag Tavern.

He was my ideal, my hero. [...] We guided a few parties here and there, taking the first party to the top of the mountain that ever reached that point with ladies, I believe, and then returned to Yreka for the winter, going back to Lower Soda over the spring snowbanks with a tremendous rush of miners that Mountain Joe had worked up by his stories of the Lost Cabin and mysterious gold mines.

Thousands on thousands of men! The little valley of Soda Creek back of Castle Crag Tavern was a white sea of tents. Every bar on the Sacramento was the scene of excitement. The world was literally turned upside down. The rivers ran dark and sullen with sand and slime. The fishes turned on their sides and died. But the enraged miners found almost nothing. Mountain Joe disappeared. Men talked of handling "Mountain Joe's boy." The game disappeared before the avalanche of angry and hungry men. The Indians had vanished at their first approach and were starving in the mountains.

The tide went out as it came in—suddenly, savagely. Deeds of cruelty to Mexicans and half-tamed Indians who tried to be friendly and take fish in the muddied waters were not rare, as the disgusted miners retired from the country either up or down the river, leaving trails of dead animals, camp debris and cast-iron oaths behind. As they went, Joe came, and the Indians came, furious! We treated them well, tried to make friends of them once more, but they would have none of it.

By the end of June, 1855, the last miner had left our section; and soon the last Indian left us to go on the warpath. Mountain Joe and I were now utterly alone, with not even a Mexican to take care of the pack-trail and do the cooking. But we kept on. [...]

Meantime, ugly stories were afloat; and ugly sullen Indians came by, now and then—Modocs on their way across to the Trinity Indians, by the pass up little Castle Creek. They would not sit down, nor eat, nor talk. They shook their heads when we talked, and assumed to not know either the Shasta or Chinook dialect. The Trinity Indians were in open revolt beyond Castle Crags, and Captain Crook from Fort Jones, near Yreka, the famous General Crook, was in the field there. He drove them up Trinity River to Castle Crags, but had no decisive battle.

One hot morning, [...] Joe suddenly dropped his pick and caught up his gun. A horse went plunging up the valley past us with an arrow quivering in his shoulder; and smoke began to curl above the pines from the burning trading-post. We hastened down, but did not see a single Indian, nor did we see another horse or mule. [...]

Blotches of flour from torn sacks here and there made a white trail up over the red foothills on the brown, sweet-smelling pine-quills, and, without a word, Joe led cautiously on, I at his heels. The savages divided soon, the party with the horses going to the right, toward the Modoc country, the party with the stores, leaving a trail of flour, to the left, toward Castle Crags. This latter Joe followed, crossing the river at a ford, and going up the left bank of little Castle Creek. The canyon shuts in very close after a time. In a narrow pass the spilt flour was suspiciously plentiful. [...]

As said before, there were and had for some time been rumors of coming trouble. Joe and I turned back from Sisson [Mt. Shasta City] to give the alarm and get help along the river. Portuguese Flat, which it took us two days to reach through the mountains, as we dared not take the trail, was the nearest post. Dog Creek, the ghost of which may be dimly seen in Delta now, was then a prosperous camp, and full of men. Judge Gibson, then the only magistrate in the country, had married an influential chief's daughter, and, by a wise and just course, had gained great authority, and had kept this tribe, the Shastas, from taking part in the great uprising which finally spread all over the Coast. The Indians had determined on a war of extermination. It ended in the utter extinction of many tribes in Oregon and some in California.

Courage was not lacking in those days, but coolness and experience in Indian warfare were wanting. Gibson had all these. So had Mountain Joe; but Joe had lost an eye by an arrow, and the other eye was not good. So he deferred to Gibson. [...] Joe and I went back, and, with such friends as we could gather, waited at the base of Castle Crags for Gibson and his men.

Amazing as it may seem, he brought but about fifty, all told Indians and white; and yet he was the only man who could have done as well. The miners were already more than disgusted with the country; and Indians rarely fight Indians in a general uprising like this. Mountain Joe could raise but ten men of his own.

Gibson led straight up Big Castle Creek, as if avoiding Castle Crags and the savages entrenched there. He kept himself almost entirely with his Indians, and hard things were said of him by the worn and discouraged white volunteers. They suspected that he was afraid to make the fight, and was trying to join the regulars under Crook in the Trinity Mountains.

At last, when our shoes and moccasins, as well as patience, were worn out, he turned sharply to the right making the entire circuit of the Castle. We rested by a deep, dark lake which the Indians call the abode of the devil, Ku-ku-pa-rick, and they refused to approach its grassy, wooded shores.

Here Gibson, leaving his Indians for the first time, passed from man to man as they crouched under the trees. He told them that there was to be a fight, and a fight to a finish; that the hostiles were not an hour distant, and that no one could turn back and live, for if we did not kill them they would kill us. He told us that they had come down out of the Castle to kill deer, and so their arrows were not poisoned, and that we could swim.

He broke us up in parties, putting good and bad together, with Indians at the head of each. He told me to go with Joe, whom he sent to make a show of attack on the side next to Soda Springs. When near the hostiles Joe put me behind a tree on the edge of a small open place, and told me to stay there. Then he went on, creeping through the dense brush, to place the other men. I put some bullets into my mouth so as to have them handy, but I do not know what I did with them. I fired a few shots after Joe opened the fight, but hit only brush and rocks I reckon. And now pandemonium! Indians do not often yell in battle; but on both sides of us now the yelling was simply fiendish. They yelled from the top of the Castle to the bottom, it seemed to me.

We had taken the enemy entirely unawares, asleep, most of them, after the morning's chase, and our first shots brought down their dozing sentinels on the rocks. Finally there was some parleying, and the yelling, the whiz of arrows and the crack of rifles stopped. Then some Indian women came out and across the little gorge to Joe and his men, and I, thinking they had all surrendered, walked out into the open. Gibson called from the rocks ahead of me and to my right: "Boys, the fight now begins, and we've got to git them or they git us. Come on! Who will go in with me?" I answered that I would go, for it was all a picnic so far as I had yet seen, and I ran around to him. But there was blood on his hands and blood on his face, blood on all of his Indians and most of the white men were bloody and hot.

The enemy used arrows entirely. They could tell where we were, but we knew where they were only when we felt their sting. Gibson led, or rather crept, hastily on, his head below the chaparral. No one dared speak. But when we got in position, right in the thick of it, our men opened. Then the arrows, then the yelling, as never before! The women and children prisoners down with Joe set up the death song, as if it was not already dismal enough. The savages bantered us and bullied us, saying we were all going to be killed before the sun went down; that we were already covered with blood, and that they had not lost a man. I had not yet fired a shot since joining Gibson, and, rising up to look for a target, he told an Indian to "pull the fool down by the hair," which he promptly did.

The battle had lasted for hours. The men were choking, and the sun was near going down. We must kill or be killed, and that soon. We must do our work before dark. The white man has little show with an Indian in battle at night.

Gibson gathered all who could or would go, and took still another place by storm. Then Lane fell, mortally hurt by an arrow in the eye. I saw Gibson's gun fall from his hand from the very deluge of arrows; then all was blank, and I knew no more of that battle.

The fight was over when I came to my senses, and it was dark. A young man by the name of Jameson was trying to drag me through the brush; and it has always seemed to me that a good many people walked over me and trod on me. I could hear, but could not see. An arrow had struck the left side of my face, knocked out two teeth, and had forced its point through at the back of my neck. I could hear, and I knew the voices of Gibson and Joe. They cut off the point of the arrow, and pulled it out of my face by the feather end. Then I could see. I suffered no pain, but was benumbed and cold as we lay under the pines. Joe held my head all night expecting that I would die. Gibson had the squaw prisoners carry his wounded down to the pack-trail on the banks of the Sacramento. They laid us down under some pines and pretty juniper trees on the west side of the swift, sweet river. And how tender and how kind these heroic men were! I was as a brother to them now—their boy hero. Only the day before I had been merely "Mountain Joe's boy."

Gibson's loss in killed was considerable for so small a number engaged. [...] Indians never give their loss, because of encouragement to the enemy; and Mountain Joe and Gibson, for like reason, always kept their list of killed and wounded as low as possible, and spoke of the battle of Castle Crags as a trifling affair. Yet General Crook, in his letter to Captain Gibson, marveled that he ever got out with a single man.

[...] There are those who care to read of savage incidents in these border battles, but such things should be left to obscurity, and I shall set down but two here. The first of these was the treatment of the dead Modoc chief, Docas Dalla, by the chief of our Indian allies. When the body was dragged before him, where he stood in the heat and rage of battle directing his men, he threw off his robe, and, nearly naked, leaped on the naked body (for it had been stripped and scalped), and there danced and yelled as no fiend of the infernal regions could have danced and yelled. He called his fallen foe by name, and mocked and laughed, and leaped up and down on the dead till the body was slippery with blood which gushed from its wounds, and he could no longer keep his footing. Yet after all it was only the old Greek and Trojan rage—the story of Homer in another form of expression; and Castle Crag was Troy above the clouds.

One more incident, as described to me by the son of this same furious chief on revisiting the battleground: This son of the chief was but a lad at the time, and so was left by his father with two Indians and a few white men, who were too lame and worn out to rush into the fight, in charge of the blankets, supplies and so forth. They were left in the little depression or dimple in the saddle of the mountain a few hundred feet above and to the south of [...] Castle Lake, and in the Modoc pass or trail.

When Gibson forced the fighting as night came on, the hostiles separated, some going down the gorge as if to reach their stores of arrows in the caves of Battle Rock (for their supply must have been well nigh spent by this time) while others stole off up the old Modoc trail that winds up above and around the lake, and in which the son of the chief and other Indians, as well as some whites, lay concealed. And here in this dimple on the great granite backbone that heaves above and about the lake, here above the clouds, amid drifts and banks and avalanches of everlasting snow, the wounded fugitives, with empty quivers, and leaving a red path as they crawled or crept on and up over the banks and drifts of snow, were met by their mortal enemies face to face.

If you will stand here facing Battle Rock to the south, and with your back to the lake, which lies only a few hundred feet to the rear, though far below, you will see how impossible it was for the wounded savages to escape down the rugged crags to the left, or up and over the crescent of snow to the right. They could not turn back; they could not turn to the left nor to the right; and so they kept on. Two of them got through and over the ridge and onto the steep slope of snow, and slid down almost to the lake, where they lay for a few moments concealed in the tall grass. But their relentless red enemies followed their crimson trail, found and tomahawked and scalped them where they lay, and threw their bodies into the lake.

[...] You will find small stone cairns set up here and there on heads of granite rocks that break above the snow. It is the custom for an Indian, when passing the scene of some great disaster, especially if alone, to place in a conspicuous position a stone by the way in memory of his dead. He never rears his monument at one time, as does the white man. He places but one stone, often a very small one, and leaves the rest to time and to other hands.

Miller concludes his tale by recounting the occasion of the thirty-eighth anniversary of the Modoc battle, when he joined Captain Gibson at the site of the skirmish. "The finger of the infinite," Miller says, "traces and retraces in storm or sun the story and the glory of their unselfish valor here while the world endures. It is enough."

MY CLOSE ENCOUNTER WITH BIGFOOT

By Monte Dodge

Few legends have transcended cultures, eras, and regions like that of Big-foot, Sasquatch, Yeti, or Ts'emekwes. Common to all is the notion of a species of shy, wild, hairy giants living in the remote wilderness. Nefari-ous? Gentle? Carnivore? Perhaps a relict population of Gigantopithecus. Periodic sightings and footprints over the years have constituted the pri-mary evidence of the existence of Bigfoot—a record that is undermined by the abundance of hoaxes and the absence of fossil records.

No contemporary location has experienced a greater concentration of encounters than the mountains and forests of northern California. In 1958, tracks were found around a road construction site at Bluff Creek along the Klamath River; and in the same region nearly a decade later, Roger Patterson and Robert Gimlin shot movie footage of a Bigfoot. Each year, accounts of new sightings are reported.

Perhaps you will find Monte Dodge's experience compelling, from when he walked along the Pacific Crest Trail in the Trinity Mountains back in 1977.

One of the wildest nights of my entire hiking career occurred near the Eagle Creek Benches, a heavily wooded, well-watered area under the watchful eye of Eagle Peak in the Trinity Alps back in 1977. When I was a kid, our family would travel from Washington State to northern California to the small town of Hoopa located in the rugged forests near the confluence of the Klamath and Trinity Rivers. I remember the Hupa Indians gathering pine nuts,

SOURCE: A version of this story was published in the magazine of the Pacific Crest Trail Association, *The Communicator* 22, no. 1 (February 2009).

fishing for salmon, and capturing eels from traditional traps that they still used along the Trinity River. During this time I also heard many of the local stories of Bigfoot from the Hupa people and from my uncle who had lived in the area for thirty years. They all were believers.

My uncle, who was a logger at the time, often worked in remote areas of the region. His experiences reminded me that the deep forests of the Trinity, Klamath, and Marble Mountains have never really been tamed. Although he had many stories, most vivid in my memory was a time he heard wild howling one evening after a full day of work. Upon investigation the following morning, he discovered large humanlike tracks close to a freshly cut area along the forest boundary. His coworkers had their own large-track stories. Other locals refused to hunt in places they were convinced were inhabited by Bigfoot. At the time I thought these were just tales to scare us kids, but in late July 1977 these tales became much more real to me.

I was hiking the old PCT route in the Trinity Mountains, along Bloody Run, a tributary of Eagle Creek. Subsequently the PCT was rerouted to the ridgelines, avoiding the lower bottomlands, and in the late 1980s this area suffered a large forest fire that decimated the ecosystem. At the time, however, it was a region of thick pine and fir forest and abundant undergrowth. The trail was seldom used in those days and overgrown enough that I struggled periodically to see my feet. That, in itself, was unnerving because it was not unusual to encounter rattlesnakes in this area.

I camped for the evening near the confluence of Bloody Run and Eagle Creek. I had already set up my tent and had my stove blazing away, when I thought I heard low voices in the distance. I turned down the stove and listened, hearing what sounded like music or someone talking across the creek and up on the opposite ridge. Then to my surprise, I heard the same low "voices" coming from the ridge above me. I turned off my stove and listened intently; I repeatedly heard the voice murmurs from across the creek and then again on the ridge above. Even after years to reflect on the experience, I have struggled to describe these sounds. It was a low grumbling like indistinct music in the distance—no melody just sound. For some reason, I got goose pimples and the hairs on my arms raised.

I packed up my camp, rolled up my tent, picked up my still-hot stove, and hauled butt out of the there. Pumped with adrenaline, I hiked by moonlight, supplemented a bit with my old flashlight. After walking a few miles and believing I was hearing rocks roll and a few sticks breaking above me, I slowed and listened. Nothing, not even a frog or a cricket chirp. I fought with my imagination, which was already working to keep my heart racing. Despite my best attempts to quell my fear with logic, when I spread out my pad and bag I lay awake most of the night with a flashlight in one hand and my buck knife in the other.

Finally, with the coming of first light, I dozed off. I suppose it surprised me when I awoke alive. All the sounds and fears where gone and the morning was beautiful. I ate a Pop Tart and a few Space Food Sticks (*the* 1970s energy bar, marketed as what astronauts ate). I put on my pack and proceeded down the trail toward the Eagle Creek Benches. Being low on water, I kept an eye out for a creek to cross the trail. I soon found one, but the flow was insufficient to easily fill my wide-mouth bottle, so I climbed up the bank to a small pool. Near this creek I saw what looked like animal tracks going down into the ravine and then up the other side. In the middle, next to the pool was a perfect, huge footprint! All of the sudden, all the stories I had heard as a child and my experience the night before hit me, and I felt like I was in a dream. In retrospect, I did not feel fear but a sense of disconnected calm. Perhaps it helped that it was daytime or that I had no sense that "It" was still nearby. I filled my water bottle, got my camera out, and took a few photos with my foot next to His or Its or Whatever's large print.

To this day, I feel that, yes, there could be a Bigfoot. I have considered the possibility of these prints being a hoax, but where the tracks were found would never have been seen from the trail unless I had climbed up a bit. This seemed inconsistent with the approach of a practical joker. Bigfoot encounters with the white people in this region go back more than a century and with Native people for hundreds of years. After my experience I am willing to concede that it could be possible that some rare ape or hominid inhabits this wilderness.

I have been climbing, kayaking, and backpacking from Alaska to Baja and everywhere in between for some thirty-two years. I have countless rich and wonderful memories from those experiences, but none exist with the vivid clarity of that evening on the PCT in the Trinities. To this day, when I return to the quiet of the deep forest, it takes little to remind me of my close encounter with Bigfoot.

AIR STREAMING OFF THE CREST

By Chuckie "Funnybone" Veylupek

*Early in the conception of this project, we began looking at online jour-
nals and blogs that documented hikers' PCT experiences. With recent
advances in technology, it has become increasingly common for thru hikers to actively blog or journal their trip as they're hiking so that friends
and family can follow them from afar. In fact, a vibrant trail community
has blossomed in this virtual and digitized wilderness, with a plethora of
online advice, discussions, and stories.*

*One of the first that really caught our attention was Funnybone's
story of his encounter with two rather unusual trail angels. Humor, often
with a dash of hyperbole and a splash of the ribald, characterizes some
of the best trail stories. Whether shared around the campfire or through
the flickering pixilated light of a computer, these wild and sometimes
raunchy tales that leave us laughing out loud are common favorites for
PCT hikers.*

By sundown, I stumbled upon Somes Bar-Etna Road, where a lone can of
soda had been placed for "You crazy PCT hikers." I was just the guy.

When I started to cross the seemingly desolate road, an older model Dodge
flatbed pickup truck roared into view from the south. The driver, a surly middle-
aged man whose belly alone was twice my size, pulled over on the opposite side
of the road and got out. He told his dogs to behave and then offered a quick hello
as he hoisted the hood to check the oil.

"Goddamn drive's gonna kill her. Say, are you wanna them loony PCT hikers passing through?"

I stopped. "I am."

"Goddamn. You peoples are nuts. I sees you all summer, passing through town like a migratin' herd of cattle." He spoke with a hoarse, raspy voice, as though he had smoked a few acres worth of tobacco in his time.

"Town?" I asked the bespectacled guy, quietly.

"Yeah," he boomed back. "I lives down near Etna. You guys are always invading the goddamn brewery all summer." He pulled out the dipstick one more time and wiped it clean in the elbow crease of his flannel sleeve.

"Sonavabitch, she's burnin' right through it! I knew it!" The two dogs, both Rottweilers—and both, like their owner, twice their intended size—sat patiently in the front seat, slobbering all over the dashboard and fogging up the windshield.

"Say. What's the attractshun to this trail, anyway?"

"Oh, I don't know. It's always been one of those things I had to do, I guess. I love the outdoors."

"I hear you," he interrupted, as he wiped his oily hands in his ZZ Top–length beard.

"I do a lot of huntin' and fishin' myself, so I can relate." He then turned to the dogs and yelled, "Mavis! Goddammit, you gonna drown poor ol' Maggie." Mavis started wagging his whole body and slobbering more, encouraging poor old Maggie to get in on the act. "Goddamn dogs own that truck I tell you. 'Course, I'm the one that's gotta pay fer the oil in her." He reached out with a greasy hand: "The name's Rodney, but I prefer being called Rod."

"I'm Ch-Chu-Chuck." I was going to say Funnybone or Chuckie, but Rod was clearly a man's man and the sobriquet Funnybone isn't worth explaining, while Chuckie is simply too cute, too effeminate and altogether too doll-like. He might've beat the living crap out of me right then and there.

"Nice to meet you Chuckie." He reached up to grab the hood and slammed it shut and then wiped his oily hands on his pants legs. I used my shorts for the same reason. "Listen Chuckie. You seem like a good feller. I could read peoples real good. I'd like you to come down and meet my ol' lady. We can cook you up a real meal—meat and potato like—and let you git cleaned up. I'd be mighty offended if you refused; you really need to git yerself cleaned up."

"Um, sure, I guess," I said. I didn't need supplies or anything, but turning down a free meal goes against every aspect of thru-hiker religion. And when he mentioned his "ol' lady," I knew I wasn't going to die at the hands of some maniacal madman from the mountains. At least not a single one.

"No guessing about it. You comin'. Thing is, you gotta sit in the back since Mavis and Maggie is too goddamn old. They's gonna roll right off otherwise."

Unlike a normal pickup truck, there was no "in the back" that I could see. There was an *on the back* and it didn't look too inviting or too terribly safe. The truck's bed was a pancake-flat rear-end with nothing to hold onto but a spare tire bolted onto the boards, and nothing to keep you from flying right off. Between each of the boards was a quarter-inch gap, not quite big enough to jam a finger into. Plus, as I was about to discover, the spare tire was so tightly bolted down there was no way to get a hand underneath it and hold on. Nothing would prevent me from rolling to my death.

But before I could reject Rod's kind offer, he'd started the truck back up, gnashed its gears into place, and yelled back, "Git on and hold on!"

I was doomed.

We started down the mountainous road and Rod slipped the old Dodge into neutral, so it could gain speed without interruption. Gain speed it did and I was soon rolling around on the back like a pinball, only with little to bounce off but the road itself. After traveling at two and a half miles per hour for weeks on end, this was altogether insane.

With each twist in the road—it was all twists—the doghouse on wheels gained momentum. It seemed Rod had forgotten about me. It also seemed all my yelling and screaming didn't help to remind him of my existence. The damn dogs drowned out my own cries and they were each barking joyfully with their heads out the passenger window. I was soon soaked in a steady stream of slobber. The spare tire was all I could wedge myself against—and then I realized I could unscrew the wing nut holding it down and fasten the Grudge's hip belt around it (*the Grudge* was my affectionate name for my vengefully heavy pack). This was easier in theory than it was in practice, and unfortunately I had little time to practice. The wing nut rusted onto the anchor bolt and would've been less secure had it been welded. With all the force I could muster, I cranked it loose and quickly jammed the Grudge underneath it, just as we dove into an off-camber hairpin turn.

The Dodge had one of those fancy rear axles with two tires on each side, hence it stuck to the road like bubblegum. I'm not sure Rod knew how much trouble I was having, since rearview mirrors were apparently optional on Dodge dualies. But the truck did have an NRA sticker, as well as a NASCAR one, both stuck off-kilter on the cracked rear window. Rod, I realized, was used to speed. And used to death.

Despite getting the Grudge's hip belt wound around the tire and tightly in place, the ride was no less dangerous. I saw my life flash before my eyes so many times I had to start counting over. This was especially the case when Rod grabbed the steering wheel with one hand and turned to shout something back to me, taking his eyes off the road for eons at a time.

"Tell me Chuckie. You like fear?" he yelled, beard flapping in the wind.

What the f—?!

"Um, no, not really," I screamed back. *But thanks for asking.*

"What? You gotta be kiddin' me. What kinda answer's that?!" he asked. "Everyone likes beer!"

"Oh, beer! I thought you said, oh, never mind. Yeah, I like beer."

"Good, 'cause I got two kinds: Coors in a can and Coors in a bottle. What'll it be?"

"A can'll do," I yelled.

He reached down under the dogs to the floor of the passenger side, losing sight of the road yet again, and grabbed a can of Coors. Then he turned back and leaned out his window once more and offered me the can.

"Thing is," he shouted, "you gotta do me a favor."

"Um, okay," I replied, without any idea of what to expect next.

"Be sure to chuck the empty can overboard when you're done with it. If my ol' lady finds these in here, she'll chew right through my ass like a Husqvarna through a sapling."

"No problem," I replied, struggling to pry open the can with my free hand. I didn't really have a *free* hand, but I managed to get the can open and spill foaming barley hops all over myself. I took a quick swig as Rod ground the transmission back into gear to decrease our speed. When he wasn't looking, I tossed the rest of the beer off to the side of the road—the first time I meant to litter my entire life—and wrapped my arms back around the Grudge. For all the wretchedness the faded old backpack had caused me, I now held onto it with a devotion she'd never known. Never again would I swear at her or throw her on the ground.

When we got to his property—nothing more than a converted Airstream trailer in a swath of missing trees—Rod slammed on the brakes and sent me nose first into the NASCAR sticker. By the time I unpeeled my face from the window, the dogs were running circles around the truck trying to figure out how to climb up and check out their guest. One of them, Maggie I presumed, was missing a rear quarter.

"Come on in Chuckie," Rod yelled. "I'll let Rhonda know we got a guest." When we entered the small smoke-filled mobile home, Rod said, "Honey, there's someone I wants you to meet."

I prayed he wasn't talking to me.

Then Rhonda turned the corner and introduced herself by saying, "What did ya drag in this time?" Almost instantly, I relaxed.

Rhonda made Rod look like a sidekick, like an elf. She had to have weighed at least four hundred pounds—about what the Grudge seemed to—and, at six-foot-four, was a good few inches taller than either Rod or me. We shook hands and sat down on a couch built for an NBA team. The dogs did the same.

A quick glance around didn't tell me any more than I hadn't already imagined: the place appeared to have been ransacked, but neither of them noticed. Hunting pictures donned the walls and a gun cabinet leaned precariously against an archaic sewing machine, right next to a not-so-archaic Husqvarna chainsaw. Their music collection consisted mostly of country artists I'd never heard of but a few classic rock bands that I had: Bad Company, Lynyrd Skynyrd, and ZZ Top.

"Chuckie here is hikin' the PCT," Rod yelled, as he rounded a small divider and went into the kitchen.

"What the hell's the B-Z-T?" Rhonda yelled back. She lit a cigarette and used the same flame to light a warped pile of wax called a candle on the coffee table in front of us.

"The Pacific Crest Trail, honey. That's that trail I been tellin' you about. I drive by it everyday. Starts down in Mexico somewhere and goes all the way up to Alaska or somethin'."

I didn't feel like correcting him, so I sat quietly and patted the dogs' heads while they searched me for new, exciting scents—I didn't disappoint. But it was hard to say who smelled worse: Mavis's coat was dank and dirty while Maggie's breath would kill any trespasser.

Rod sat down in his captain's chair, kicking his work boots off and adding to the musty aroma. He flipped the TV on, found a tape-delayed auto race, and asked, "What's fer dinner hon?"

"How should I know, I ain't makin' it," Rhonda quipped. Then came the most annoying sound I'd heard since Big Bear's fire siren—her laughter. It wasn't so much a laugh as a partially derailed train sliding by with every one of its wheels squealing and screeching and throwing sparks. The dogs didn't flinch.

"Goddammit woman!" Rod yelled, jokingly. "We got a guest."

"I'm just teasin'," Rhonda said, "I already made it." I didn't laugh, but unfortunately she did, only to stop to take a puff of cigarette and say, "Plus, I got a little somethin' extra." If her laugh was dreadful, the coughing fit that followed was life threatening.

Rhonda pushed herself from the couch and went to work. We were eating minutes later. Rod was right—it was meat and potatoes. I got the feeling that's what they ate every night. There was no dining room table since there was no dining room, so we sat right there in front of the TV with plates in our laps. The dogs had clearly been trained—they never so much as salivated even though the chow was barely a few inches from their noses.

The entire time we ate, I suffered a gas attack of unprecedented severity. I tried to hold it in, but the strain of restraint was killing me. Little by little, I let small explosions go, hoping the meal, or the lingering cigarette smoke, might drown out the soul-sucking stench. I also figured I might be able to blame the dogs if anyone could indeed smell things. Shortly after one silent explosion, Rod yelled at the dogs, "Maggie! Mavis!"

It was working beautifully.

So I let out some more. It's not that I had a choice. I had to: I was miserable. The food was fabulous, but I couldn't enjoy it under such distress and discomfort.

"Maggie! Mavis!"

Eventually I felt like saying something to the dogs, but it wasn't my place to, so I just sat there eating and slowly seeping. Little by little, the pressure lessened itself, only to rebuild that much quicker. I thought for a minute: It had to have been the macaroni and cheese lump I ate earlier.

"Maggie! Mavis!" Rod yelled again, while flipping through the channels.

The couch wasn't absorbing any of it but instead seemed impenetrable, which was odd, as comfortable as it was. When dinner was done, I let out a few more bombs and heard the same response, "Maggie! Mavis!" Only this time, Rhonda did the complaining as she got up to collect dishes and dessert.

I felt bad using the dogs as my scapegoat but they weren't *my* best friends, not after forcing me to risk my life on the back of the old rig during the ride down. And as anybody (*everybody*) who's ever suffered a gas attack can tell you, misery is *your* company and misery loves that company. It was my own private air stream and I was looking for any way out.

"Maggie! Mavis!"

The candle's flame was roaring.

Fearful I might be caught, I tried not to shift or move, when finally the smell was simply too overpowering. Many more and the (aptly named) Airstream trailer might've looked more like the Hindenburg. Rod got up from his recliner and yelled once more at the poor pooches: "Maggie! Mavis! Jeeezus Chriiist! Get on up off the couch before he kills you with those!"

My death couldn't have come soon enough.

"Well," Rod said, "I'd say you need to git yerself cleaned up, Chuckie. The bathroom is just right there. Help yerself. Towels are under the sink."

The dogs never budged the entire time.

THE KLAMATH KNOT

By David Rains Wallace

In this excerpt from The Klamath Knot: Explorations of Myth and
Evolution, *David Rains Wallace explores the fourth dimension—deep
time—which makes this mysterious section of the Pacific Crest Trail's
corridor even more haunting. As Wallace describes, the Siskiyou region
contains many prehistoric features not found in the surrounding Sierra
and Cascades. The dark and diverse forests, steep terrain carved by lush
and overgrown canyons, and fern-filled understories encourage hikers to
contemplate the mysteries of human evolution, the origins of life, and
other secrets hidden in the darkness of time. Here, hikers see such a variety
of plant species—from trees to flowers and fungi—that each mile of trail
teems with life.*

*The PCT lies in the eastern Klamaths, giving hikers a clear view of
Preston Peak and a fog-enshrouded view of the enigmatic Siskiyous. As
Wallace describes, walking this winding path through a landscape so rich
with evolutionary stories is like visiting a vast ancient library.*

Ten years passed before I went back to the Siskiyous. During that time I
walked into a number of wild places, and acquired what I thought was a
fair knowledge of western mountain wilderness: of the climb from chaparral or
sagebrush in the Upper Sonoran Zone; through Douglas fir, ponderosa pine,
and white fir in the Transition Zone; past lodgepole pine, red fir, or Engelmann
spruce in the Canadian Zone; to stunted whitebark pines and heather in the
Alpine Zone. I went to a few places where there were still grizzly bear tracks as

well as black bear tracks. So I didn't really expect to find much that was new when I started up the [...] trail into the northern part of the high Siskiyous [...] with my down sleeping bag, gas stove, contour maps, and other sophistications. But the Siskiyous still had some things to show me.

I knew the Siskiyous are among the richest botanical areas of the West, and I soon saw evidence of this. [...] Ravines contained so much blossoming azalea that the forest often smelled like a roomful of fancy women, and rhododendrons were in flower on one flat bench. There were more orchids than I'd seen anywhere. California lady's slippers hung over one rivulet like tiny Japanese lanterns dipped in honey, and I found three species of coralroot, red and orange orchids that have no green leaves, lacking chlorophyll. Farther up the trail, where snow melted recently, pink calypso orchids had just burst through the pine duff.

The forest that overshadowed these flowers was the most diverse I'd seen west of the Mississippi. Besides the Douglas fir, tan oak, madrone, golden chinquapin, and goldencup oak I had expected just east of the coastal crest, I found ponderosa pine, Jeffrey pine, sugar pine, western white pine, knobcone pine, and incense cedar. Moist ravines were full of Port Orford cedar, a lacy-foliaged tree with fluted bark like a redwood's. The diversity became confusing; it seemed I had to consult my tree field guide every few minutes.

As I climbed higher, I kept expecting this unwonted diversity to sort itself out into the usual altitudinal zones, waiting for white fir, ponderosa pine, and incense cedar to close ranks against the confusion. But it didn't happen. Douglas fir kept playing its polymorphous tricks, its foliage sometimes resembling the flattened needles of white fir, sometimes dangling like the branches of weeping spruce. I got a stiff neck looking up to see if cones hung downward, denoting Douglas fir, or stood upright, denoting white fir (or perhaps silver fir, grand fir, or noble fir, three other species found in the Klamaths).

Broad-leaved madrone and tan oak disappeared obligingly after I reached a certain altitude, but then new species appeared. I found western yew, a sturdy little tree resembling a miniature redwood, and Sadler's oak, another small tree whose serrated leaves reminded me of the chestnut oaks I'd known in the Midwest. I passed a grove of lodgepole pines, and these austere trees, which typically grow on bleak, windswept terrain, looked out of place in all the effulgent variety. The trees were sorted out somewhat according to soil conditions, but these distinctions were patchy and vague, offering cold comfort to my organizing instincts.

After two days of walking, I stood on the slopes of Preston Peak, which is 7309 feet above sea level at its summit but seems higher as it thrusts abruptly above the forested ridges. I was surprised, on looking around at the snow-stunted trees on the glacial moraine where I stood, to find they were the same species that had accompanied me from the Klamath River. [...]

Clearly, there was something odd about the Siskiyou forest. For so many species to grow all over a mountain range simply doesn't conform to respectable western life-zone patterns. It is more like some untidy temperate deciduous forest or tropical rainforest, species promiscuously tumbled together without regard for ecological proprieties.

The high Siskiyou forest is a rare remnant of a much lusher past. Fossils of trees almost identical to those of the Siskiyous have been dug from twelve-million-year-old, Pliocene epoch sediments in what are now the deserts of Idaho and eastern Oregon. Fossils of trees not at all unlike Siskiyou species have been found in forty-million-year-old sediments in Alaska. In that epoch, the Eocene, a temperate forest surpassing any living today covered the northern half of this continent from coast to coast. Redwoods, pines, firs, and cedars grew with hickories, beeches, magnolias, and other hardwoods not found within a thousand miles of the Pacific Ocean today, and with ginkgoes, dawn redwoods, and other trees that don't even grow naturally in North America anymore. It is hard to imagine such a forest: it sounds like poets' descriptions of Eden. After the Eocene, though, the climate became cooler and drier; and this gradually drove the forest southward, and split it in half. Deciduous hardwoods migrated southeast, where the summer rain they needed was still available, while many conifers migrated southwest to cover the growing Rocky Mountain and Pacific Coast ranges. Ginkgoes and dawn redwoods fell by the wayside during this "long march," which has resulted in our present, relatively impoverished forests, where trees that once grew together are separated by wide prairies and plains.

There is still one area west of the Rockies, however, where rainfall and temperatures approximate the benign Eocene environment: the inner coastal ranges of southwest Oregon and northwest California, the Klamath Mountains. In the Klamaths, winters are mild enough and summers moist enough for species to grow together that elsewhere are segregated by altitude or latitude. Several species that once grew throughout the West now survive only in the Klamaths. Perched on my Siskiyou eminence, I again felt suspended over great gulfs of time. [...] Looking out over the pyramidal Siskiyou ridges, I was seeing a community of trees at least forty million years old.

Later that day something hair-raising happened. There were still some patches of snow, and I had walked across one on the way to my campsite. After dinner I wandered back past that patch and found, punched deeply into each of my vibram-soled footprints, the tracks of a large bear. It probably had been foraging in Rattlesnake meadow, heard me coming, and took the trail downhill to escape my intrusion. A simple coincidence, but it caused a sudden feeling of emptiness at the pit of my stomach, as though I were riding a fast elevator. It seemed the lesson begun ten years before was proceeding: from a realization that the world is much greater and older than normal human perception of it, to a reminder that the human is a participant as well as a perceiver in the ancient continuum of bears and forests. I was used to walking in bear tracks by this time; it was instructive to find that a bear also could walk in mine.

[...] I had many sleepless hours to wonder why I kept going to places like the Siskiyous when so many civilized places were so much easier to get to. I'm not all *that* crazy about exercise. Wilderness areas are certainly among the most beautiful places on the planet, but I wonder if this alone is enough to explain the fascination many people feel for them, or the difficulties and real suffering they endure to reach them. [...]

I wondered if my motives for going into wilderness might be more obscure, and more profound, than I had realized. While part of me was going into the mountains seeking the pleasures of exercise, self-reliance, accomplishment, and natural history, it seemed that another part was looking for things of which I had only a vague conscious awareness, as though a remote mountain or desert releases some innate human behavior, a kind of instinctive predilection for the mysterious.

So many major structures of belief have arisen at least in part from experiences in wilderness. This was to be expected with the oldest structures, such as animism and shamanism, since the entire world outside a Paleolithic camp was wilderness. But why should all the major religions of the modern world include a crucial encounter with wilderness—Moses, Jesus, and Mohammed in the desert mountains, Siddhartha in the jungle? And why should the predominant modern view of the original development of life have arisen from the five-year wilderness voyage of a Victorian amateur naturalist named Charles Darwin? There evidently is more to wilderness than meets the eye—more than water, timber, minerals [...] psychic raw materials from which every age has cut, dammed, or quarried an invisible civilization—an imaginative world of origins and meanings—what one might call a mythology. [...]

The Klamath Mountains are an exceptionally rich storehouse of evolutionary stories, one of the rare places where past and present have not been severed as sharply as in most of North America, where glaciation, desertification, urbanization, and other ecological upheavals have been muted by a combination of rugged terrain and relatively benign climate. Klamath rocks are older than those of the California and Oregon coast ranges to the south and north or those of the Cascades in the east. They are more intricately and tortuously folded, faulted, and upthrust, forming a knot of jagged peaks and steep gorges less modified by civilization than other areas, even though they are only a day's drive from large cities. [...]

The relatively low elevation of the Klamaths, compared to the Cascades or Sierra Nevada, has caused them to be overlooked. Naturalists often say that the Klamaths are a combination of Sierra Nevada and Cascades ecosystems because the Klamaths contain species found in both other wilderness regions. This is a little like saying that a person is a combination of his brother and sister because he shares genes with both siblings. The Klamaths have a character of their own, although not perhaps as ingratiating a character as the graceful volcanic cones of the Cascades or the clean alpine country of the Sierra. There is something wizened about the Klamaths. Their canyons do not have sparkling granite walls and wide river meadows as do the U-shaped, glaciated canyons of the Sierra. Klamath canyons are preglacial, and uncompromisingly V-shaped. They've never been scoured into spaciousness by the ice flows. They seem to drop down forever, slope after forest-smothered slope, to straightened, boulder-strewn bottoms so noisy with waters and shadowed by vegetation that they may bring startling dreams and uneasy thoughts to campers.

More than any other wild region I've known, the Klamaths have a venerable quality which is not synonymous with "pristine," "unspoiled," or other adjectives commonly applied to natural areas. Certainly the Klamaths are as unpolluted as any American place these days. But these adjectives imply something of the smoothness and plumpness of youth, whereas the Klamaths are marked by the wrinkles and leanness of great age. Although their peaks and high plateaus have been marked by glaciers, they are at heart preglacial mountains, with elements of flora and fauna that reach back farther into the past than any place west of the Mississippi River. The Klamaths seem so old, in fact, that I'd call them a grandparent of the Sierra and Cascades instead of a sibling. [...] I hope [...] they will remain an outstanding vantage point into what I perceived during my first visit as the fourth dimension of life.

A TASTE OF JEFFERSON

By Rees Hughes

Somewhere in the Trinity Mountains or perhaps the Marbles, the Pacific Crest Trail crosses the murky border into the state of Jefferson. Although the state of Jefferson movement has a long and varied history, it gained momentum in late 1941 when angry residents of five rural counties of northern California and southern Oregon announced a short-lived secession, proclaiming that this region would secede each Thursday. The highway was blockaded in Yreka, speeches were made, and photos were taken, but the fervor dissipated with the attack on Pearl Harbor. Nonetheless, the embers of disconnect have persisted and have flared up periodically since. Recent disputes over the water of the Klamath River and old-growth logging have rekindled the Free State movement and the Jefferson state of mind.

Signage outside the post office indicates that you have entered Seiad Valley, state of Jefferson. While this is certainly part publicity stunt, there is no question that there is something different about these remote reaches of the mighty Klamath River valley. California feels like it is a long way away. Seiad Valley is also no ordinary trail town—a fitting home to the "pancake challenge," one of the great PCT traditions.

Walking north along Grider Creek into the little community of Seiad Valley, one of those wide-spot-in-the-road, don't-blink-or-you'll-miss-it towns, I was not totally surprised to see signs confirming our arrival into the rebellious "state of Jefferson." Descending from the wild beauty of the Marble Mountains with my lifelong trail companions Rocky and Pierre, the final six miles had wound past a curious mix of "Beware of Dog" warnings and weathered homesteads, fecund gardens and satellite dishes, and the rusting detritus of what must have been a once grand civilization. I was not quite sure whether I had arrived in an idyllic trail town or had been transported to the set of *Deliverance.*

William Brewer, California's first geographer, called this area "a delightful spot—it seems an oasis in a desert" when he passed through a century and a half earlier documenting the existence of Chinese gold miners, Native peoples, as well as white settlers. But despite the beautiful setting and the fertile bottom-land, he reported that the Reeves family, whose ranch then filled much of the valley, was eager to sell out, as they felt "caged up from the world." Certainly those hardy souls who made this valley home today must still have a genuine sense of independence and self-reliance and a passion for isolation.

Contemporary Seiad Valley isn't much more than a collection of houses distributed above the floodplain of the Klamath River, with the welcome show-ers and shade of the RV park and the adjacent cinderblock post office, store, and café. Just as in Brewer's day, the deep valley with its surrounding peaks remains spectacular. The café, which I had heard about for years, seemed mod-est and unassuming given its legendary place among PCT walkers. The much heralded "pancake challenge" is anticipated no less than reaching Deep Creek Hot Springs, Forester Pass, Timberline Lodge, or Stehekin.

Five one-pound pancakes eaten in two hours and your breakfast is free. Five eye-popping pancakes as large as a dinner plate. It seemed so simple.

Challenge is to PCT hikers what blood is to sharks. The gauntlet of chal-lenge is why we have PCT speed records, competition to minimize base pack weight, winter hikers in the Sierras, and side trips to bag nearby peaks. It fol-lows that food would also be subject to conquest. By the time many PCT hikers reach Seiad Valley, their confidence is high, very high. The body is strong, the diet insufficient, and the hunger insatiable.

I have been hungry since birth and was especially ravenous after the previ-ous ten days on the trail. I am tall and lanky and had survived this long by willingly finishing the uneaten portions from the plates of friends and family over the years. I had always prioritized quantity over quality when it came to calories. This pancake thing seemed the perfect match for my aptitude.

As we dropped our packs and prepared to enter the Seiad Valley Store and Café, I found it inconceivable that my appetite would be bested by anything served at such a small eatery. How could the proprietor know that I had stra-tegically been making preparations for miles? Drinking copious amounts of water to stretch my stomach. Reminding myself to approach the task slowly.

Visualizing success. Confident that I was poised to become a name whispered reverently along the length of the trail.

My golden-brown pancakes were delivered with a side of syrup. Somehow they looked bigger in life than I had imagined—a little like an ocean swell viewed from the trough. And yet, I had survived lightning storms in Desolation Wilderness and a midsummer snowstorm on the PCT east of Rainier. This was a mere nothing. I enjoyed the first bites—warm and sweet comfort food. It was a welcome alternative to granola, dried fruit, and powdered milk. I devoured the first layer in but a few minutes. It was difficult to imagine anything standing between me and an empty plate. I may have even been guilty of a boast or two, and casting an eye to the sausages on Rocky's plate. "Bring it on."

By the time I began to attack the second layer, my senses had dulled. Instead of savoring bites, appreciating the taste and aroma of breakfast, I became more mechanical in my approach. But my speed was steady. Yet, as I neared the end of "el Segundo" (I thought it might help if I named each pancake) I had become aware of a long forgotten feeling in my stomach—the creeping fog of fullness.

I decided this was nothing a short walk around the premises wouldn't remedy.

I returned to the task at hand, pulling my chair back to the table. However, no longer was I thinking of the remaining stack of three as comfort food. The professionals of food excess at the Nathan's hotdog-eating contest use water to soak the buns; I tried water too. It did make the bites go down easier. Conventional wisdom suggests that the moisture compresses the dough so that it requires less space in your stomach. As I finished my third pancake it was unmistakable. I was full.

The only thing on my side was the clock. Seventy-five minutes more, one way or the other, and I would be through. A visit to the toilet helped.

I became aware of a new pressure. In addition to my fellow hikers, several patrons lent their support and encouragement. An ancient woodsman, perhaps a prophetic apparition, with his suspenders stretched to the breaking point, and his toothless companion nursed along a third round of coffee just to enjoy the spectacle. Rocky cautioned, "Just take your time."

I flashbacked to Paul Newman's downing of fifty eggs in an hour as Cool Hand Luke. "Get mad at them damn eggs," exhorted George Kennedy. The increasingly public nature of my quest propelled me well into the next pancake. I imagined discreet wagering among the assembled, although even the most loyal would recognize that the pancakes were a heavy favorite. As I neared the end of the fourth slab of the damn dough, the exhortations of the café patrons had become insufficient incentive.

I started to become aware that my mind was working against me. "Why didn't I just get the omelet?" "Why did I have to make such a big deal about this?" "I've heard about people's stomach's exploding from eating too much." I scanned the walls, imagining the prospects of flapjack debris adhering everywhere as I became the first culinary suicide bomber.

My plate had been room temperature for some time and the once supple pancakes seemed to have assumed the consistency of soft pine. I tried eating smaller bites but after ten minutes had trouble detecting any difference in the size of the fifth pancake. Time was proceeding agonizingly slowly.

I felt hands on my shoulders, massaging them vigorously. It was my cornerman with his smelling salts, cotton swabs, and an ice pack. I was the heavyweight with head down, towel covered, filled with self doubt while being prepared for the twelfth round. There was no hope of victory. I knew it and those cheering me on knew it. But the bell rang and I answered the call. I took a few frantic bites, stabbing wildly at the plate, hoping desperately for a knockout.

"Rees," Pierre's voice revived me. I wondered how long I had been staring at the remaining pancake hoping that it would magically vaporize. Or that I would. I slowly sighed. My valiant effort was over. I paid the bill but declined to take the remnants of "the Terminator" with me in a doggie bag, and I staggered out.

It could have been worse. Someone reminded me of the thru hiker, perhaps apocryphal, who had arranged a joyous rendezvous with his family at the Seiad Valley Store and Café. Partway through the challenge this cursed fellow violently regurgitated several pounds of pancake ignominiously across the table before him.

Although the number of individuals reputed to have successfully conquered the pancake challenge varies, there is no disagreement that the number is small.

Unfortunately, the clean t-shirt I had purchased with the "XX" on the front, the double-cross icon of the state of Jefferson, no longer fit. I hoped that it wouldn't take more than a day or so for my body to return to its earlier condition. The ache that permeated my belly reminded me of my quixotic journey of the morning. The thought of carrying the extra weight up the daunting climb out of Seiad Valley to Lower Devils Peak made a "zero" day very attractive.

But, it was time to get on. I knew my discomfort and my embarrassment were only temporary.

I shouldered my pack. The trail, appropriately, slinks out of town alongside Highway 96 before abruptly turning north and up. I thought about Brewer's climb up this same ridge long ago. He had been accompanied by two men from Reeves' ranch, one of whom brought a bugle. Brewer commented that "every little while [he] awakened the echoes of the silent mountains with its notes." As the day waned and I looked down from the abandoned Lower Devils Peak lookout on the diminutive settlement, my failure receded into insignificance. I imagined myself sitting like Brewer, with this magical view of the distant ribbon of the Klamath River and the layered ridges of the Klamath Knot before me. I could even imagine the soulful notes of a cornet reverberating off the shoulder of the ridgeline to the north.

WHEN DEER GO BAD

By Susan "Backpack45" Alcorn

Salt. It is so important that the word salary comes from the Latin salarium, *the money provided Roman soldiers for the purchase of salt. It is one of the primary electrolytes in the bodies of animals and is necessary for optimal bodily function. Backpackers can carry salt tablets to swallow, packaged electrolytes to add to water, and high-sodium snacks to balance the body's loss from persistent sweating. Insufficient sodium results in a craving, a longing, a passion for salt that may drive a person—or an animal—to almost unimaginable lengths to get it. Normal fears and caution get cast aside when you're desperate enough. Susan Alcorn's story is one of unrequited desire and unexpected consequences.*

While backpacking on the Pacific Crest Trail, I've worried about rattlesnakes in the Mojave, fretted about bears in the Sierras, swatted at mosquitoes in Tuolumne Meadows, and searched for ticks near Belden, but never once did I consider that we would meet up with deer gone bad.

In late summer 2007, Ralph ("Timecheck") and I did a long PCT section hike from Burney Falls to Ashland—three hundred miles of gorgeous scenery ranging from the 129-foot thundering waterfall at Burney Falls State Park, to the heavily glaciated jagged gray peaks of Castle Crags, to the rugged and aptly named Marble Mountains. During this hike, we saw zero bears, but more scat than ever before; one rattlesnake, as big around as your arm and the largest we've seen to date; and perhaps two dozen deer.

One night, while camped close to the Marble Valley Guard Station, we heard a strange breathing sound and then a commotion outside the tent. I

Source: A version of this story was published in the magazine of the Pacific Crest Trail Association, *The Communicator* 19, no. 6 (December 2007).

held my breath and tried to figure out what it might be. Being the brave soul that I am, I insisted that Ralph check it out. He looked, saw nothing with the dinky little pinch light that we had, and crawled back into the comfort of his sleeping bag and quickly fell asleep. Hardly reassured, I lay awake, listening intently before finally managing to fall asleep. In the morning we studied the trail and found prints of deer, horses, and humans on the trail—certainly nothing unusual. We wondered if a horse had wandered away from someone camping nearby.

The next night we were farther north—near Buckhorn Springs, still in the Marbles. We could see smoke, and occasionally flames, from a nearby wildfire. It was two ridges away and the PCT had not been closed, but I was scared. As evening came, the layers of smoke settled closer to the ground and I found that even more worrisome. The visibility became so poor that we could no longer see how close the flames were. I looked around at the nearby pines, the rocky outcroppings not too distant, the steep slopes where a fire might quickly sweep through, and determined that if the fire were to come closer I'd run for the rockiest area.

We were camped farther from the trail than we had been the night before but close enough so that anyone hiking by would see us and be able to update us on the fire. Around 10:00 PM, I was awakened by what sounded like footsteps coming down the trail. "Hi! Who's out there?" I called. No answer. Did someone coming along the path not see us?

"Ralph, did you heard that noise?" I asked.

"No," he replied with a deep yawn, "but it's probably just a hiker walking late." I rolled over and went back to sleep.

At 4:00 AM, footsteps again. This time closer and on the side of the tent away from the trail. Was a ranger coming by to evacuate the area?

"Who is it?" I called out. No answer. Did Bigfoot really exist? I woke Ralph and we both looked outside. Nothing. Why would someone come so close to the tent but not respond? It made no sense. I lay awake as my imagination worked overtime. What kind of creature might be out there? I envisioned the worst while Ralph continued to sleep. As I rationalized away some of those fears, once again I started worrying about how close the fire might be.

We surveyed the area in the morning. Several holes, perhaps a foot in diameter and six inches deep, had been dug. We could see clearly deer prints in the dirt. Then we realized that the holes were in the spots where we had peed. Ah ha, salt! The deer was salt-starved!

Two days later we were past Seiad Valley, at the location described by the *Pacific Crest Trail Data Book* as "spring in soggy ground" (mile 1672.5). Kangaroo Springs was just half a mile farther. We had stopped late in the day to choose our campsite. While Ralph collected water from the spring, I noticed a couple of deer in a nearby meadow and spent a few minutes photographing them. We decided it would be a good idea to pee farther away from the tent so that we'd have a good night's sleep.

Only minutes after climbing into the tent, we heard the deer approach. We looked out: there were two nearby, examining our site. We heard the clatter of metal as they nosed our cook kit. We watched them for a while and then tried to ignore them—difficult, because we could hear them munching on the grass alongside the tent. My main concern was that one would trip on a tent line and fall on us. When either of the deer got close, we yelled at them to go away—but they hardly budged. They obviously weren't afraid of people. It was going to be a long night.

Suddenly there was a strange movement in front of the tent. I looked out and saw a full-grown doe just on the other side of the mesh. It jerked back, turned and ran.

"It's taking my hiking pole!" I yelled. Ralph leaped out of the tent, "bare ass nekkid" as they say, hollering and running after the errant deer. Fifty yards away, the deer finally dropped it and Ralph returned triumphantly with my pole.

The next morning, I inspected the items that had been outside of our tent overnight. I wiped the deer slobber off the pole's strap and then the pole itself— it was none the worse for wear. The stuff sack that contained our cook kit was also stained with deer drool—unappetizing. I now make a point of keeping the straps of my hiking poles within sight whenever we go to bed.

I guess we were lucky. I've since learned that ours was not an isolated event. We later heard about a thru hiker in Oregon whose shirt was stolen from her campsite by a deer—after that, I was hesitant to use a clothesline. And back in July 2005, thru hiker Scott Heeschen acquired his trail name, Buck Larceny, after his encounter with deer near Stover Creek (mile 1339). During the night, deer dragged away not only his hiking poles (one was never found) but also his backpack during multiple "raids" on his camp.

So be forewarned that it may not be the mountain lions, the bears, or Bigfoot that should strike fear into your heart as you enter the backcountry, but those unassuming mammals of the family Cervidae who have taken the wayward path.

A GENERATION BETWEEN THRU HIKES

By Jerry Smith

One of the most unique features of the Pacific Crest Trail is the lasting and looming presence it holds in both the lives of individual people and in the collective culture of the West. Thanks to its increasingly long and rich history, the PCT has been hiked by multiple generations of single families and multiple times by single individuals. While the gear may have changed, the trail improved, and the number of hikers increased over the decades, the experiences of PCT hikers both past and present are much the same: camaraderie and solitude, wild grandeur and beauty, physical hardship and enduring happiness. Jerry Smith captures his multigenerational experience—and how the PCT has both changed and remained the same—in this story of his two thru hikes, one in 1976 as part of the Mayberry Gang and the other twenty-five years later, in 2001, as TrailBird.

Our decision to use Seiad Valley and the Klamath River as the geographic terminus of the first volume of the Trailside Reader *was somewhat arbitrary. It is not the middle of the trail for thru hikers and it is no more an ending or a beginning for section hikers than any other trail town or access point. However, the Klamath River does serve as a physical boundary, mirroring the nearby state line.*

We felt that Jerry Smith's unique perspective, possible because of the years separating his thru hikes, does provide a transcendent view of the PCT experience. His story seemed big enough to both close this volume and segue into the next. As Smith rightly notes, although we and the hiking culture may change over the years, the one thing that always remains the same is the deep meaning and value we find in our time on the trail.

My first thru hike was in 1976, and once finished I got on with college and other things. I married and settled into a career in the US Navy, but I was wrong in thinking that my PCT experience would sit idle as a memory. Many of the physical components of the hike—backpack, pictures, stove, walking stick—were stored away, and my retired boots had long since become bookends on my shelf of PCT books. However, memories of my 1976 hike continued to surface in daily life. To this day, stepping into a hot shower takes me immediately back to Camp Oakes outside of Big Bear and how incredible the first, and one of the few, showers of the hike felt. I will occasionally hear a sound that reminds me of the familiar power burn of a healthy Svea stove—that sound, and oatmeal (which I probably didn't eat for a year after that first hike), are lasting memories of 137 trail breakfasts.

With the hike ten years behind me, in 1986, I was stationed at the Naval Postgraduate School working on my master's degree. The curriculum was intense and I spent most free hours studying, usually with close friend and fellow naval officer Dave Lyon. During one of our marathon study periods, I got up and went outside. When I returned some minutes later, Dave asked me what was up. I explained that every May 1 at 10:25 AM I try to be outdoors—on the date and time when I started my hike in 1976. I remember he put his book down and surprised me by saying we should hike the PCT someday. "Sure, why not," I think I said. After graduation, our naval careers bounced us around to different parts of the world, but on occasion we did bump into each other and the idea would resurface. After I retired, my family began a cross-country drive from Virginia back to Oregon. Somewhere in Ohio I called Dave, who had settled in Idaho since retiring, and asked if he was up for a hike in six months. And so it was that on April 27, 2001, fifteen years since the study-session discussion and twenty-five years since my first PCT hike, we set out.

Surprisingly, I found I had mixed emotions about returning to the trail. My first hike harbored so many happy memories that I didn't want them to be diluted or diminished. But this feeling arose only in the planning stages and was immediately gone with my first step back on the trail—I remember having a silly broad smile as we departed the border monument and hiked along a chaparral-lined trail on a beautiful blue-skied morning.

During my quarter-century absence both myself and the trail had seen several changes. My age wasn't much of a factor, but I did now carry a thicker sleeping pad and had prepared this time around by hiking seven hundred training miles in the previous six months. I'd completed no physical preparations for the hike in 1976, hoping the advantage of youth would get me through—it did, but not without a painful two-week breaking-in period. As for the trail, it had been dedicated as a continuous route from border to border in 1993, and I found the routefinding much easier and the trail markers abundant. I used the Wilderness Press guidebooks on both hikes and read every word—in-depth daily in 1976 to stay on track, whereas in 2001 the guidebook maps supplemented with the data book sufficed most of the time. In 1976, we had anticipated that the first section of well-established trail would be in the Mount San Jacinto area, but when we got there deep snow covered most stretches of trail. After a cross-country 7200-foot descent directly off Fuller Ridge to Snow Creek, we found our first substantial trail on our climb up Mission Creek. In 2001, thanks to intervening years of trail construction, we found ourselves on well-established trail from the border northward.

One of the immediate and most noticeable differences between 1976 and 2001 was the number of hikers. In 1976 we saw one hiker as we drove out to the border, and throughout the summer we would occasionally meet up with one or two. I started that first trip with Scott Shuey, and Heath Hibbard joined us at Anza, having lost his partner due to injury. Sierra City was a surprise, with seven thru hikers in town during the bicentennial celebration—this was the largest gathering we experienced. In northern California we hoped we would have the opportunity to meet Teddi Boston who was hiking southbound solo, but we likely missed her when we detoured to camp on the summit of Lassen Peak. In contrast, for our start in 2001 we waited our turn to get a photo with the monument. It was a rare day in the coming months to not meet another thru hiker, and at most resupply stops we would join a dozen or more.

Budget also played a big difference in the hikes. I did my first thru hike during a break from college and I needed to make due with a small budget. With all of our supplies purchased and packaged beforehand, we expected—incorrectly—that little funds would be needed once on the trail. The little we had was quickly spent trying to satisfy the well-documented appetites of thru hikers. We had no extra funds for luxury expenditures like lodging, so around towns we had to be creative. On the outskirts of Warner Springs we spent the night next to a cemetery; while staying over in Burney we camped under the bridge downtown; and at Stevens Pass we settled in for the night under a semi-trailer to get out of the rain. On more than one occasion we hiked through a town with no money between the three of us. We learned quickly not to eat in restaurants but instead to buy a package of hotdogs or Bisquick and cook up our own cheaper meal. Hiking into Tuolumne Meadows, for our first day off, the three of us each carried a load of firewood on top our packs. We bought a package of twenty-five hotdogs, roasted and ate eight each, and then drew straws for the last one. Clean laundry was also a luxury, and I remember washing clothes only two times in 1976. In 2001, with cash and credit cards at the ready, I enjoyed a different and more pampered hike with a shower ratio likely five times greater.

Trail angels have become a part of the thru hiker's experience; although we received occasional assistance in 1976 it was much less than in 2001. This might be due to few knowing what we were attempting back then—sitting in front of the store in Cascade Locks in 1976, a forest ranger asked where we were hitchhiking to. When we said we were hiking the PCT, he didn't know what we were talking about. Present-day thru hikers are aware that upon crossing the Antelope Valley Freeway they are approaching "PCT exit 455" for a visit at the Saufleys, and in another day they might be guests at the Andersons. This section is rich with trail angel kindness, but in 1976 it was quite the opposite. Three separate times in the small town of Acton we were warned about the upcoming Annan Ranch, whose new owner would likely show hostility rather than hospitality. Six miles north of the freeway, the temporary PCT route went directly through this property and passed next to the ranch house. We had been told that armed confrontations were not uncommon, so when the dirt road reached the gate, posted with warning signs, we entered the property but cut cross-country away from the road and temporary route. We stayed up on the ridge along the southern side of the ranch before rejoining the PCT later—without incident.

I tried not to bore Dave with too many "back in '76" reflections and noticed something interesting when I did. When I warned him about the extreme cold nighttime temperatures in the High Sierra, we experienced mild temperatures instead. There were no frozen water bottles for us in 2001. When I mentioned the upcoming 100-degree-plus heat in northern California, we instead enjoyed unseasonably cool temperatures. And, way in advance of Washington, I made sure to make several references to the coming days of rain and possible snow—and then all our days through Washington were beautiful. We experienced very little precipitation of any kind during the entire hike—a total of only four hours of "in raingear hiking" compared to weeks in 1976. I was once again reminded that a PCT experience is not only different for everyone but is also different from year to year.

However, some things on the trail had changed little over the years. Mosquitoes come to mind immediately. They were bad on both hikes, and I got no satisfaction thinking that some of the latest generation were likely made possible by the bites I had suffered decades earlier. Also, each hike had about a dozen rattlesnake encounters, but now the snakes seemed to lounge more on, and across, the trail. On several occasions during my second thru hike I had to encourage one to move on by nudging it with my hiking pole. In 1976, during our first attempt at night hiking to avoid the daytime temperatures of the Mojave, we were approaching Jawbone Canyon when I stepped on what I thought was a stick—until it wrapped around my lower leg. I was able to shake it free by jumping around, but Heath and Scott, who saw little of the encounter due to the dark, questioned my story. Not until I got my flashlight out did we discover a sidewinder, who was still unwilling to rattle, under a nearby bush.

Planning for my first thru hike was done in a vacuum compared to the information available today. Scott and I didn't know who else would be on the trail until we started. I read the few books available and purchased the two guidebooks. I read in Eric Ryback's book that he had used only five resupply points, so I thought we would take it easy and use nine. To calculate a sensible start date I spent hours at the university library going through historical temperature and snowpack data. A May 1 start looked like it would get us to the Sierras in early June and allow us through the high passes as the snow hopefully receded. Arriving at the border, we found a handwritten cardboard sign tacked to a fence post identifying the spot as the southern terminus of the PCT. Hikers before us had added their names and it appeared we had likely begun near the back of the pack.

Although heavy packs are usually assumed the norm for thru-hike attempts in the earlier decades, in 1976 I started out with a thirty-five-pound pack, including water and seven days worth of food. What caused the largest pack weight fluctuation were the nine resupply points compared to twenty-four in 2001. In 1976, our longest stretch between resupply was twenty-one days from the small community of Weldon to Tuolumne Meadows, with a Mount Whitney side trip. In contrast, the longest stretch in 2001 was the nine days from Kennedy Meadows to Mono Hot Springs.

Although I had replaced much of my gear since 1976, I did have a few items that made both thru hikes: my compass, aluminum cooking pot, and a small pair of scissors. In the interim, fleece had replaced wool and I added two items absent from my first trip: a water filter and a large supply of sunscreen.

The piece of equipment that I hadn't planned on taking was my old Kelty Tioga pack. In preparing for the 2001 hike I had researched and tested many packs but didn't find the right one for me. A few months before our start date, I searched the basement for my old pack. Its weight was comparable to many of the internal-frame packs I'd tried, I'd forgotten what a good fit it was. Not only would this be the second PCT thru hike for the both of us, but this trusty pack had also made a 1977 thru hike of the Pacific Northwest Trail as well as many shorter hikes. It completed all hikes without flaw and still has the original shoulder straps and hip belt.

In 1976, we referred to one another collectively as PCT hikers, and trail names were fairly common on both my thru hikes. In 1976 the three of us were called the Mayberry Gang, and in 2001 a fellow thru hiker gave me the name TrailBird. What was different in 2001 was the unique vocabulary developed and widely used by thru hikers to better communicate trail life: zero days, camel-up, slack packing, flip-flopping, nero days. And somewhere along the way the suffix -let was added onto a multitude of words: the familiar *creeklet* spawned *ridgelet, blisterlet,* and so on to describe something of lesser magnitude. My favorite new trail word became *smileage.*

I started the trail the first time thinking of the incredible places I'd see and the experiences waiting. After the hike I found my lasting memories to be of the hikers who shared the adventure and of those who helped us along the way. Now, years later, when going through pictures of either hike, I notice that I quickly scan them and pause at the ones with hikers. The vistas along the way are grand, but the people are exceptional. One of the benefits of a second thru hike was realizing this forthcoming gift beforehand.

During the twenty-five years between thru hikes I had a recurring dream, probably several times a week, of being on the trail. However, once on the PCT again my hiking dream was gone. I mentioned this to another thru hiker and her reply made perfect sense: "You are *living* the dream," she said—and I believe that to be true.

CONCLUSION

The idea of the literary pilgrimage—a reverent journey to visit locations from a favorite piece of literature—is not a new one in Western culture. In fact, the archeological discovery of Troy, by Heinrich Schliemann in 1868, stands as a famous example of this tradition. Schliemann, as well as archeologists today, constantly return to Homer's *Iliad* to gain information on the location of the city, the size and shape of its buildings, and the topography of the surrounding area, using the story as a kind of map of the territory. In recent years, however, there has been a growing interest in the literary pilgrimage by both popular audiences and academic scholars. Whether one is a tourist walking the streets of Sherlock Holmes's London with stories and guidebooks in hand, or a hiker enjoying a walk around Walden Pond, the impulse is the same—to connect the trail with the tale and to walk through both story and place with the mind and the feet.

There has always been a deep connection between stories and journeys, for they share much in common. A narrative unfolds before us in much the same way as a voyage, and upon completion a journey often transforms into a story. The notion of the pilgrimage is particularly fitting for such a process, for a pilgrimage is both an external and an internal journey, an exploration of the world and the self. Similarly, walking the PCT has, for many hikers, the qualities of a spiritual experience: transformation, inspiration, insight.

Many of the authors collected here have made just such a connection in their stories, noting similarities between walking and meditation and recalling significant moments of philosophical insight and spiritual connection during their times on the trail. This deep connection between the story and the journey, between the inner and outer experience, was the original impetus for *The Pacific Crest Trailside Reader*. Because the PCT is America's longest National Scenic

Trail and also one of the greatest loves of our outdoor lives, we wanted to leave other PCT hikers with a legacy they could take with them on their own per-egrinations and pilgrimages, something that could stand as a testament to the significant personal and cultural influence the PCT has had in our history.

Americans have no Holy Wall to journey to in our country. There is no single and special place consecrated by thousands of years of history. But we have established and cherished pilgrimages nonetheless. For many of us, the PCT is both a pilgrimage route and a sacred location. And like the pilgrims of old, we embrace the journey and honor its significance by experiencing it as directly and fully as possible, by walking each and every step of the way.

Many of the authors included here are themselves, pilgrims, faithful devotees of the PCT. Walker Abel notes this deep connection in "Wilderness Boundary," where he reflects on the psychological threshold that we cross when we physi-cally cross into the wilderness. He writes of "a sense of having returned home" because "trails such as the Pacific Crest are pathways into a latent and inherent side of ourselves that welcomes us when we activate it again." We return to the PCT, both in person and through story, because it is a homecoming, a reunion with our larger, nonhuman family. As Abel explains it, we return to "feeling ourselves part of something bigger than just the human realm. It is both a hum-bling experience and yet also one that is profoundly affirming of the self."

Wallace Stegner notes this critical value of wilderness in his letter that we reprint from *The Sound of Mountain Water*. He observes that simply the idea of wilderness "is a resource in itself . . . an intangible and spiritual resource." In addition to being our evolutionary home, where both our bodies and our emotional psyches have evolved, Stegner notes that wilderness has "helped form our character" as a nation and a people. "It has no more to do with recreation," he writes, "than churches have to do with recreation." Many westerners have noted, like Stegner, that for many Americans our Sistine Chapels and holy cities were not built by men, but rather directly by the hand of God, and they carry names like Yosemite Valley, Lake Tahoe, and Mount Shasta.

Of course, in order to make a pilgrimage to any of these holy places the faithful must, at some point, leave the car behind and walk. This act alone, the required divorce from the human and industrial realm, is one of the key components that makes the journey sacred. Hank Meals, in his essay "Walk-ing," reflects on our evolutionary history of bipedalism and notes that "walk-ing is fundamentally exploration and as such is part of the human psyche." He continues, observing that "technology moves forward with efficiency and achievement as its goals but leaves the soul starving for beauty and grace. For walking to be nutritious you have to leave the landscape in."

It is our fervent hope that readers will find both the geographical organization of the *Trailside Reader* and the stories themselves to have succeeded in keeping the landscape in. Whether you explore the Sierras and Cascade crests of California in the first volume or you continue northward into the second volume to explore the forests of Oregon and the great white north of Washington, we hope these stories will resonate with the power and inspiration, as well as the joy and laughter, that is found on the trail. For just as it threads its way up the backbone of the American West, the Pacific Crest Trail has also woven its way into our history and our hearts, giving us these stories and many more to treasure and share.

CONTRIBUTING WRITERS

WALKER ABEL is director of the Sierra Institute, a branch of Humboldt State University in Arcata, California, that offers environmentally oriented field programs. He has been teaching for the Sierra Institute since 1988, leading groups into wilderness areas around the country, including the Sierras and along the PCT. He thinks drinking snowmelt from the cup of a hand is a perfect gesture.

SUSAN "BACKPACK45" ALCORN is an author and long-distance hiker who has completed more than 4000 miles of the PCT and Camino routes in France, Spain, and Portugal. Her most recent books are *Camino Chronicle: Walking to Santiago* (2006) and *We're in the Mountains Not Over the Hill: Tales and Tips from Seasoned Women Backpackers* (2003), both published by Shepherd Canyon Books.

MARY HUNTER AUSTIN (1868–1934) is known as one of the first authors to recognize the beauty and wildness of the arid Southwest, writing lovingly and lyrically about the deserts of southern California and Nevada at the turn of the twentieth century. Austin was an experienced adventurer, traveling by stagecoach and horseback throughout regions now transected by the PCT, she lived at times with the Piute and Shoshone, as well as with the Basque sheepherders in the region. She is most well known for such works as *The Land of Little Rain* (Houghton, Mifflin and Co., 1903), *Lost Borders* (Harper & Brothers, 1909), and *California: The Land of the Sun* (A. and C. Black, 1914).

LINDA "BLUE BUTTERFLY" BAKKAR is from Washington State and attempted a thru hike of the PCT in 2008. She left the trail in the Sierras due to a stress fracture but returned in 2009 to complete another 600 miles. Being outdoors is her passion, and she has been fully encouraged by her three grown sons and her husband of over forty years.

DUFFY AND ANGELA BALLARD hiked 2300 miles of the PCT in the summer of 2000 and in 2003 recounted their adventure in the award-winning book *A Blistered Kind of Love: One Couple's Trial by Trail* (The Mountaineers Books, 2003). Angela served as the editor of *The Communicator*—the primary voice of the Pacific Crest Trail Association—for six years. Duffy is an emergency department physician. They live in northern California with their two children.

ANDREW BECKER is an avid climber, peak bagger, and trail runner. His reporting has appeared in the *New York Times*, *Washington Post*, *Los Angeles Times*, as well as on PBS's *Frontline/World* and National Public Radio. Becker lives in the San Francisco Bay area with his family.

CHARLES BERGMAN writes frequently on endangered species, wildlife, and animal issues. He admits to a special affection for his book *Wild Echoes* (Alaska Northwest Books, 1990). He teaches at Pacific Lutheran University in Tacoma, Washington.

NATASHA CARVER is a walker, writer, and dreamer.

MIKE CIPRA is a writer, educator, and environmental activist who lives in Death Valley, California. His short stories have been featured in the *Awkward One* and *Awkward Two* anthologies (Awkward Press, 2009, 2010) and in the *Danger City I* and *II* anthologies (Contemporary Press, 2005, 2006). He has testified before the US House of Representatives regarding the future health of America's national parks, and his nonfiction—focusing on twenty-first-century environmental challenges and policy—has appeared in newspapers and magazines throughout the West, including the *Los Angeles Times* and *The Sun Runner Magazine*.

DAVE CLAUGUS is an avid backpacker who has been hiking in the Sierra Nevada for almost fifty years but more recently began section hiking the PCT. When not hiking, he lives in Sacramento, where he enjoys the company of family and friends and operates his own electronic waste recycling business.

SAMUEL LANGHORNE CLEMENS (1835–1910) was also known as Mark Twain, Quentin Curtis Snodgrass, and Thomas Jefferson Snodgrass. With over twenty novels and travel books to his name, dozens of short stories and essays, as well as plays and countless articles, he is perhaps one of the West's most well-known and unruly authors. When the Civil War effectively closed down the Mississippi, Clemens lost work as a river boat captain and headed out West as a newspaper journalist, living first in Virginia City, then San Francisco, and later traveling up and down the West Coast.

NORMAN CLYDE (1885–1972) is arguably the Sierras' most accomplished mountaineer ever. He is recognized for making over 130 first ascents, setting a speed-climbing record of Mount Shasta, and for being the "pack that walks like a man" due to the legendary size and weight of his pack, which often held five cameras, several books, and even a cobbler's hammer and anvil for repairing clients' boots. An early leader of the Sierra Club High Trips and member of several search and rescue teams, as well as author of a number of naturalist articles, Clyde holds an iconic position in Sierra Nevada history.

CARYN DAVIDSON is a park ranger at Joshua Tree National Park and the park liaison for the Artist in Residence program. For the past fifteen years she has developed and presented environmental education programs for students in grades K–12. Her work has been published in the *L.A. Weekly*, *The Stone Magazine*, *GEO*, and *The Journal of the Los Angeles Institute of Contemporary Art*.

DAN DEQUILLE was the pen name of William Wright (1829–1898), an author, journalist, and humorist who wrote extensively about silver mining and the people and culture of the eastern Sierra. Like his friend Samuel Clemens, Wright originally came west to prospect for gold in the late 1850s but abandoned mining and turned to writing. For over thirty years he was on the staff of the *Virginia City Enterprise*.

JIM DODGE is in Humboldt State University's Faculty Early Retirement Program. He is now way too old to plant trees all day or backpack twenty miles, but he still enjoys playing in creeks, looking at stars, and trying to tighten his grip on the obvious.

MONTE DODGE thru hiked the PCT in 1977. He works as a freelance photographer and an engineer for the Burlington Northern Santa Fe Railroad in Wenatchee, Washington.

MAURICE DOREAL (1898–1963) was the name adopted by Claude Doggins as head of the Brotherhood of the White Temple, an organization currently headquartered in Sedalia, Colorado. Doreal founded the Brotherhood in 1930 and spent much of his life writing the *Brotherhood Lessons* and a series of pamphlets on a wide variety of occult-related topics.

"NO WAY" RAY ECHOLS (1942–2006) was an experienced hiker with over fifty years' travel in the mountains worldwide. His vivid and whimsical stories of the PCT are collected in *A Thru-Hiker's Heart* (Tuolumne Press, 2009).

SUZANNE "TAILWINDS" FINNEY has been active in such disparate fields and pursuits as theater, electron microscopy, aviation, horse riding, shooting, and scuba diving. Finney earned a degree in theater arts from UCLA and a graduate degree in drama from California State University, Sacramento. She holds a commercial certificate and instructor ratings for hot-air balloons, a variety of airplanes, and helicopters. She retired in 2007 to hike the PCT the following year. She presently lives near Grand Rapids, Michigan. Her advice to others, no matter what the pursuit, is "If I can do it, you can do it."

RYAN FORSYTHE is a writer and artist from Cleveland, now living in southern California, where he is completing an MFA in creative writing at San Diego State University. His writing has been published by Lonely Planet, the *Oberlin News-Tribune*, *Hostels.com*, and *Mandala Journal*.

GARY FUNK hiked the PCT in 1975 with his brother, Steve, experiencing an adventure they still talk about today. Featured in Gary's story, friends Mark Dobransky and Marty McCormick listened to the brothers' stories (and believed them) and decided to hike the PCT in 1977. The Funk brothers hiked several sections with them that year as they completed their thru hike. In 1979, the four skied the Continental Divide Trail starting in March. Over thirty years have passed since that time and they still look forward to their annual hiking trip together.

ANDY HAMMOND and his wife, Joanne, are charter members of the Oregon-California Trails Association (OCTA) and have been researching the mid-nineteenth-century western migration for over forty years. They have retraced most of the old wagon roads from Nebraska west to Oregon, Utah, and California; have mapped the 1851 Beckwourth Trail for the National Park Service; have received numerous awards for their work; and have coauthored two books: *Following the Beckwourth Trail* (self-published, 1994) and *The Look of the Elephant: The Westering Experience in the Words of Those Who Lived It, 1841–1861* (Oregon-California Trails Association, 2009).

GEORGI "FIREFLY" HEITMAN was raised in Portland and Salem, Oregon, and is a member of the Mills College class of 1960. She has been a resident of California since 1967 and has lived in Old Station since 1993 with her husband, Dennis. She was a longtime Boy Scout volunteer, Girl Scout leader and camp director, and ultimately a Girl Scout executive, and she has devoted her abundant energy to being a trail angel since 1999. She has two daughters, Jennifer and Nikki.

DAVID HORTON is a professor of kinesiology at Liberty University in Lynchburg, Virginia. He is the former speed-record holder for the Appalachian Trail, Long Trail, and the PCT. He holds the third-fastest time in the trans-America footrace and has run over 113,000 miles in training and racing.

REES HUGHES has been section hiking the PCT since 1981. Growing up in Kansas he found the lure of the mountains irresistible, leaving the flatlands first for Seattle and then, for the last twenty-five years, northern California, where he lives with his family. Despite dalliances with ultralight hiking, he still finds a tent and a book worth the weight.

JACK KEROUAC (1922–1969) is perhaps best known as an icon of the Beat generation and for his novel *On the Road* (Viking, 1957). He published a number of novels and collections of poetry, such as *The Dharma Bums* (Viking, 1958), *The Subterraneans* (Grove, 1958), and *Mexico City Blues* (Grove, 1959). Kerouac is often noted for writing "spontaneous prose" (an unadorned and unrevised stream of consciousness) and for promoting "the rucksack revolution" (a simple and rootless wandering life).

ZENAS LEONARD (1809–1857) was born in rural Pennsylvania. He left the family farm at the age of twenty-one and became a mountain man, trapping for fur and exploring throughout the West. By 1835, Leonard had returned to Missouri, where he established a store and trading post. It was there that he began compiling his journal notes. Leonard published his account in the *Clearfield (Pennsylvania) Republican* newspaper, which was later expanded into a book-length manuscript. Leonard operated the trading post until his death.

COREY LEE LEWIS makes his home with his two sons, Hunter and Bodie, in the heart of Redwood Country on the North Coast of California. Author of *Reading the Trail: Exploring the Literature and Natural History of the California Crest* (University of Nevada Press, 2005), Lewis is a longtime trail builder, hiker, and lover of the PCT.

BENJAMIN FRANKLIN (B. F.) LOOMIS (1857–1935) was one of the first and most significant of Lassen Volcanic National Park's benefactors. Born in Illinois, Loomis traveled west in a covered wagon as a young boy. For most of his adult life, Loomis lived in the shadow of Lassen Peak, where he initially made wood shakes and ultimately owned and operated a sawmill, general store, and hotel. In 1898, Loomis began his avocation of photography, generating a substantial collection of images that he housed in his Louisa Mae Loomis Memorial Museum at Manzanita Lake. Loomis deeded the museum and the surrounding forty acres to Lassen Volcanic National Park in 1929.

BARNEY "SCOUT" MANN thru hiked the PCT in 2007 with his wife, Sandy "Frodo" Mann. They observed their thirtieth wedding anniversary on top of Forester Pass, the trail's high point. Scout is a San Diego-based writer and retired attorney.

TOM MARSHBURN, after his stretch on the PCT, went on to graduate with a degree in physics and to complete a graduate degree in engineering physics at the University of Virginia. His PCT hike engendered in Marshburn a love of climbing, and he later scaled peaks in Canada, the Pacific Northwest, Mexico, and South America. His love of exploration continues as a NASA astronaut.

CHARLOTTE E. MAUK was secretary of the Sierra Club from 1943 to 1968 and a frequent participant in the club's famous High Trips into the Sierras. In 1948 she edited the book *Yosemite and the Sierra Nevada* (Houghton Mifflin Co., 1948), which combined the work of two of the Sierras' best-known artists:

photographer Ansel Adams and author John Muir. Mauk was one of a small group of people who helped to push the Sierra Club to national prominence after World War II.

HANK MEALS is a longtime resident of the Yuba River watershed, where he works as a historian, photographer, and writer. He finds the northern Sierra a source of pleasure, inspiration, and knowledge.

JOAQUIN MILLER (ca. 1840–1913) is the pen name of the colorful "Poet of the Sierra," Cincinnatus Heine Miller. A prolific writer and adventurer, Miller moved with his family to the Willamette Valley when he was a young boy, and he worked a variety of rough and tumble jobs in the West, ranging from a camp cook to a Pony Express rider. He was married three times, once to a Modoc woman, and according to fellow writer Ambrose Bierce was "the greatest-hearted man he ever knew" and "the greatest liar this country ever produced."

BRADLEY JOHN MONSMA has hiked trails and kayaked rivers throughout the western United States and Canada. His book, *The Sespe Wild: Southern California's Last Free River* (University of Nevada Press, 2004), explores the environmental and cultural history of Sespe Creek, its endangered species, and its management dilemmas. His writing has appeared in *Surfer's Journal, Pilgrimage, ISLE, High Country News*, and numerous anthologies. He is a professor of English at California State University, Channel Islands.

JOHN MUIR (1838–1914) has often been dubbed the father of both our national park and national forest systems and is recognized as the founder of the Sierra Club. Muir was an unparalleled mountain man and natural historian who discovered a variety of new species and proved that the Sierras were carved by glaciers. Muir was also an accomplished author, writing such well-known works as *My First Summer in the Sierra* (Houghton, Mifflin and Co., 1911), *The Mountains of California* (The Century Co., 1894), *Our National Parks* (Houghton, Mifflin and Co., 1911), *The Yosemite* (The Century Co., 1912), and others.

SUZANNE ROBERTS's books include *Shameless* (Cherry Grove Collections, 2007), *Nothing to You* (Pecan Grove Press, 2008), and *Plotting Temporality* (Pecan Grove Press, forthcoming). "The Ghost of Muir Pass" is from her memoir, *Almost Somewhere: 28 Days on the John Muir Trail* (forthcoming). Roberts currently lives within walking distance of the PCT in Lake Tahoe.

CHRIS ROBERTSON grew up in British Columbia. She completed her PhD in literature and environment at the University of Nevada, Reno. Robertson lives in Reno with her husband, John, and their cats, Molly and Sophie. She teaches writing and literature at Bemidji State University in Minnesota.

Krystal Rogers holds a triple bachelors degree in international studies, art, and French from Humboldt State University in Arcata, California. She has lived in Switzerland and Senegal, and she loves to experience new people and explore new places abroad and at home. She has been a lover of the outdoors ever since her first time camping. Rogers grew up in Sandy, Utah, and currently works as the youth educator for the Wasatch Community Gardens in Salt Lake City.

Eugene A. Rose is both an accomplished mountaineer and author of mountaineering books focused on the Sierra Nevada. In addition to *High Odyssey* (Howell-North Books, 1974), he also wrote *Magic Yosemite Winters* (Cold Stream Press, 1999), *Yosemite's Tioga Country* (Heydey Books, 2006), and *The San Joaquin* (Quill Driver Books, 2000). An expert skier and winter mountaineer in his own right, Rose wrote about the snow-covered crests of the High Sierra and those rugged mountaineers skilled enough to brave them in their ice-cold beauty.

Moses Schallenberger (1826–1909) was raised by his married sister Elizabeth Townsend after his parents died, when he was six. He was seventeen when the Stephens-Townsend-Murphy journey west from Missouri began. Following his winter in the Sierras, which is recounted in *The Opening of the California Trail: The Story of the Stevens Party from the Reminiscences of Moses Schallenberger* (University of California Press, 1953), Schallenberger clerked in Monterey during the gold rush, inherited the Townsend estate following the couple's death, adopted their infant son, and farmed there until his death.

John Henry Smihula, originally from New York, teaches English and humanities at the University of Nevada, Reno. He is also a documentary filmmaker, producing films such as *Hidden in Plain Sight*. His favorite place to be is high in the mountains during a boisterous summer thunderstorm or the first snowfall of the season.

Jerry Smith returned to Oregon after serving twenty-four years in the US Navy. He lives in Corvallis with his wife, Sue. Smith is currently employed by the city and volunteers as an instructor of wilderness navigation and as member of the county search and rescue team. He has dreams of another long trail.

Gary Snyder makes his home on the San Juan Ridge of the Yuba River watershed. Trail crew member, logger, fire lookout, member of the Beat generation, and contemporary environmental poet, philosopher, and activist, Snyder won a Pulitzer Prize for his poetry collection *Turtle Island* (New Directions, 1974). Since then he has also become widely recognized for his environmental philosophy and essay writing, collected in such works as *The Practice of the Wild* (North Point Press, 1990), *A Place in Space* (Counterpoint, 1995), as well as collections of poetry such as *No Nature* (Pantheon, 1992) and *Mountains and Rivers without End* (Counterpoint, 1996).

THEODORE S. SOLOMONS (1870–1947) was born in San Francisco and was an early and influential member of the Sierra Club. From 1892 to 1897 he mapped the Sierra north of Kings Canyon, naming both Mount Goddard and the Evolution Valley. He is best known for having originated the idea for "a crest parallel trail" in the Sierra Nevada, which eventually became the John Muir Trail.

JONATHAN STAHL AND AMANDA TYSON STAHL, the "Sunshine Couple," hiked the PCT in 2007 to celebrate their engagement. While hiking through the desert in southern California, Amanda "Moonshadow" and Jonathan "Oats" decided to plan their wedding to coincide with the last stop on the PCT in Stehekin, Washington. They currently reside in eastern Washington with their daughter, Sierra Jade.

WALLACE STEGNER (1909–1993) was born in Iowa and authored over twenty books and countless essays. He is often thought of as a bard of the rural West and Midwest. One of his most well-known novels, *Big Rock Candy Mountain* (Duell, Sloan and Pearce, 1943), covers this territory, while his Pulitzer Prize-winning novel, *Angle of Repose* (Doubleday, 1971), is set in the California, Colorado, and the Idaho frontier. His writing has done much to solidify the West's mythic place in American culture.

CHUCKIE "FUNNYBONE" VEYLUPEK has hiked the PCT in its entirety on two occasions and vows he will do so at least as many times more. However, he currently lives too far from the trail, near Boulder, Colorado, and may have to walk there first.

DAVID RAINS WALLACE is an award-winning author of such books as *The Dark Range: A Naturalist's Night Notebook* (1978) and *The Klamath Knot: Explorations of Myth and Evolution* (1983), both published by Sierra Club Books. He has been a visiting lecturer at such schools as the University of California, Davis, and Oregon State University, and has become an important voice for our western environment. A prolific and eloquent nature writer, Wallace regales readers with scientific stories infused with mythology and philosophy that both inform and inspire.

BEN WIELECHOWSKI is a Northern Michigan University graduate, and he alternates between college instruction and adventure, trying to reach his end goal of loafing.

ALAN W. WILLENDRUP majored in history and journalism and received his masters degree in history from California State University, Chico. "The Volcanic Eruptions of Lassen Peak and Their Lingering Legacy," excerpted in this volume, was his master's thesis.

INDEX

ABOUT THE EDITORS

COREY LEE LEWIS was raised on frequent and extended camping, backpacking, and horsepacking trips in the Rocky Mountains of Colorado and Wyoming. Family tradition and practice defined summer as a time for being at high elevations, jumping in cold streams fed by snow-melt, and reveling in the smell of sage, pine, and campfire smoke. Born in Fort Collins, Colorado, Corey moved with his family to a small farm in eastern Kansas when he was ten years old; he has been returning to the western mountains ever since.

Corey first encountered the PCT in 1998 while earning his PhD from the University of Nevada, Reno and working for the Nevada Conservation Corps. The long trail immediately took hold of his heart and became a major feature in both his professional work and personal life. For eight years, Corey led trail crews working on and around the PCT, and taught field-based college classes in environmental studies along its length. His first book, *Reading the Trail: Exploring the Literature and Natural History of the California Crest* (2005), discusses the methods he developed during these years for uniting experiential education and conservation along the trail.

Corey teaches environmental writing and literature at Humboldt State University and continues to lead students in the field. He returns each season to the high country of the PCT with his two sons, Hunter and Bodie.

REES HUGHES has been section hiking the PCT since 1981. Growing up in Kansas he found the lure of the mountains irresistible so he traded the flatlands for Seattle, the Olympics, and the Cascades. He has walked his way through some of the most stunning regions on Earth—from the top of Kilimanjaro to the arid interior of Australia, from the pilgrimage route up Sri Pada

in Sri Lanka to the picturesque Cornish coast, from the Himalayas to the Andes—but he insists there is nothing he has found to equal the Pacific Crest Trail's unique blend of access, wildness, and diversity. And, despite dalliances with ultralight, he still finds a tent and a book to be worth their weight.

The evolution of Rees' trail names reflects the manner in which he has aged with the PCT these past thirty years . . . from Boris to Uncle Rico to Mr. Question to Team Geezer. He hopes, however, that he is more akin to fine wine or cheese than a threadbare shirt or the old horse relegated to the pasture.

Rees has lived for the last twenty-five years in Northern California, with his wife, Amy, and their two daughters, Chisa and Mei Lan. He retired from Humboldt State University in 2008.

THE MOUNTAINEERS, founded in 1906, is a nonprofit outdoor activity and conservation organization whose mission is "to explore, study, preserve, and enjoy the natural beauty of the outdoors . . . ." Based in Seattle, Washington, it is now one of the largest such organizations in the United States, with seven branches throughout Washington State.

The Mountaineers sponsors both classes and year-round outdoor activities in the Pacific Northwest, which include hiking, mountain climbing, ski-touring, snowshoeing, bicycling, camping, canoeing and kayaking, nature study, sailing, and adventure travel. The Mountaineers' conservation division supports environmental causes through educational activities, sponsoring legislation, and presenting informational programs.

All activities are led by skilled, experienced volunteers, who are dedicated to promoting safe and responsible enjoyment and preservation of the outdoors.

If you would like to participate in these organized outdoor activities or programs, consider a membership in The Mountaineers. For information and an application, write or call The Mountaineers Program Center, 7700 Sand Point Way NE, Seattle, WA 98115-3996; phone 206-521-6001; visit www.mountaineers.org; or email clubmail@mountaineers.org.

The Mountaineers Books, an active, nonprofit publishing program of The Mountaineers, produces guidebooks, instructional texts, historical works, natural history guides, and works on environmental conservation. All books produced by The Mountaineers Books fulfill the mission of The Mountaineers. Visit www.mountaineersbooks.org to find details about all our titles and the latest author events, as well as videos, web clips, links, and more!

The Mountaineers Books
1001 SW Klickitat Way, Suite 201
Seattle, WA 98134
800-553-4453
mbooks@mountaineersbooks.org

The Mountaineers Books is proud to be a corporate sponsor of The Leave No Trace Center for Outdoor Ethics, whose mission is to promote and inspire responsible outdoor recreation through education, research, and partnerships. The Leave No Trace program is focused specifically on human-powered (nonmotorized) recreation.

Leave No Trace strives to educate visitors about the nature of their recreational impacts and offers techniques to prevent and minimize such impacts. Leave No Trace is best understood as an educational and ethical program, not as a set of rules and regulations.

For more information, visit www.lnt.org, or call 800-332-4100.